THE CHEY AND BLACK HILLS STAGE AND EXPRESS ROUTES

by

AGNES WRIGHT SPRING

PLATE I

Post Sutler's store, Fort Laramie

To the Memory of
the Owners and Operators
of the
Cheyenne and Black Hills Stage
and to the
Pioneers who traveled
the Cheyenne-Deadwood Trail

Contents

Illustrations

---

*Plates 2 to 17 follow page 372 of the text.

Photographs unless otherwise stated are from the Russell Thorp collection, Cheyenne, Wyoming.

Preface

Although there were numerous trails through various gateways into the Black Hills during the gold rush days, we offer here only the story of the Cheyenne and Black Hills Stage and Express routes, over which there went thousands upon thousands of passengers, tons upon tons of freight and express, and millions of dollars worth of "treasure."

The Cheyenne-Deadwood trail was not, as the name might imply, just a single two-rut track. From time to time it spread out, branched and diverged to meet the changing conditions. This route was fraught with the danger of Indian attacks, hold-ups by road agents, the peril of swollen rivers, cloudbursts, and blizzards, and innumerable other vicissitudes.

Over this trail for more than a decade, a ceaseless rumble of wagon wheels reverberated across rolling plains, through valleys, and into the foothills as innumerable gold hunters, freighters, carpenters, merchants, soldiers, adventurers, and others surged toward a new Eldorado.

Under the guidance of such men as Jack Gilmer, Monroe Salisbury, M. H. Patrick, and Russell Thorp, sr., the "stage went through."

Shoulder to shoulder with these sturdy stage men, worked the superintendent, division agents, stage drivers, stock tenders, blacksmiths, freighters, station keepers, and "shotgun messengers," who kept the wheels rolling until the whistles of trains turned the rattle of spokes into just an echo of the past.

The writing of this story of the Cheyenne and Black Hills Stage and Express routes has been a pioneering adventure, as the territory was uncharted and only slightly explored. If there appear to be discrepancies as to the mileages along the old trail, it must be kept in mind that accurate surveys had not yet been made. Data pertaining to many phases of the story, especially the outlaws, has had to be winnowed from "reminiscences" of pioneers, newspaper files, and men who knew the facts "first hand" in the long ago.

I am indebted to Russell Thorp for originating the idea of the story and for the use of his spendid collection of photographs including original Jackson sketches, original records, scrapbooks, and other source data.

I am most grateful to the university of Wyoming for a research fellowship made possible by Henry Swan, Russell Thorp, and the late R. S. Ellison.

Much valuable data has been obtained during many years through personal interviews with the following pioneers: WYOMING , *Alcova*–Mrs. Boney Earnest; *Basin*–Harry Williams; *Casper*–Judge A. C. Campbell; *Cheyenne*–Hon. Joseph M. Carey, Hon. William C. Deming, Mrs. Thomas F. Durbin, Mrs. Harry Hynds, Will H. Kelly, Judge T. Blake Kennedy, Ernest A. Logan, Mrs. John MacGregor, William Scanlon, Luke Voorhees, and Fred E. Warren; *Devils Tower*–Clint Wells; *Fort Laramie*–John Hunton; *Gillette*–C. P. (Dub) Meek; *Laramie*–N. K. Boswell, Robert Hall, Edward A. Vincent; *Newcastle*–Mrs. E. P. Dow; *Rawlins*–Gov. John Osborne, John

Friend. COLORADO, *Denver* – P. A. Gushurst; *Fort Collins* – Mrs. A. W. Scott. SOUTH DAKOTA, *Deadwood* – George V. Ayres, Mr. and Mrs. John S. McClintock, D. M. McGahey; *Hill City* – Chris Holley.

I wish to acknowledge the faithful and accurate assistance in research work of Miss Mabel M. Peck of Cheyenne; and to thank the following for their co-operation: Ina T. Aulls and her staff of the Western History department, Denver public library; Miss Mary Marks, librarian, university of Wyoming; Lola Homsher, archivist of the university of Wyoming; Miss Mary McGrath, state librarian of Wyoming; C. I. Leedy, Rapid City, South Dakota; Edwin G. Burghum, Concord, New Hampshire; Florence J. Crutcher, St. Louis public library; James H. Furay, New York City; Clarence Paine, Oklahoma City; Jerome K. Wilcox, university of California library; Mrs. Eleanor Bancroft, Bancroft library; and Miss Lucile Gilmer, Salt Lake City, Utah.

To Archer T. Spring, I express sincere appreciation for two extensive and most interesting trips into the Black Hills along the old trail once traveled by the swaying Concord coaches.

AGNES WRIGHT SPRING

Denver, october, 1948

Gold in the Black Hills

"Gold in the Black Hills!"

Teamsters left their horses half-unhitched; soldiers
quit their card games; half-breeds rose from their heels
and left the protecting shade of the old sutler's store
at Fort Laramie (*see plates* 1, 7) that sultry day in
august 1874. Eagerly they crowded around a trail-
weary rider, as he stepped from his saddle. He was
Scout Charley Reynolds[1] straight from the heart of the
Black Hills, with the first official confirmation of the
existence of the precious metal there.

At once Reynolds sought the telegraph operator. The
message, which went out over the wires, from General
George A. Custer, then in charge of the Black Hills
expedition, flashed like a rocket across the nation.

From city to hamlet, from hamlet to farm those
magic syllables echoed. They swept across the plains,
leapt great rivers, and spanned oceans, to set men's
blood tingling with anticipation. Old '49ers who had

[1] Charley Reynolds, one of General Custer's most experienced scouts, was
said to be the "best shot on the Missouri river." In her book, *Boots and
Saddles,* Elizabeth Custer, wife of the general, wrote of him: "The one whose
past we would have liked best to know was a man most valued by my husband. All the important scoutings and most difficult missions where secrecy
was required were entrusted to him. We had no certain knowledge whether
or not he had any family or friends elsewhere for he never spoke of them.
He acknowledged once, in a brief moment of confidence, that he was a gentleman by birth." Reynolds was killed on june 25, 1876, at the battle of the
Little Big Horn in which Custer also fell.

plodded across the plains to California and home again, began to polish the rust from their gold pans; coal miners, then out of work by the thousands, took new hope; men everywhere began to dream new dreams. This was the news they had been hoping years to hear. Gold in the Black Hills!

With the nation in the throes of a business depression or "panic," as the result of the post-Civil War inflation, the rumors of new gold fields swept far and wide as if "Heaven-sent."

For some time General Phil Sheridan had been recommending the establishment of a military post in the Black Hills proper, in order to have better control over the Indians. Obtaining authority to have a "Military reconnaissance" made, he had sent General George A. Custer, with about 1,000 men, from Fort Abraham Lincoln, Dakota territory, on july 2, 1874, into the Hills.

After the first discovery of gold had been made near Harney's peak in so-called Custer's park,[2] Custer and some of his men had accompanied Reynolds to the south fork of the Cheyenne river, thence the scout had struck out about midnight on august 3, with only a hand compass to guide him. Fort Laramie, estimated to be about ninety miles to the south, was his destination. Across unfamiliar, parched badlands, along dim Indian trails, but more often picking his own way in order to keep out of sight of roving bands of red men, Reynolds had forged on.

And now, through lips swollen from sun and wind, and under eyebrows crusted with alkali dust, the scout told his listeners how Ross and McKay,[3] two prac-

[2] Also spelled Custar's park.
[3] Horatio Nelson Ross and William McKay.

tical miners, with the Custer expedition, had come into camp on French creek, with a little yellow dust wrapped up in the leaf of an old account book. It had been examined with the microscope, washed with acid, mixed with mercury, cut, chewed and tasted, until everybody was convinced that it actually was gold. That is, everybody except Geologist Winchell of the party, who had been off climbing mountains that day and who was highly miffed at not having been officially consulted as to the value of the "find."

"The general had forty or fifty small particles of gold on his table at one time," Reynolds told his listeners. "Every one in camp went to digging. Every man who could get a stand in with the camp cooks got hold of pans, tin dishes, old buckets, pot hooks – anything to try their luck in the sands of the creek. Some even used tent pins. They were all looking for 'colors' when I left."

Fort Laramie reeled with excitement as men planned how they could elude the military and make their way into the forbidden Indian country at once.

And while the white men talked and planned, smoke signals spiraled and mirrors flashed from hilltops in the vast country between the Big Horns and the Black Hills of northeastern Wyoming territory. This was the land that had been set aside by two treaties for the red man's hunting grounds. The Indians were alarmed and angry as they ringed their campfires along the willow-fringed banks of Clear creek and Tongue river, or counseled at the Red Cloud and Spotted Tail agencies south of the Black Hills.

For a month their scouts had been watching every move made by General Custer and his great column of one thousand armed men as they pushed southwestward from Dakota into Wyoming, then circled northeastward into the heart of the sacred Hills.

Hatred smouldered in Sioux eyes as the heavy wheels of the five score white-topped wagons crushed the lush grasses of their hunting grounds, and the hoofs of more than two thousand animals crunched through the sage across their hunting trails. "The Thieves' trail," the red men muttered stormily.

They had been told that the Great White Father was searching for a place to establish a military post to protect them from white intrusion. But they felt deep in their hearts that the white men were breaking the trail to rob them of the hidden treasure of the Hills.

Rumors of gold in the Black Hills had been heard for many long years, but the few white men who had ventured in there either were driven out of those timbered uplands by the red men before they had started to mine, or they had been killed on the spot.

Because of the inaccessibility of the Black Hills, as compared with other localities in which gold existed, and because the Hills were included in the lands set aside for the Indians in 1851, the great tide of gold hunters flowed to California and ebbed, then to Colorado, to Nevada, to Oregon, into New Mexico and Arizona, up to Idaho, and over into Montana, while the wealth of the Black Hills lay practically undisturbed.

Just when the first prospecting was done in the Hills is not of record. Remnants of rusted picks and shovels with handles decomposed; a wagon chain dangling from a lofty pine, imbedded in the tree trunk with years of growth; a log chain hidden eight feet under ground; old stumps bearing ax marks; a wheel barrow made of ash fallen apart and practically in dust; decayed sluice boxes, buried from six to eight feet under the earth; a prospector's pit with a sturdy young oak growing out of it; old shafts and timbered tunnels; and similar discoveries in later years gave mute testimony to the fact that miners had been in the country at some early date? When? And who were they? Who could say?

The cover of an old notebook, found near two skeletons in the Bear Lodge area, bore the date "1832." A sandstone slab found by Lewis Thoen, on Mount Lookout near Spearfish, South Dakota, bore a crudely inscribed message which read in part:

. . . came to these Hills in 1833 seven of us . . All ded but me Ezra Kind Killed by Ind. . . Got all our gold 1834 . . got all the gold we could carry. . .

In 1836, old Jim Goodle, Seth Grant, and Jim Bridger reported that they saw gold nuggets that came from the Black Hills, which had been taken by Crow Indians from the Uncapapas and Minneconjous. Some two years later Owen Rubble, a trapper, displayed a shot pouch filled with nuggets which he claimed had come from the upper waters of the Yellowstone river.

Father De Smet, the Belgian missionary, who had spent much time among the Sioux, had long since explained to them the uses and great value of gold among the whites. He had told them that it would spell their doom if the white man came into their country. The missionary exacted a promise from the red men that they would never reveal the location of the gold.

Long before the Black Hills were developed, De Smet, as a dinner guest of Robert Campbell, the trader, in St. Louis, Missouri, remarked that there was a "place in the Rocky mountains so rich in gold that if it were publicly known would astonish the world." He also stated that there was a valuable platinum mine between the Yellowstone and Cheyenne rivers.

Before 1860, several exploratory parties, chiefly topographical in purpose, penetrated this huge, unsurveyed frontier country later embraced by northeastern Wyoming and southwestern South Dakota. Members of some of the parties made statements as to the decided evidences of gold in many of the streams therein. Leaders of the parties, however, were afraid that their men would get the gold fever and would desert in the Indian country, if they knew of the "finds," so kept the information about the gold traces as secret as possible. Some even denied them vigorously.

But when John M. Bozeman, in defiance of the treaty of 1851, laid out a short-cut road in 1863, from Fort Laramie to the booming gold camps of Montana, that diagonally traversed the country lying east of the Big Horns, prospectors at once began to turn their eyes eagerly toward the Black Hills. Especially were they encouraged over the future when they learned that United States troops were on the march north over the so-called Bozeman road, in 1864. Here, they reasoned, would be protection from the Indians.

Accordingly, for a brief time, a few gold seekers, including "Bob" Bailey and John ("Portugee") Phillips, ventured to branch off from the Montana trail, to pan for colors in Crazy Woman's fork,[4] Clear creek,

---

[4] According to the Cheyenne *Sun,* the Indian name for Crazy Woman's fork was: wi-ya wi- tko- tko-pa. Wi-ya, it was said, stood for woman, wak-pa was river. The rest denoted crazy. This creek is in Johnson county, Wyoming, and should not be confused with Crazy creek in Park county.

the Pineys and even as far as the south fork of Powder river and the Belle Fourche. It was only a short step farther to the inner Black Hills.

For years stories had been told of Indians bringing gold nuggets into Fort Laramie, which they "swapped off" for powder, lead, and other things. Many white men contended that the Indians had taken the gold from prospectors who were returning from California. Others surmised that they had found it in the Black Hills.

Jim Bridger was of the latter group. He had guided parties, including Sir George Gore, through the forbidden country, and he knew that gold was there. He could not resist talking about it.

On october 11, 1865, Will H. Young, a sojourner at Fort Laramie, recorded the following in his diary:

Tonight has been cold and we sit by the snug fire listening to Major Bridger's gold stories. Major Bridger and Gunn created lots of fun with Indian dances.

A few men listened to Bridger's stories and envisaged vast treasure lying undiscovered in the recesses of the mysterious hills. Most of his listeners, however, took Jim's stories with a grain of salt, as he had a well-established reputation for tall tales. Why should anyone, these doubters asked, believe his stories about gold nuggets in the streams of the Black Hills, any more than they should believe in mountains of glass and a place where "all Hell bubbled up?"

But when a few years later the wonders of the Yellowstone National park were explored and were found to be as Bridger had described them, "Old Gabe," as Jim was called, was credited with truth.

He had scarcely finished telling his tales about gold, when two Swedes came to Fort Laramie, one blustery winter night in 1865, and asked the post sutler's clerk, Charley Clay, to keep for them some baking powder cans, which contained $7,000 worth of coarse gold. They claimed that with five companions they had been working a gold claim in the Indian country; had built a cabin; and were preparing for winter, when they had been attacked by Indians. Only the two of them had escaped. They had made their way to Fort Reno on Powder river and thence to Fort Laramie.

The Swedes were reticent to talk of the location of their mine. It might, according to their description, be either in the Black Hills or in the Big Horn mountains. Early in the spring of 1866, the two men left Fort Laramie and headed north with their cans of yellow dust. That was the last heard of them. Thus began the legend of the Lost Cabin mine, which has come down through the years of Wyoming history.

Fired with enthusiasm at the sight of the actual gold, which the Swedes had brought in, and which had been in the sutler's safe all winter, Colonel William G. Bullock, for many years agent to Post-sutler Ward at Fort Laramie, recalled various incidents. Only three years before, Swift Bear, a Sioux, had asked Bullock why he didn't go over to the Hills and get some gold. Also, John Richards (Reshaw, Reichard), a well-known squawman, had told Bullock about his son getting gold from the Indians who frequented the hunting grounds near the Hills. Too, Bullock recalled having traded with a squaw who produced a gold nugget from her mouth and asked for a stick of candy in exchange.

After the Swedes started north, Bullock began to

organize a mining expedition. He succeeded in enlisting one hundred and fifty men and was ready to start out when an order was issued by the military, forbidding the expedition. An extensive Indian war was feared, the authorities said, if such a party went into the Hills.

Men had been prospecting the South Pass region in west-central Wyoming since 1860, but had been so harassed by Indians that little had been accomplished. There, not far from the old Oregon trail, in 1842, gold had been discovered by a trapper with the American Fur company. Men persisted in their search, however, and during the summer of 1867, rich strikes were made in that area.

With the rush to South Pass, attention for a brief time was focused away from the Black Hills. Gulches near Atlantic City, Miner's Delight, and South Pass City hummed with activity. Next, the treaty signed at Fort Laramie, in 1868, with the Sioux, forbade white men to enter that part of Wyoming territory north of the Platte river and between the eastern slopes of the Big Horns and the Black Hills. The Bozeman road was closed. All entrance to the Hills from the south and west was barred to gold seekers.

White men, however, continued to strain at the leash and refused to accept the treaty as an ultimatum. During the winter of 1869, Judge William L. Kuykendall,[5] a leader in civic affairs in Cheyenne, proposed the organization of a large Black Hills expedition of a semi-military character, much more pretentious than that planned three years before by Colonel Bullock.

---

[5] In 1876, Judge Kuykendall presided over the "Miners' Court" at Deadwood, D.T., which tried Jack McCall for the murder of Wild Bill Hickok.

In response to a small notice which Kuykendall placed in a local newspaper, eager-eyed men packed McDaniels theatre. The organization of the Black Hills and Big Horn Mountain association, with Judge Kuykendall as president, and Colonel Farrar, secretary, was quickly perfected. Recruiting began at once. Luke Murrin, pioneer saloon owner and businessman of Cheyenne, as superintendent of the new association, went to Chicago about the middle of april, 1870, to arrange railway rates from there to Cheyenne for all interested.

Letters from men in many states began to pour into the little frontier town, which because of its rapid growth, called itself the "Magic City of the Plains." In a brief time, two thousand men were booked, pledged to join the expedition at Cheyenne, to arm with repeating guns, with one thousand rounds of ammunition, and to supply themselves with six months' rations.

In support of the Sioux treaty, however, President U. S. Grant caused an order to be issued prohibiting the expedition from going to the Black Hills. Later the order was modified and the men received permission to go as a group to the South Pass country, since that was not in the restricted Indian area.

Under Kuykendall's leadership the party which dwindled to one hundred and twenty men, after the shift in destination, left Cheyenne and went as far north as the Meeteetse country. Among them was Henry Comstock, discoverer of the famous Nevada lode, which bears his name. They failed to make a strike.

The unsuccessful outcome of the Kuykendall expedition did not decrease the gold fever in Cheyenne. With stories continually filtering through about individuals who had gone into the Black Hills and who had made rich strikes, Cheyenne businessmen began to grubstake miners to prospect territory nearer at hand, until the Hills should be opened.

During the early 'seventies, prospectors went into the Laramie mountains (often referred to as the Black Hills by early travelers), into the far reaches of the Medicine Bow range, and also along Horseshoe creek, and La Bonte.

Not once though did they forget that the real Land of Lure lay off to the northeast, just beyond their reach. Cheyenne newspapers kept the coals of desire fanned to glowing embers by constantly urging the government to open up the country north of the Platte river to exploration and settlement.

The word which Charley Reynolds brought to the world via Fort Laramie on that august day in 1874, was what the whole country wanted to hear. It was a signal for renewed attacks on the barred gates of the Forbidden Land of Gold. Cheyenne, over night, became a seething cauldron of unrest and expectant activity.

Cheyenne: Magic City of the Plains

By 1874, Cheyenne, the "Magic City of the Plains," then only a seven-year-old frontier town, had scarcely shaken off the title of "Hell-on-wheels," which it had acquired in 1867, as the rip-roaring temporary end of track, of the Union Pacific railroad.

In fact, only recently the Boston *Globe* had remarked:

> But one man has died at Cheyenne with his boots off since the town first sprouted, and he had them in his teeth and was crawling out a bedroom window, when an avenging pistol ball let daylight shine through him.

In like vein, the editor of *The Daily Central City* (Colo.) *Register* wrote:

> The Governor of Wyoming has appointed Thanksgiving in that Territory upon the same day as the National Thanksgiving. This is wise. The people of Wyoming (if they have not been misrepresented) would hardly give *two* days to prayer and solemn devotion.

With the arrival of the Union Pacific rails, in november 1867, Cheyenne had become a hub or cross-roads and a melting pot of the west. Day and night, crowds of men had milled up and down the streets: buffalo hunters, trappers, traders, railway workers, engineers, Indians, soldiers, mule skinners, bull whackers, stage drivers, gamblers, actors, miners, ruffians, and "men of the country,"[6] with their dusky wives.

In the earliest days, saloons and amusement places, of which there were legion, had vied for patronage. In order to attract attention some operated large-sized Barbary organs, imported from Germany, which played opera airs with full orchestration; one had a huge diorama; another, a picture of a Civil War scene, done in oils by a "master artist."

Vice had run rampant until the Vigilantes had taken a hand. Said one visitor of this so-called, wild, hell-roaring inferno of the plains, "the very atmosphere of Cheyenne seemed to vibrate with a constant zest of unrivaled emotions, tingling with petulance and vice."

To men who had been living in isolated cabins and dug-outs, in tepees or railway boxcars, or who had been sleeping in the sagebrush, with only the stars for a canopy and in constant danger of Indian attacks, the protection and accommodations of early Cheyenne, seemed adequate. A French gentleman, one Louis L. Simonin, however, was amazed to find the guests of the Dodge house sleeping in one large room with "no less than thirty beds, most of which were occupied by two sleepers at a time."

And he wrote home that,

In the common lounging-room where everyone cleaned up, one had to share the same brushes, the same combs, and even the same towel. I rolled the soiled linen, spotted with dingy stains, until I found a clean place, and then bravely rubbed my face. What could I do? It is the custom of the country.

Monsieur Simonin also said:

How rough and crude in appearance they are, all these men of the

---

⁶ So-called by the Indians because they were white men who had married Indian women. The whites called them "squawmen."

Far West, with their long hair, their felt hats with the broad brims, their ill-kept beards, their clothing of nondescript color, their great leather boots in which their pantaloons are engulfed. But what virile characters, proud, fearless! What dignity, what patience! No one complains here. If things are not better, it is because they cannot be, and no one finds anthing therein to blame.[7]

Nevertheless from the time the first tent pegs were driven and the first shacks thrown up, there had been an undercurrent of permanency, despite the fact that the majority of the first residents moved on up over Sherman hill, in the spring of 1868, as the rails were extended westward. Men and women who remained on the banks of Crow creek put down permanent roots. They had not just "floated" west, but had come west to build.

And while there still were those who milled day and night through the ankle-deep dust or mud of the streets of the Magic City in search of drink or diversion, the more substantial citizens were bringing order out of chaos, in the civic life of the little new border settlement.

On the very night when a howling mob of men edged the ringside at a bloody prize fight, that is reported to have gone one hundred and twenty-six rounds, a small group of Cheyenne's citizens met and perfected the organization of the first public school in that remote part of Dakota territory, which in less than a year became Wyoming territory.

Had Simonin visited Cheyenne in 1875, at the beginning of the gold rush, he would no doubt, have been amazed at the Brussels carpets and "elegant" mirrors and furniture in the new Inter-Ocean and other hotels.

[7] "A French Picture of Cheyenne, Wyoming, in 1867." Trans. from the French by Wilson O. Clough. *The Frontier Magazine,* march 1930, p. 240.

Before the Union Pacific railroad penetrated what is now Wyoming, the overland mail and telegraph route from Julesburg, Colorado to Fort Laramie, followed the old Oregon trail, past Scottsbluff.

As soon, however, as the rails reached the mushrooming little settlement called Cheyenne, the mail and express were sent westward by train from Julesburg to this new terminus. Thence they were relayed to outposts by any means available.

On december 20, 1867, the Cheyenne *Leader* announced that:

A line of stages is now run between Fort Russell and Fort Laramie. It carries the mail from this point to Laramie, Fetterman, and Phil Kearny. We learn that the road is now being re-stocked, new coaches put on, and new arrangements being perfected.

Upon the arrival of the telegraph line in Cheyenne from Laporte, Colorado, the previous october, a government telegraph line was constructed to parallel the new military highway to Fort Laramie.

There were at that time only two cabins along the route which later became the Black Hills trail. The first, built in 1866 by a man named Bailey, was at the crossing of the Chugwater, about fifty-two miles from Cheyenne. The second, built by James Bordeaux, as a road ranch and trading post in 1867, was fourteen miles north of the Chug. A few tepees of white men with Indian wives were along the Chugwater and Laramie rivers. Otherwise the rolling plains, hills, and valleys that lay between Fort D. A. Russell and Fort Laramie were primitive roaming grounds of the Indians.

The so-called "stages" which carried official passengers, mail, and express during the late 'sixties and early 'seventies, were government ambulances "managed" by soldiers. One left each fort every other day and met on the "Chuck" (Chugwater). Civilians who desired to ride made application to the quartermaster at Camp Carlin (Cheyenne depot) near Fort D. A. Russell, or at Fort Laramie.

Although the mail contract provided for the carrying of mail only to the military posts, the driver was permitted to carry loose mail to the road ranch proprietors at Chugwater and Bordeaux. This included mail addressed to men in camps in the vicinities nearby.

These camps were temporary winter "hangouts" of small freighters, or men who owned one or two teams of oxen or horses. After the cold weather prevented long hauls, the freighters usually went into camp, where they could turn their stock out to graze and keep an eye on the animals. One of the largest of these "hangouts" was on the Sybille (Sebeal) about twelve miles west of Bordeaux. It was the scene of much drinking, gambling, carousing, and even of a couple of murders.

Indian depredations in eastern Wyoming in the general vicinity of Fort Laramie during the spring of 1868 were numerous. In various raids the red men burned the buildings of the few ranches on Cottonwood, Twin Springs, and Horseshoe creek, but left the road ranches at Chugwater and Bordeaux, on the Fort Laramie stage route, unmolested.

Although the Indians made no direct attacks upon the stages or their stopping places during that first year in which the mail line was operated, evidences of their deviltry were sufficiently close to the stage route to keep the drivers and stock tenders on the alert.

At that time there were at least a thousand Sioux around Fort Laramie every day, trading buffalo robes, antelope skins, an occasional mountain lion hide, or a few beaver pelts for powder, lead, and Indian cloth. According to W. G. Bullock, sutler's agent, they brought in four thousand hides that season.

With the seat of government at Yankton, Dakota territory, hundreds of miles away, the citizens of the new railway town, Cheyenne, began to clamor for a territory of their own. Astonishingly enough, in only about a year from the time the first surveyor's stakes for a town site were pushed into the grass roots of those rolling plains, a new territory was created from parts of Dakota, Utah, and Idaho. It was called Wyoming.

And while the citizens of the new commonwealth were, on july 25, 1868, shooting firecrackers and celebrating their good luck, scouts were combing the foothills of the Big Horns to bring in Red Cloud and his tribesmen from their favorite hunting grounds, to affix their signatures to the treaty then under way.

The signing of the 1868 treaty with the Sioux, however, was like snapping shut a padlock on the Cheyenne gateway to the Black Hills. White men were forbidden entrance into the Indian country. The Indians were not permitted to cross to the south bank of the Platte river. This meant that they could no longer trade at Fort Laramie, where they had been trading for more than three decades. Disappointed and bewildered, they moved eastward and went into camp near the site of the present town of Henry, Nebraska.

Small bands of unruly young warriors ignored the treaty and raided ranches south of the river. They ran off horses, since they could move them quickly; and slaughtered the slower-moving cattle on the spot where they found them. They murdered herders, freighters, and soldiers, if they discovered them alone or in small, unprotected groups. The Sioux chiefs, who had signed the treaty, insisted that they were unable to curb these young marauders.

It is readily understandable, in the face of such conditions, why many residents and newcomers in Cheyenne, who were chafing to explore the Black Hills, feared to venture very far northward.

Politicians went ahead as if no treaty had been signed. Territorial Secretary Edward M. Lee told the first Wyoming legislature in 1869, that gold was known to exist in large quantities in the vicinity of the Big Horn mountains and along the Black Hills.

"Heretofore," said Lee, "its development has been retarded by Indian occupancy, but now movements are progressing that will result in opening up this richest gold region yet discovered."

Just what the "movements" were he did not explain.

During the winter of 1869-70, the Quartermaster's department, United States Army, made one four-day round-trip every week from Camp Carlin to Fort Laramie, with the mail. That winter Indians jumped and scalped a courier who was returning to the herders' camp on the Sybille with mail from Bordeaux. He was said to have been the son of Tutt, the first post sutler at Fort Laramie.

Shortly afterwards, a band of marauders attacked a camp of freighters and half-breeds at Point of Rocks, two miles below the Chugwater stage station. In trying to make a getaway with some mules and horses, one of the invaders was killed. His body was found by the ambulance driver near the stage road when the mail came along from Camp Carlin the next morning.

Ranchmen and settlers gradually occupied the valleys near Cheyenne. Steadily in the early 'seventies they pushed north to the Chugwater, to Horse creek, and on to the Laramie river and its tributaries. Many of these pioneers became in some way connected with the Cheyenne and Black Hills stage line.

By 1874 the government was having much difficulty in keeping both the whites and the reds under control as cattlemen with large herds had reached the North Platte river and had joined the gold seekers in clamoring for entrance into the Indian country, north of the river, where hundreds of valleys lay knee-deep in rich, untouched forage.

During the months just preceding Custer's official announcement of the discovery of gold on French creek, there had been much discussion as to the moving of the Indian agencies from northwestern Nebraska to new locations on the Missouri. The Indians were sullen, restless, and resentful. Raids on horses and mules south of the North Platte river became more numerous and several white men were attacked and killed. So many depredations were committed that the whole territory was in a constant state of alarm.

From the Laramie plains to the Wind river country and on over to the North Platte and Laramie rivers near Fort Laramie, during the early spring and summer of 1874, stories were current of murder and plundering.

At the time Charley Reynolds brought the message to Fort Laramie that gold was lying in the gulches to be had for the taking, hundreds of thousands of men were out of work all over the United States. Construction programs had been halted. Banks had failed. Railways were in the hands of receivers.

The depression-ridden populace paid little attention to that part of Custer's official report which stressed the fact that the expedition had not remained long enough at any one camp to make a satisfactory examination of deposits of valuable minerals and that "until further examination is made regarding the richness of the gold, no opinion should be formed." All that the people kept in mind was the news of *gold in the Hills*.

The government did everything to stem the gold-crazed tide. From numerous official sources came denials of the finding of the precious metal.

General Phil Sheridan issued orders to all commanders of frontier posts to curb the contemplated rush to French creek. He instructed Brigadier General A. H. Terry, commander of the department of the Platte, to burn all wagons, to destroy all outfits, and to arrest all leaders attempting to enter the Sioux country.

But the public ignored all deprecatory reports and chose to believe only the glowing ones. The prohibitive military orders merely served to whet the desire of men to go after the gold.

Lying in the heart of a vast, rolling plains area, Cheyenne was on an almost direct line between the flourishing little city of Denver, one hundred and fifteen miles southward, and Fort Laramie on the Oregon trail, about ninety-eight miles to the north. Too, it was practically midway between the Missouri river and Great Salt Lake. It was ideally situated as a focal point for transportation, in the great mountain and plains area.

Like a great magnet the little frontier settlement drew from every direction, men intent upon searching for golden dust in the glittering streambeds of that forbidden Indian country to the northeast. Women also came, many of them. But for the most part they dug their gold in less rugged terrain.

North out of Cheyenne there was later established one of the best known thoroughfares of the west, the famous Black Hills trail, over which rolled the wheels of the Cheyenne and Black Hills stage line to Custer City and then on to Deadwood—a line whose history is filled with struggle, adversity, and superb achievement.

The Black Hills trail was not, as the name might imply, just a single two-rut track nor just one route. From time to time it spread out, branched and diverged to meet the changing conditions.

Over this trail for more than a decade, a ceaseless rumble of wagon wheels reverberated across the plains, through the valleys, and into the foothills, as thousands upon thousands of gold hunters, freighters, carpenters, merchants, soldiers, and adventurers surged toward a new Eldorado. Rugged individualists they were. Each strove to wrest from the virgin territory, through his own will and brawn, economic independence.

The Mystic Gates

The Indians did not, as was generally supposed by their eastern sympathizers, spend much time in the high Hills. In the autumn they ventured into the lower foothills for lodge poles, or to hunt, or to gather wild fruits and berries. In the summer, however, when as sometimes happened, a violent wind, accompanied by rain and lightning, swept over the hills, twisting, splintering, and uprooting the great trees, the red men were sure that this was a display of wrath on the part of the Great Spirit, who they believed sat enthroned under one of the lofty peaks.

Why then, if the red men did not live in the Black Hills nor dig the gold, should they object to white men going there to prospect, the gold-seekers wanted to know. To the Sioux such invasion spelled the doom of their best hunting grounds, the grazing lands of the buffalo. To gain entrance to the Black Hills from the south and west it was necessary to cross these lands.

Opinion throughout the nation as to the opening of the Black Hills to settlement was divided. There were many persons, including Quakers, who sympathized with the Indians and felt that the white men had no right to intrude on the lands designated for the red men by treaty terms. They accused government officials and Indian agents of grafting in beef contracts, of oppressing the Indians, and of spreading malicious reports.

Others thought that since the Indians had broken the treaty by raiding and killing, that the white men should drive them on to the reservations and keep them there. Some blamed congress for holding up appropriations and declared that the Indians were forced through starvation to pilfer. Others vigorously denied this. They said that the Indians were being amply supplied and had merely "entered upon a course of savage depredations out of pure cussedness."

There were plenty of individuals, who, with their own eyes, had seen the Indians kill innocent white women and children; who had had their stock run off by them; and who personally had clashed with the red skins. They were in favor of cutting the beef issue low and in striking as hard as possible to punish the Indians and to make them submissive.

Cheyenne newspapers plunged into the maelstrom of controversy.

Few, if any persons, called attention to the fact that the residents of Wyoming, Dakota, and Nebraska were following the pattern set by their forefathers in pushing the Indians from one frontier to another, in order to occupy their lands. Pioneers had been doing just that from the Atlantic coast toward the west and from the Pacific coast eastward. What men of the west were trying to do now was nothing new in the annals of America.

For generations the red man had been pushed on and on by civilization. Now he was surrounded on all sides. He was making his last stand in the Black Hills and in the great basin east of the Big Horn mountains. He was battling for his property and his very existence.

With little regard for the claims of the Indians,

ambitious citizens in many western towns realized the importance of having their locality become the gateway to the gold country.

Sioux City, Iowa already had promoted expeditions and had for several years been agitating the opening of the Black Hills. Yankton, Dakota territory had declared itself the most logical gateway. Grand Island and Kearney, Nebraska were growing railway towns with ambitions. Sidney, Nebraska, to the south of the Red Cloud agency, proclaimed that it was the "nearest point to the Hills." Laramie City aspired to be on the "direct route" by promoting a cross-country road that by-passed Cheyenne. But Cheyenne forged ahead and became the most widely heralded outfitting center and place of departure for the new gold fields.

Even before the Custer expedition went into the Hills, Cheyenne consistently demanded that northeastern Wyoming be opened to settlement. The "Magic City of the Plains" vociferously proclaimed the excellence of her hotels, her newspapers, theatrical performances, gorgeous atmosphere, and health-giving climate.

Through the influence of Cheyenne citizens, a bill was introduced into congress early in 1874, to grant a right of way to the Cheyenne, Iron Mountain and Helena railroad, through the territories of Wyoming and Montana. The bill carried an amendment which provided for a road from Cheyenne to Red Cloud agency on White Earth river, only fifty miles from the Black Hills.

Shortly after the bill was proposed, the Cheyenne and Fort Ellis Transportation company, with a capitalization of fifty thousand dollars was organized in

Cheyenne. Under its articles of incorporation the company was authorized to "build roads, bridges, collect toll, transport freight over any portion of the route and to transact other business as may be desired."

Nothing concrete, however, came of either company's plans. The office of Indian affairs in Washington immediately blocked the building of a wagon road through the Indian country as "highly inexpedient and dangerous to the peace of the frontier."

A bright ray of hope had appeared on Cheyenne's horizon in the summer of 1872, when General Ord had approved the construction of a military bridge[8] across the North Platte river at Fort Laramie, not to cost more than fifteen thousand dollars. In transmitting the original plans for the bridge to Congressman Steele of Wyoming, General Ord attached this comment:

"As you were so instrumental in having this bridge built, and it was for the benefit of Wyoming, I have not deemed it advisable to recommend any removal from Fort Laramie of the site, though by recent explorations which I directed, there is found a short and direct road, 125 miles to Red Cloud from Sidney, crossing the North Platte near Court House Rock."

Had General Ord not approved the building of the bridge in Wyoming, the Cheyenne to Deadwood route and the Cheyenne and Black Hills stage line might have had an entirely different history, or, perhaps, none at all.

Autumn of 1874, following the arrival of Charley Reynolds in Fort Laramie, with his momentous news,

---

[8] The bridge, which became a political football for many months, was completed in the winter of 1875 and was officially accepted in february 1876, after Captain Stanton of the u.s. Engineers, had tested the structure by running thirteen army wagons loaded with stone on to one arch at a time of the three 150-foot spans. The bridge is still in use (1948).

was a busy one in Cheyenne. Army officers, Indian peace commissioners, and innumerable gold hunters crowded the hotels.

A few of the prospectors hoped to make their way as soon as possible northeast to the Indian agencies, and then to slip away into the Black Hills. Others were disposed to wait in Cheyenne until legal entrance was permitted.

Excitement rose to fever heat when the military suspended all civilian telegraphic communication between Cheyenne and Fort Laramie. Such action apparently was taken to protect military movements in the field, but all sorts of wild rumors floated about.

Wagon wheels were at once called into service by news hungry Cheyenne editors, who established what they referred to as the "Bull Train express." For some weeks the only direct news that reached Cheyenne from Red Cloud agency and Fort Laramie came through letters in the mail or by "word of mouth" of the bull whackers of the freighting outfits.

Irritated by the military "silence," Editor Glafcke of the Cheyenne *Leader* said,

No power on the face of the earth can keep the miner out of a country where he knows gold can be found. . . the best route is via Red Cloud agency from Cheyenne.

About a month later, Glafcke was a bit more cautious. He urged that no one go off "half-cocked." He assured his readers that everything was being done by men of influence and standing in Washington, "to bring about immediate favorable action on the part of governmental authorities."

Men who were familiar with the country that lay

between Cheyenne and the Hills were anxious to go into the new Eldorado during the autumn months, when the water in the streams would be low and suitable for fording with teams or pack animals. They felt, too, that the Indians by that time, would be in winter quarters and would not be trailing back and forth between the Big Horns and the agencies.

Cheyenne citizens selected a committee of nine[9] to promote the interests of the city in developing the newly discovered mining country.

Although the route to the Hills was now under close military surveillance, Cheyenne businessmen were making preparation to divert the flow of traffic through the gates of the "Magic City of the Plains," when the hegira of gold hunters should be free to head for the reputed Golconda.

At every opportunity Cheyenne pulled all possible "wires" to keep the government mail and transportation line open to Fort Laramie and to the Red Cloud and Spotted Tail agencies on the lower end of the proposed route to the Hills.

When the postmaster general closed the mail route from Fort Randall, Dakota territory to Spotted Tail's agency (Whetstone), Cheyenne was successful in having a mail service established direct from itself to that location. It was considered only about fifty miles from Whetstone to the edge of the Black Hills.

Mail left Cheyenne each monday morning at seven and arrived at the agency the following saturday at six o'clock in the evening. The return trip was made between 7 A.M. on monday and 6 P.M. on saturday.

Since Fort Laramie was not on the new mail route,

---

[9] A. R. Converse, I. W. French, George Cassels, W. L. Kuykendall, G. W. Corey, H. Haas, D. McLaughlin, Charles F. Miller, and Herman Glafcke.

General Ord directed the continuance of a weekly stage between Cheyenne and the fort, saying that it had "grown to be a necessity." John Mayfield of Cache la Poudre, Colorado, who obtained the contract, soon turned it over to J. C. Abney of Cheyenne.

Everything at that time pointed to the establishment of a regular stage road direct from Cheyenne to the Hills, via the Indian agencies, just as soon as the gold rush should begin. Little, if any, consideration was given at that time to the idea of a more direct route north from Fort Laramie.

It remained for freighters to break that Fort Laramie trail late in 1875 and early in 1876 which became the world-famous stagecoach road known as the "Cheyenne and Black Hills trail."

In the weeks immediately following the return of Custer's Black Hills expedition to Fort Abraham Lincoln in 1874, bands of excited northern Indians returned to the agencies with tales of miners sneaking into the Hills. Councils were held and the Indians were anxious and angry, but they did not know what to do.

To disturb them more, a young professor named O. C. Marsh, curator of the museum at Yale university, and a well known paleontologist, bent upon exploring the Bad Lands north of the agency, in search of fossils, arrived at the Red Cloud agency. Red Cloud obstinately refused to allow Marsh to go into the designated country, as he believed the professor was after gold.

"If you want to get bones," Red Cloud said, "I'll take you where you can find plenty."

And he took the easterner to the place at the agency where cattle had been slaughtered. He at last though, did permit the "bone hunter" to go into the Bad Lands, upon the promise that he, Marsh, would take a message from Red Cloud to the Great White Father in Washington.

Thereby hangs a long tale of political intrigue, Indian cunning, the trickery of some squawmen, a story of musty sugar, unpalatable coffee, lank cattle, and rotten tobacco. All of which it is said fitted into a scheme to get rid of Secretary of the Interior, Columbus Delano.

But that is a story in itself and is not closely related to the story of the Black Hills stage line, except that it did take up the attention and time of officials and statesmen, who might otherwise have been devoting their efforts to more constructive work in respect to the settling of the West.

Cheyenne editors, eager to keep the "Magic City of the Plains" in the limelight, stressed the fact that the route to the agencies was open the year around, "with the best of roads, plenty of wood, water and grass . . . and whisky in abundance . . . a line protected by military posts almost to the base of the Black Hills."

Inquiries concerning the Hills poured into the officials at the Red Cloud and Spotted Tail agencies on every mail, until in september, the postmaster general authorized the Cheyenne post office to increase mail service to the Spotted Tail agency from a weekly to a semi-weekly. George M. Brown, then the mail contractor, made arrangements accordingly.

At the risk of losing their scalps, some prospectors sneaked into the Hills late in that autumn of 1874, but as winter approached, they drifted back to civilization for supplies and shelter. Each, however, brought back actual proof of "finds" in dust and nuggets.

In november, Cheyenne experienced her first real pangs of jealousy, when it was rumored that a mail contract would shortly be let to Camp Sheridan, near the Spotted Tail agency, by way of Sidney, Nebraska, instead of through Cheyenne.

The "Honorable board of county commissioners" of Cheyenne's Laramie county, lost no time in authorizing the survey of a new road to the Red Cloud agency, with a view to shortening the distance then being traveled. J. Westley Hammond of the surveyor general's office immediately surveyed a new "lower road." It was 145 miles in length and was, in december, declared ready for use by the way of Reel's ranch, Pole creek, Spring creek, LaGrange's ranch, Horse creek, Campbell's ranch, North Platte river, Spoon Butte creek, Running Water, the crossing of the Fort Laramie road, Spring branch (tributary to White Earth river), to Red Cloud. A mail route soon was in operation over this road.

While this new northeasterly road was being laid out from Cheyenne, there was slowly struggling toward the Black Hills, through Nebraska and Dakota, a small party of determined gold seekers, known later as the "Gordon party." In this group, organized in Sioux City, Iowa in early october, were twenty-eight adventurers, including Mrs. Annie D. Tallent, her husband, and ten year old son.

Scarcely had their wagon wheels rolled to a stop on French creek, than word was carried to the outside by Indians and also whites, that a stockade was being built and that miners were at work.

Troops sent from Camp Robinson, Nebraska and from Fort Randall, Dakota territory, to bring out this party, were unsuccessful because of a terrific blizzard.

The storm which struck the cavalrymen was one of the worst ever recorded in that area, with the thermometer registering forty degrees below zero. The suffering of some of the "boys in blue" was said to have been almost beyond description. Twenty-four empty saddles went back to Camp Robinson while ambulances were sent to bring in the men who were too badly frozen to ride. Forty men were hospitalized for frozen limbs.

Old timers said that not since the winter of 1848-1849 had they known such snow drifts north of Fort Laramie, nor could they recall ever having heard the wind "get up and howl" as it did for about ten days around the close of the year.

On january 8, 1875, a Cheyenne householder, Isaac A. Bard, noted in his diary:

Fearful cold. Froze one ear going to the post office and back. Rose had her house plants all frozen last night. Buckets froze fast in the well. . . Ice is one inch thick. . . Apples froze hard in the cellar. . . Our pet robin was frozen stiff last night.   . .

Cheyenne was crowded with marooned freighters, army officers, and would-be prospectors. "Chin music" was plentiful, with the Black Hills the main theme, as men grouped around the huge pot-bellied cast iron stoves in the stores, hotel lobbies, and saloons. All were eager for a Chinook to whisk the drifts out of the gullies so they could head northeastward.

Tons upon tons of freight accumulated at Cheyenne depot (Camp Carlin), two miles from Cheyenne, while freighters endeavored to round up their work cattle, which had been scattered by the storms.

A substantial committee of Cheyenne businessmen [10]

10 F. E. Warren, A. H. Swan, A. R. Converse, P. S. Wilson, J. Joslin, J. R. Whitehead, E. P. Snow, D. McLaughlin, M. E. Post, and Luke Murrin.

ranging from storekeeper, cattleman, banker, jeweler, and lawyer, to saloon keeper, laid definite plans for developing the Black Hills mining region and endeavored to answer the hundreds of inquiries pouring in from every direction relative to available transportation, routes, outfitting possibilities, distances, danger from Indian attack.

One hundred men, organized in Ogden, wrote that they were ready to start for the Hills via Cheyenne; three hundred men were waiting impatiently in Salt Lake City; and in the vicinity of Evanston, Wyoming dozens of idle coal miners milled around hoping to hurry eastward "at the drop of the hat."

There was a greatly increased undercurrent of forward-looking business activity in the little "Magic City of the Plains," which now comprised about three thousand inhabitants, exclusive of transients.

Cheyenne was proud of her five churches, a good public school and a private one, two hardware stores, three large grocery houses, three retail establishments, a confectionery store, bakeries, a jewelry store that had an international reputation for excellent workmanship, three blacksmith and wagon shops, boarding houses, tailor shops, barber shops, to say nothing of the liquor and cigar stores, saloons, and places of amusement. Its leading hotels were: Dyer's, the American house, Planter's house, and the Railroad house. Its business houses did a much larger business than those in many western towns of similar size, because of the huge nearby government supply depot, Camp Carlin, and Fort D. A. Russell, a fifteen company military garrison, just three miles away.

B. M. Ford, a colored man, who had run the Ford

house since Cheyenne's early days, was busy completing plans for a fine modern three-story structure, the Inter-Ocean hotel. B. Hellman, men's outfitter, who catered to cattlemen, freighters, railway men, and townsfolk, left for New York City to buy a large spring stock. Included on his list to be purchased was a considerable stock of "buckskin undershirts and drawers."

The leading grocers, Pease and Taylor, began putting in extra stocks of everything from fancy groceries, flour, feed and grain to fence posts, and baled hay. I. C. Whipple, another pioneer grocer, whose store and stock had been wiped out by fire six months previous, was now ready for business in a new building that was heated with a "hot air heating plant." As mayor of the "Magic City," Whipple was identified with every progressive movement and was convinced that Cheyenne would be a permanent key city.

Converse & Warren, who handled everything in the general furniture line from milk crocks to carpets, added what they thought outfitters for the Hills might need.

Henry Houseman, hardware dealer, spent busy hours estimating how many picks, shovels, and gold pans he should include in his spring orders. George D. Fogelsong & Company doubled their stock of California woolens, heavy boots and shoes, and other "furnishing goods."

But most important of all, Abney, Tracy, Ward, and others, who were running livery stables, began scouting the country for all available horses and work cattle suitable for transportation purposes.

Early in march 1875, the citizenry of Wyoming territory gave a brilliant reception in Cheyenne, in honor of John M. Thayer, former United States senator from Nebraska, who had arrived to succeed Governor John A. Campbell, as the chief executive of Wyoming.

Unlike so many so-called "carpet baggers," who had been awarded western political plums, Governor Thayer was familiar with Wyoming's people and their problems. He had been running cattle on the Laramie plains, near Rock creek, in Albany county, for four years. He believed implicitly in the great future of the western country and began an active campaign to open up that part of Wyoming now closed under Indian treaty.

Cheyenne was pleased not only with the new governor, but was also enthusiastic over the recent announcement that General George Crook would succeed General Ord, as commander of the department of the Platte. Since Crook had been successful in subduing the Apaches, it was felt that his appointment foreshadowed an aggressive and vigorous policy on the part of the government, against the Sioux. This, it was hoped, would speed entrance into the "Land of Gold."

Congress had under consideration an amendment to the Indian appropriation bill, by which it was proposed to pay the Sioux fifty thousand dollars, if they would surrender the lands north of the Platte river and east of the summits of the Big Horn mountains, in the territory of Wyoming, claimed by them under treaty stipulations.

When the amendment was presented, a newspaper reporter, in all seriousness asked, "Does the government have that much money?"

Few imagined that almost two years would elapse before the legal surrender of the Black Hills.

Go North, Young Man!

After the february thaws, the road down White
Earth river to the agencies was reported clear of snow.
Wagon wheels again rolled northward out of Cheyenne.
In addition to the sugar, flour, bacon, and other Indian
"goods," there was being transported to Fort Laramie,
the material for the new bridge over the North Platte
river.

Early in march 1875, two members of the Gordon
party, Thomas McLaren and Charles Blackwell, who
had made their way on foot from the stockade on
French creek, arrived at Fort Laramie. They proved
through the actual display of gold dust, that the persistent rumors concerning their new diggings were true.
They reported that their companions were settled in a
comfortable stockade, but were short of rations and
mining tools.

Closely following their arrival, others came into
Fort Laramie from the stockade. All had fine specimens of ore and claimed to have found gold "everywhere."

As soon as the reports from the various new arrivals
went out over the telegraph wires and appeared in
print in the newspapers, Cheyenne was deluged with
inquiries. Mayor Whipple telegraphed to Washington,

D.C., that there was "great excitement in Wyoming." He urged that the Indian country be opened at once.

The government replied that it was planning to bring a delegation of Sioux to Washington immediately, to treat for the cession of the Hills and the hunting rights in Wyoming.

Upon receipt of such reassuring news, the Cheyenne *Leader* ran big headlines:

Glorious News from Washington – The Black Hills and Northern Wyoming To Be Opened – Nine Cheers for Everybody in Washington! Let Old Glory Wave! Northw'd Empire Takes Its Way.

On that same evening the court room in Cheyenne was "crowded to suffocation," as gold-fevered men listened to J. Newton Warren, newly arrived from the Gordon stockade, tell of his experiences on French creek. Warren brought the meeting to a high pitch with the announcement that he was enlisting two hundred to three hundred men for an expedition, which he would pilot to Custer's valley, as soon as outfitted. He hoped, he said, to be able to leave in about twenty days. Volunteers swarmed to join him.

But before the designated twenty days elapsed, the secretary of War issued an order to "prevent any further expedition from going into that part of the Indian territory known as the Black Hills country, as long as the present treaty exists."

And up in Fort Laramie, two arrivals from the Gordon stockade, J. J. Williams and Dan McDonald, were "detained" by the military and taken back as guides for Captain Mix and his men, who were dispatched to bring out the miners on French creek.

In the meantime the demand for transportation to Red Cloud agency, "the jumping off place" to the French creek area, had become so great, that Hoshier & Cinnamond took over the mail line then being operated by Todd Randall, an agency trader. On march 8, the new owners launched what they termed the "Pioneer stage line to the Black Hills," under the name of The Spotted Tail Express and Stage company. H. S. Tracy, one-time sutler at Fort Morgan, Colorado was the Cheyenne agent for the company.

The first stage out, which left the headquarters at the Great Western Corral at O'Neill and Twenty-fifth streets, on march 8, 1875, carried three "gold prospectors." They boasted that if they could find a way to traverse the fifty miles from the agencies to the Hills, there would not be enough troops in the department of the Platte to find them.

The stages on the new line left Cheyenne at two o'clock every monday and thursday afternoon and returned on tuesday and saturday. This time schedule was in effect until the following august, when Tracy bought Cinnamond's half of the stage line. The company then operating as Tracy and Hoshier, changed the Cheyenne leaving time to seven o'clock in the morning.

Although the mail had been transported to the agencies for several years, the carrying of express and passengers by a regular stage was an innovation.

Men knew that orders had been issued by the government forbidding them to enter the Hills, yet, with about the same amount of reason as each individual hoped to pick up huge gold nuggets along every stream bed, each hoped that Washington would play the role of an expert locksmith and would swing open the doors of the Hills over night. They did not reckon with the slow moving temperament of the Sioux.

For some time a number of business men in Cheyenne had felt that the shortest and best route to French creek would be due north from Fort Laramie, instead of by the way of Red Cloud agency. Thence to Raw Hide Buttes, Old Woman's fork and Beaver creek, then along the old Custer trail to the diggings in Custer's park. It was established that the distance by this route would be about 182 miles to the south fork of the Cheyenne, as compared with 195½ miles by way of Red Cloud agency.

The following tables appeared in the Cheyenne *Daily Leader*, march 15, 1875, showing comparative estimated distances.

		Miles	*Total*
Cheyenne to	Pole creek, Schwartze ranch	18	
	Horse creek, Fagan's ranch	11	29
	Chugwater, Phillips's ranch	24	53
	Hunton's ranch (Bordeaux)	14	67
	Owen's ranch	4	71
	Eagle's Nest	7	78
	Six Mile ranch	14	92
	Fort Laramie	6	98
	Spring Branch	12	110
	Raw Hide	12	122
	Running Water	15	137
	Headwaters Old Woman's fork	12	149
	Down this stream to Lightning Cr.	12	161
	Down Beaver creek	12	173
	Down So. Fork of Cheyenne at Black Hills	9	182

Distances on the "Lower road," crossing the North

Platte river at Nick Janis's ranch, about thirty miles east of Fort Laramie:

	Miles	Total
Cheyenne to Reel's ranch	18	
Pole creek	2	20
Spring creek	20	40
La Grange ranch	4	44
1st Crossing of Horse creek	1	45
2nd " " " "	11	56
Campbell ranch	3	59
3rd Crossing of Horse creek	14	73
North Platte river	6	79
Spoon Butte	16	95
Niobrara Butte	21	116
Ft. Laramie road	13	129
Spring branch (Trib. White Earth)	5	134
Red Cloud agency	11½	145½
Black Hills	50	195½

J. C. Abney, manager of a weekly mail and stage line on which he accommodated passengers from Cheyenne to Fort Laramie, expressed willingness to extend his line north to the Hills, as soon as the government would give permission.

No longer now was it a matter of interesting men to join exploring expeditions; the question at hand was one of actual transportation, as soon as the Sioux treaty should be abrogated.

Soon after Captain Mix and his men escorted the Gordon "intruders" out of the Hills, the military authorities decided to headquarter troops on French creek, to keep all miners out.

Immediately upon learning of the proposed garrison, the Cheyenne press said: "The man or company who will put a line of stages from this city to Montana via

Custer's park, the new military station, will make a for-
tune in a few years."

On march 20, 1875, a group of Cheyenne businessmen met to consider the organization of a transportation company to operate over the proposed new direct-
north route, instead of by way of the agencies. And thus,
the seed was planted for the establishment of the later
world-known Cheyenne and Black Hills trail.

In hoping to win all possible consideration from the
authorities in Washington, Cheyenne tried for a time
to restrain the gold hunters from going into the Hills.

In reply to a query from the general ticket agent of
the Union Pacific at Omaha about transportation companies at Cheyenne "that will carry passengers to the
Black Hills," the editor of the *Leader* said positively:

Citizens of Cheyenne do not propose to get up organizations to do
illegal acts and violate the laws and treaties of the United States.

But soon afterward, when a telegraphic dispatch
from Omaha announced that a coach and four from
Sidney, Nebraska would be put on at once to the Hills,
by one George W. Homan, jr., Editor Glafcke of the
Leader, seized his pen and wrote:

If the Union Pacific and Omaha can induce miners to go past Cheyenne and stop at Sidney, then will its merchants vend whiskey and
bacon, and flour and whiskey, and whiskey and yeast powders, and
picks and whiskey, and whiskey and shovels, and beer and whiskey,
and whiskey and beer to the "millions" of miners who will be obliged
to outfit at that place, before starting for Sidney. Sidney will not be
able to outfit the myriads of people who will flock to it as a departing
point, so Omaha will have to, and thus reap immense gains and
profits. . . We are incredibly informed that one of these days three
great corporations, Union Pacific railroad, Omaha and Sidney will

put on a "stage" line from Sidney direct to Harney Peak. Already a buckboard has been secured to this end, which has been transported to Sidney, over the u.p. from Omaha on a "special" flat car right side up with care. A distinguished citizen of Omaha is now in Cheyenne and vicinity, looking to the purchase of four bronchos, to be harnessed to this buckboard, and when this purchase of stock shall take place, then the "stage line" will be in existence. . . The quartette of bronchos, gaily caparisoned will be brought out prancing and amid the plaudits of a motley crowd, lashed to the buckboard. . . The passengers will climb aboard the springy plank with blankets and picks, and shovels, and rockers, and long-toms, and short ones, and guns and ammunition; . . the prominent citizen of Omaha will settle himself on the for'ard end of the buckboard as the jehu and at the word "All aboard!" will grapple the ribbons, and taking the north star for his guide across the trackless, sandy waste, will give rein to his bronchos. . . Then will the air be rent with the deafening screeches of the steam whistles and the jubilant cheers of the multitude at Sidney. Away will fly the bronchos and the "stage" and soon they will disappear from the view in the clouds of alkaline dust and drifting sand back of Sidney. . . A nice jiggity jog ride to Harney Peak.

But the above mentioned "distinguished citizen of Omaha," George W. Homan, proprietor of the City Omnibus line in that city, who had been in the transportation business there for five years, had not yet made up his mind as to the exact location of his proposed stage line.

He had just returned to Omaha from Chicago, where he had obtained from the Union Pacific railroad assurance that it would "stick by him" wherever he established his route. The company agreed to sell the stage ticket, to advertise the route, to pro-rate with Homan on through fares from the east to the Black Hills and to encourage travel by way of his stage, regardless of where it ran.

Homan wrote to A. R. Converse, Cheyenne businessman, explaining the backing which he had obtained from the railway and stating that he would consider starting his stage from Cheyenne, rather than from Sidney, if the Wyoming businessmen would extend to him substantial aid such as that offered by the Sidneyites.

Homan informed Converse:

Have also seen General Perry and the officials of this department. They agree to protect my line either from Sidney or Cheyenne, providing the government permits me to put it on. I prefer Cheyenne to Sidney, but the latter you know, is the shortest route. . . If things are satisfactory, I will agree to run a four-horse stage line from Cheyenne to the Black Hills, daily or twice a day, if the travel justifies it, to build my own stations, to stock the line with American horses and put everything in first class order as soon as government will permit.

Headed by Converse, a number of Cheyenne merchants considered Homan's proposition, but they were not enthusiastic about having an "outsider" subsidized by Wyoming money. Many felt that a stage line to the Hills should be established by Cheyenne's own citizens, as soon as feasible.

Homan, however, was not easily discouraged. He asked the Laramie county commissioners to appropriate five thousand dollars toward construction of a stage road. The commissioners promptly agreed. They suggested that perhaps part of an old freighting road between Fort Laramie and Fort Pierre via the Niobrara river, which had been used some years previous, could be put into shape. This old road, well known to the military and to early day freighters, led north twenty miles from Fort Laramie to the Raw Hide creek area, thence twenty-five miles to the crossing of the Niobrara, and paralleled Old Woman's fork of the Cheyenne river.

The wheels of the sixty gu.............t wagons and the hoofs of the horses that were ridden and driven by the four hundred men in the geological expedition, then going into the field from Fort Laramie, under the leadership of Professor Walter P. Jenney, helped to grind into the sagebrush and ravines part of this old trail. It later did become an important segment of the Black Hills stage route.

With the backing of the Laramie county commissioners[11] at Cheyenne, Homan, believing that the Hills soon would be opened, made definite arrangements to put on a daily line of stages from Cheyenne northward to the western slope of the Hills, without delay.

He arranged with Jack Hughes, an experienced stageman of Denver, for the purchase of ten stagecoaches and began lining up horses. By may 27, 1875, he had all preliminary plans perfected to establish the line of stages to Harney's peak in Custer park.

While Homan was busy organizing the proposed new line, the words "Cheyenne," "Wyoming," and "Black Hills" were on men's tongues in every mud hamlet, village, "ranche," town or city of the country, especially in those along the Union Pacific, Kansas Pacific, Central Pacific, and Colorado Central railways, where thousands of men were hoping soon to try their fortunes in the new gold fields.

Large expeditions were being organized in Boston, Milwaukee, St. Louis, Philadelphia, Chicago, Mem-

---

[11] A memorandum of agreement between George W. Homan, Jr., and G. A. Draper, chairman of the board of county commissioners, was filed in the county clerk's office at Cheyenne, june 2, 1875.

phis, San Francisco, Brooklyn, New Orleans, New York City, Harrisburg, Lebanon, Lancaster, and in many other places.

The outstanding Black Hills promoters at that time were: Colonel C. C. Carpenter, commander of the Jessie Scouts in the "late unpleasantness," who was operating from 1200 Clark avenue, St. Louis; J. S. White of Philadelphia; and Dr. William Wright and D. K. Allen, of the Boston Black Hills expedition. Added interest was aroused at the Boston meetings by William F. (Buffalo Bill) Cody and Kit Carson, jr., friends of Allen.

It was predicted that fifteen hundred men would leave Kansas City in may for Cheyenne, as special through-trains could be made up there.

Some communities, fearing to be tricked by sharpers, raised money and sent fellow townsmen to scout conditions at Sidney and Cheyenne.

Rivalry between Cheyenne and other "ports of departure" increased. Sioux City, Iowa held the spotlight of the Missouri valley excitement, because some members of the Gordon party had returned there direct from French creek in Custer park.

Along the Union Pacific route, Sidney, Nebraska was not the only aspirant just then to being a gateway to the land of gold. North Platte and Columbus strove to be "rallying points." In Columbus, a large brick building facing the Union Pacific tracks bore a sign painted in black letters on a white ground which read: BLACK HILLS AND COLUMBUS MINING CLUB AND TRANSPORTATION COMPANY.

Cheyenne fumed, blustered, and fretted over such rivalry and prayed that the Sioux delegation, scheduled to go to Washington, D.C., to discuss treaty terms, would hurry up and get going. But there was considerable delay while the Indians waited for first one chief and then another one to come into the agencies from their various camps.

At last the Indians reached Cheyenne on may 10, and put up at the Railroad house. In the evening they visited McDaniels' theatre and gave vent to their delight with the performance with many "Hows" and "Ughs." Spotted Tail, one of the most interested spectators, had been a theater visitor on previous occasions. He also had become an enthusiast over the "snow in summer" sold at the Ellis Ice Cream parlor.

As the delegation, including Red Cloud, Spotted Tail and Mrs. Spot, and many others of the "breech clouted gang," as the Cheyenne press called them, departed for Washington, to have a big talk with the Great White Father, Cheyenneites hoped they would take a few quick puffs of kinnikinnick, put their X's on the dotted line, and be back on their reservations by the time all of the ice was out of the streams in the Black Hills.

But no sooner had the Indians reached Washington than they sent back to the agencies for additional interpreters. They told the Great White Father how dissatisfied they were with their Indian agents. They demanded millions of dollars for the Hills. They were disgruntled over their hotel accommodations. They declared they were getting nowhere in their negotiations.

The government officials were suspicious of the half-breed and "squawmen" interpreters, whom they termed "mischief makers," and were trying to be firm with the Sioux, but also were getting nowhere.

After pow-wows with President U. S. Grant, Secretary of the Interior Delano, and various other high officials, the Indian delegation left Washington early in june (1875) in bad temper. The matter pertaining to the opening of the Hills remained unchanged. Tomorrow would inevitably be filled with delay.

Bitterly the western newspapers referred to the members of the delegation as "Thieves with feathers in their hair," "Old stick-in-the-mud," "Man-afraid-of-his-horses-voices," "Old man-with-a-peeled nose," and the "Noble red men who have been to Washington to eat strawberries, drink whisky, and visit bawdy houses."

President Grant, it was reported, had done all in his power to bring the Indians to an agreement concerning the relinquishment of the Black Hills, but they refused to sign any paper because of the lack of agreement among the several bands of the Sioux and because they said they wanted to go home and "talk things over" with their people. They refused to be rushed into anything.

The Indians were excellent "copy" and their stopovers in New York and Chicago made many columns in the news. One outstanding feature of the return trip was a visit to Gilmore's garden in company with Buffalo Bill.

Back again in Cheyenne, the Indians expressed much pleasure at the entertainment provided for them by James McDaniels. In addition to having them as his theater guests, McDaniels gave each Indian a $5.00 note and numerous presents of clothing from B. Hellman's store.

And in order that each chief might go back to his people "in style," the government arranged through

Ward & Mason of Cheyenne, to present to each one, an outfit costing $100, including a horse, bridle, saddle, blanket, and lariat.

The government appointed a commission to carry on treaty negotiations with the Sioux, which meant that many weeks would elapse before the Hills possibly could be thrown open to settlement. The weeks might become months or even years.

Although George Homan was ready and anxious to start the wheels of his stage line to rolling, he held up his plans pending the Indian commissioners' parley.

While the Indians had been pow-wowing in Washington, there were tragic days that spring and early summer of 1875 for the "pilgrims," as the newcomers to the west were dubbed. At that time, Wyoming territory experienced unprecedented weather. There was rain on sixty-seven consecutive days. For a period of about three weeks the sun was scarcely seen at all. There were also severe thunderstorms, followed later in the season by terrific hail storms. During one such storm a Cheyenne resident reported that, "a gold pan outside was stove full of holes. Largest hail I ever seen." On june 2, it snowed for several hours at Fort Laramie.

More than one thousand men in wagons, on horseback, or on foot slogged and sloshed over the Cheyenne-Fort Laramie road in may. During june, Cheyenne was crowded with men in parties varying from five to twenty in number, who outfitted daily. All headed northward. They hoped that encouraging news from Washington soon would permit them to cross the Laramie river Hillward.

The various divisions of Colonel Carpenter's big

eastern expedition, which reached Cheyenne under the leadership of William (Idaho Bill) Sloan,[12] Captain McBrine, Lieutenant Blackwood, and the Colonel himself, went over the rain-soaked roads to a camp about three miles from Fort Laramie, near the Coffey and Cuny ranch. There they huddled around dismal, spluttering campfires, waiting for the "go ahead" signal.

But there were many who did not wait. Some swam the Platte or bribed the ferryman at Fort Laramie[13] to take them across. Some paid freighters of Indian goods to hide them in wagons and thus negotiated the treacherous high-tide stream without being detected by the military.

After the Sioux returned from Washington and it was apparent that negotiations for the Hills would be prolonged, Colonel Carpenter disbanded his expedition. Many of the men returned to their homes in the "states," disgruntled and disillusioned. Others, including the Colonel, struck out for the Hills "on their own."

By conservative estimate, at least six hundred to eight hundred men had evaded the authorities and were engaged in prospecting and mining in the Hills by july. Many of them kept close enough to the Jenney exploration party to be within the protecting shadow of its military escort, led by Colonel R. I. Dodge.

Dodge and his soldiers did not disturb the miners. And when, on july 17, Professor Jenney sent word to

---

[12] William (Idaho Bill) Sloan, born at Johnny Grant's American Fur company's camp no. 15, at American falls on Snake river, had spent thirty-two years of his life in the west and in British Columbia. He was considered a most able man to pilot Black Hillers.

[13] S. B. Davis said he paid ten dollars for crossing the Platte on the ferry at midnight, june 26, 1875.

Cheyenne that he had "discovered gold in paying quantities in gravelbars on both Spring and Rapid creeks," a bulletin was posted at McDaniels theatre in the city, fireworks were set off, and the citizens of the town hilariously congratulated themselves upon the good word.

But Captain Edwin Pollock and the troops assigned to patrol the southern part of the Hills, against the invasion of white men, continued to execute their orders to the letter. They constantly pursued the miners, arrested them, in some instances placed them in close confinement on hard tack and water, and took them as quickly as possible to Camp Sheridan, Camp Robinson, or Fort Laramie. There the soldiers turned them over to the civil authorities.

Curiously enough, the civil authorities released the prisoners without bail. Hence the interlopers usually retraced their steps immediately to the Hills. One prospector said later that he had been captured and sent out of the Hills four times in three months, but guessed he could stand it as long as the military could.

Cognizant of the game of hide-and-seek which the military was playing with the miners, and how next to impossible it was to keep men out of the region by this pursuit-and-capture method, General George Crook went into the Hills to map out a plan of action. He mingled with the miners and even panned out gold.

The general was inclined to be more lenient with the trespassers than Captain Pollock had been, because he knew that more than four hundred of the horses, which had been stolen recently from settlers along the line of the Union Pacific, had been trailed to the Sioux reservation. When Crook reminded the prospectors that they were violating the treaty by being in the Hills, they pointed out to him how the Indians had violated the treaty hundreds of times in their predatory excursions. He knew they spoke the truth.

The general decided to reason with the men and to put them on their honor. He issued a proclamation that all must be out of the Hills by august 15. He suggested that they hold a miners' meeting on august 10, to make provision for their future interests, and then leave voluntarily.

Crook's firm but fair policy, backed by his word, did more in a few days than the troops had accomplished in weeks. Some of the men, knowing that they must leave their prospects for the time being, organized societies based upon Masonic lines. The members took oath not to reveal any discoveries to others. Some regular mining districts already had been organized, including the Jenney Mining district and the Buckeye Mining district.

Colonel Richard I. Dodge, who attended the miners' meeting in Custer valley on august 10, said:

Here was a most motley collection of citizens of all ages and conditions of manhood, voluntarily relinquishing the bright anticipations and promises of wealth, cheerful, and if not contented, willingly acquiescing in the execution of an obnoxious law. Here were men with bottles and vials of the precious grains, as evidence of their success in mining, leaving rich prospects and in their opinion, sure pecuniary independence. Far outnumbering the scanty force of troops, completely armed, inured to all the hardships and dangers of the frontier, they would have been no despicable enemy to encounter even in a pitched fight, on open ground . . . never have I seen a body of men which gave me a grander idea of the inherent value and true worth of American men, and American institutions.

Dodge reported that sixty-five of the miners organized a mining district, elected officers, drew up rules and regulations and then on their honor left their fields of gold. Dodge continued:

By sunrise the morning of august 12, not a man or animal was to be seen. The valley, so lately bustling with life, was still and solitary. Thin wreaths of smoke, arising from expiring campfires, were all that remained to tell of the swarm of people which crowded the valley only the day before.

The miners fixed forty days as the margin, after the opening of the Black Hills, for claim holders to return and repossess their claims.

A townsite, which had been laid out in a grassy basin on French creek, later became the terminus of the through Cheyenne and Black Hills stage line. It was named Custer City.

Joseph Reynolds of Georgetown, Colorado, who had bribed his way into the Hills in may, with a freighter of Indian supplies, made hurried arrangements with Case Brothers to haul out the 2,250 pounds of quartz, which he had mined. In Cheyenne he sampled the ore and then sent it to Georgetown, Colorado to be tested. The highest grade samples yielded seventeen dollars per ton of quartz. This was said to have been the first large shipment of ore transported on wheels, out of the Black Hills, for treatment.

As hundreds of miners turned their backs on their prized prospects, Captain Edwin Pollock[14] of the Ninth Infantry, assumed command of the new post in Custer valley, called Camp Harney. Pollock finished

---

[14] Retired from the army in 1885, Captain Pollock soon met his death by falling down stairs in the Inter-Ocean hotel in Cheyenne.

building a log structure that had been started by Dr. D. M. Flick, and occupied the cabin as headquarters. He was assisted by one troop each of the Second and Third Cavalry.

For the next three months, until about november 17, Pollock and his men scoured the Hills for gold hunters, made a number of arrests, and performed their assigned duties in a creditable manner. In november the troops went into winter quarters at Fort Laramie.

When the members of the Indian Peace commission reached Red Cloud agency early in september, they found about twenty thousand Indians, with great herds of ponies, camped for miles and miles around and along the banks of White Earth river. There was much bickering over the location of a council grounds, quarreling among tribes, and resentment among the Indians at what they said was government pressure being brought to bear to hurry their deliberations.

It was reported that Spotted Tail (Old Spot), wanted six million dollars for the Black Hills plus "eighty years' boarding, clothing, and washing for the members of the tribes thereof. How!" Another chief wanted seventy million dollars. The commissioners felt that the demands of the Indians were exorbitant and out of all reason.

The situation soon became critical. The commissioners feared for their lives, but matters were kept in hand through the intervention of friendly Indians.

Writing about events of the third day at the council, one of the eye witnesses said:

Little Big Man came to the ground naked, threatening to kill a white man. A lot of the hostile young bucks got behind the cavalry and loaded their rifles, and things looked a little mixed. Sitting Bull, to whom the president presented a rifle this spring, stepped into the circle with his gun in one hand and a war club in the other and said he would kill the first Indian who fired a shot.

After strenuous efforts to persuade the Sioux to cede the Hills, the commissioners admitted defeat and departed. The Indians, who refused to talk, trailed to their tepees in bad temper.

And as the frost of autumn colored the hills and valleys with golds and bronze, bands of marauding Indians began serious depredations below the North Platte river and sometimes within forty miles of Cheyenne. They raided stock ranches, killed and scalped herders and shot twenty-five head of work cattle in an attack on a freight outfit near Bridger's Ferry on the North Platte.

Commissioner Smith of Indian Affairs admitted that the "experience of the past summer proved the utter impracticability of keeping American citizens out of a country where gold exists, by any fear of a cavalry patrol or by any consideration of the rights of the Indians." He also said that he felt that the "display of military force in the Black Hills operates as the surest safeguard of the miners against the attacks of the Indians. . . Some of the miners have brought suits against the military officers for false imprisonment, and much embarrassment to both the Army and the Interior department is the result."

Despite General Crook's orders and requests, a party of thirty miners, including T. H. Mallory, secretary of the Buckeye Mining district, crossed the Platte above Fort Laramie in september and arrived in due time on Iron creek in northeastern Wyoming even while the commissioners were counseling with the Sioux.

How many men pushed their way into the Hills

that autumn will never be known. When the Denver *Tribune* in october, reported that "four citizens will start for the Black Hills this week," the Cheyenne *Leader* announced that "Four are leaving Cheyenne *every minute.*" And that was just about true!

Typical of the experiences of many of the "sooners" who pushed their way north in that early winter of 1875, was that of George W. Stokes, one of a party of four who penetrated Dakota in december.

This little party followed Jenney's expedition's route. Stokes said:

At the Custer stockade, near the present site of Custer City, South Dakota, and along French creek, we left several groups already settled for the winter and ventured into the unknown but supposedly richer gold fields to the northward.

We four partners had laid in a six months supply of miners' and soldiers' rations at Denver and Cheyenne, except fresh meat. On the way from the railroad we had been eating buffalo and antelope and we knew that the hills sheltered plenty of black and white tailed deer.

Over the divide we at once struck Spring creek, reputed to be the best prospecting stream visited by Jenney. Ten miles down we found several prospect holes offering some encouragement, so we made a midday camp and found a meadow half a mile wide washed by a considerable stream that debouched into Spring creek, with plenty of spruce and jack pine at hand. After dinner we looked over the land, voted to move in and Palmer's Gulch was born.

Everybody rejoiced. The tired horses rolled in the belly deep sun cured grass. We had fuel, water and protection from the northeast winds and were a half mile from the only road, but out of sight from it. Nothing bothered us except the inevitable snows and ice of Dakota. We had a wall tent, two axes, a four foot cross-cut saw, hatchet, plenty of picks and shovels and a keg of assorted nails to work with.

Two of the party were expert ax men. Another killed a couple of blacktails – mule deer – before dark the next day. I snaked in logs, which were quickly notched. Sheets of slate were got out for the chimney and stiff clay dug for mortar and floor covering. We used a pair of horses with lariats to parbuckle the logs after four tiers had been rolled or lifted by hand. A section sawed out of a log in each cabin prepared the way for a canvas covered window.

We cut up parts of the wagon bodies to make doors and two boot legs provided the material for the hinges. Rude benches and dining tables were made from split puncheons. Poles and balsam boughs were first class materials for bunks; upon these we placed sweet smelling mattresses of hay and covered them with our wagon sheets. The roofs were made of straight poles covered with spruce boughs and overlaid with clay, and the soft soil floors were vigorously tamped with moist clay . . . two very satisfactory cabins were our homes for nearly six months. Before the first real snowfall we moved into them, happy and carefree.

On december 23, I made, I think, the first washboard used north of Fort Laramie. Taking a two-foot piece of pine I split and hewed off the sap and heart until I had a slab a foot wide and an inch and a half thick. With a pencil I drew lines across the slab half an inch apart; then with saw and pocket knife I notched out a fairly effective washboard. My fellows did me high honor and that washboard worked practically three eight-hour shifts for the next few days.

With that pride which presages fall, I attempted a Christmas pie. Thinking to surprise the boys I suggested that one of the partners, who had been a hotel man, take a saddle horse and bear our Christmas greetings to a neighbor down the gulch; and in some way I managed to get rid of the other two. Then I brought out the dried apples, sugar, baking powder, and, of course, flour.

Having no butter, I used deer fat. With this abundant material I built a pie entirely satisfactory to my eye and hid it pending the return of my mates and the approach of the dinner hour. Later I learned that dried apples were usually subjected to a preliminary cooking before being incorporated into a pie; also that a tin cup full of venison lard was a little more than one pie required. So any credit I gained by means of my washboard fell before the gibes of the more expert cooks.[15]

[15] Casper (Wyoming) *Daily Tribune*, july 27, 1922.

The Wheels Roll Hillward

Although the Indians had not yet surrendered the Hills, Judge William L. Kuykendall of Cheyenne, on november 11, 1875, introduced into the territorial legislature "An act to locate and establish a territorial wagon road from Cheyenne to the Black Hills of Wyoming and Dakota."

This bill, which became a law on december 1, declared, "the present traveled wagon road from Cheyenne, by way of Chugwater creek and Fort Laramie, to Custer City, in the Black Hills . . ." to be a territorial road, and provided that upon the petition of 100 residents of Laramie county, the county commissioners should appoint a road commissioner to "proceed to locate, or supervise the location of such road, over the nearest and most practicable route . . . on the west side of said Black Hills, if a good, practicable route therefor can be obtained."

An appropriation of two hundred dollars was authorized to take care of the expenses of the road commissioner.

On the same day that the road bill passed both houses of the legislature, W. M. Ward introduced a bill in the council to legalize the contract of the county commissioners with George W. Homan, jr., for the establishment of a daily line of stages between Cheyenne and the Black Hills and the Big Horn country.

The bill was approved by the council and passed by the house unanimously on december 8, 1875.

Because Laramie county, of which Cheyenne was the county seat, as well as the capital of the territory, stretched from the southern boundary of Wyoming almost four hundred miles up to the Montana line, the legislature decided to create a new county in the north-eastern part of the territory. This new division named Crook, which was made from northern Laramie county, included some of the "diggings" on the western slope of the Black Hills in the Sand creek area. The county, however, existed in name only until it was organized ten years later.

Upon being notified of the favorable action taken by the legislature, Homan, then in Omaha, announced that he had purchased one hundred and fifty good American horses for his new line and that he intended to start the stages early in the spring. He also said that General Phil Sheridan had assured him that the travel "will not be interfered with by the soldiers."

In the meantime, the only means of sending mail to and from the Hills was by entrusting it to freighters or anyone willing to carry it.

Starting on thursday morning, december 23, V. Dunlap, who claimed to have carried mail the previous year from Sioux City to the Black Hills, announced that he was establishing a pony express between Cheyenne and the new mining camps. He proposed to go through in five days. He asked that mail be deposited at Dyer's hotel. How long the "express" existed is not of record.

One great boon to the Black Hills travel was the completion of the iron bridge over the North Platte river at Fort Laramie in december, which was officially

THE WHEELS ROLL HILLWARD

accepted within two months. The bridge was looked upon as a magic key to the forbidden land of gold.

It had been one thing to sneak into the Hills on foot, "on the dodge" from the military. It was an entirely different matter for wagons to rumble across the new bridge, thence across the sacred hunting grounds! And rumble they did! That is, the wagons of the freighters.

Among those who hauled loads of merchandise from Cheyenne to the heart of the Hills with four-horse teams and wagons during the last months of 1875 were: Emil Faust, H. B. Young, W. H. Cole, and L. D. Waln, who had outfitted with Whipple and Hay, also Cuthbertson and Young. Waln carried freight at five cents a pound and passengers for ten dollars each. Cole's load of twelve thousand pounds of assorted merchandise, contained among other things, rice and "other necessaries of life" for Hop Lee, Ding Dong, Heap Wash, and Hang Jeff, so-called "Celestial chuckleheads from the Flowery Kingdom." Al Hong and Hong Lee went along with full laundry outfits.

Close in their tracks went Dick Dunne's six ox-teams, with a sawmill and supplies for M. V. Boughton; medicines, dental and surgical instruments for Dr. James Lehane; and a stock of store goods and hardware for James Droney of St. Louis.

By the time the wheels came to a stop in the Hills, log cabins were being completed in Custer, Hillyo, and on Rapid creek. Men going north, met other men coming south with pack animals carrying coarse gold, which had been acquired at the diggings in amounts running up to twenty dollars a day.

Early in december, the commissioner of Indian affairs ordered the Indian agents along the Missouri river to notify the Indians in the unceded territory that if they did not come into the agencies before january 31, 1876, they would be regarded as "hostiles." This order did not reach the agents until late in december. The messenger to the Indian camps up in the Big Horn country did not get back to Red Cloud agency until early in february. Because of the winter weather, the Indians remained in their camps in the north and did not come in to the agencies at the designated time.

Throughout the eastern states, "evangelists," including such enthusiasts as Captain Russell, George H. Newton, Colonel C. C. Carpenter, and Capt. J. M. Cummings, were telling of the expeditions being recruited to go to the Hills. Handbills by the thousands were being distributed in every direction. Nothing now could stem the tide of gold seekers which was to roll toward the Hills during the next few months.

Although Cheyenne had experienced three disastrous fires in 1875, she quickly rebuilt and soon boasted new brick "blocks," including thirteen two-story buildings and a number of brick residences. There still were, however, many structures which were described locally as having "Queene Anne fronts" and "Mary Ann backs." Some had stovepipes protruding from window panes instead of going up out of the roofs. The severe winds were blamed with forcing such means of ventilation.

Cattlemen by 1876 were enlarging their herds and were pushing them to the very fringe of the Sioux country; mining interests were being developed in numerous localities in southern and west-central Wyoming. Fort D. A. Russell and Fort Sanders hummed with activity as horses were shod, wagons were put into order, and troops made ready to campaign in the Big Horn country, in pursuit of all "hostile" Indians, who had not returned to their reservations, as ordered.

During those busy days the hotels in Cheyenne vied for patronage. The proprietors employed energetic runners or criers to attract business as the trains pulled into the depot. Joe of the Railroad house was said to lead his crowd by "ten pound Websterian words." Bernard, with the persuasive eloquence of a Calhoun drew patrons to Ford's Inter-Ocean, which was "in style and magnificence fully equal to the Grand Central in Omaha." The "straight forward story told by the Dyer's hotel bus driver was not in vain" (*see plate* 2) and the prolific distribution of the Eagle hotel cards had its effect.

The limited equipment of Tracy and Hoshier, who were then operating the semi-weekly stage between Cheyenne and Spotted Tail agency, was quite inadequate to take care of transportation demands.

On january 6, 1876, J. C. Abney, owner of one of the largest livery stables in Cheyenne, advertised as follows:

Those who want to start for the Black Hills this morning can be accommodated by Mr. Abney. He has room for a number of passengers, who will be permitted to walk behind his team; passage $5.00 each. Apply at the Elkhorn livery office.

On that same morning, a terrific blizzard struck Wyoming, but Abney loaded a wagon with "blacksmith's tools, crackers, apothecary shop, bacon and three Chinamen," who were planning to "establish a 'washee house' at the mines." W. A. Dearie and Henry Boltz, in charge of Abney's outfit went over "Pollock's

Cut-off," which turned right about three miles north of Sage creek and proceeded to Red canyon by way of what later became Edgemont, South Dakota, instead of taking the longer agency route. They reached Custer in twelve days.

In the meantime, while George W. Homan, jr., was busy in Cheyenne and along his proposed stage route, making arrangements with various ranchmen to maintain stage stations south of Fort Laramie, J. W. Dear, a trader at the Red Cloud agency, who was reputed to be a "man with a nerve of iron, most enterprising and honorable," made plans to establish "road ranches" north of the fort to be used as stage stations and to accommodate travelers. Whether Dear intended to sell or lease them to Homan is not clear.

The building of stations in that northern area was the boldest stroke yet undertaken by anyone, as the proposed stage route lay in the direct path of the Indians' hunting trails. There was at that time not a dwelling along the proposed route between Fort Laramie and the mining camps.

Since Dear was familiar with the Indian character, it was felt in Cheyenne that he "knew what he was about." His plans called for the first road ranch to be built about fifteen miles north of Fort Laramie on the site called Government Farm; the next, thirty miles north on Running Water (Niobrara); one on Old Woman's fork of the Cheyenne river; the fourth, on Horse Head creek, and the farthest one on Cheyenne river, from which point it was said Custer City could be reached in a day and a half.

It was suggested that Homan call the new stage line "The Centennial Stage line," in honor of the anniversary of the Declaration of Independence.

Because he was not entirely satisfied that his way stations would be safe from Indian attack, and also because no government mail contract could be let until the Sioux relinquished their title to the Hills, Homan hesitated in starting the line.

Cheyenne businessmen, irked at his delay, emphasized the fact that the Indians had not disturbed the miners thus far. They said that they considered the proposed stage route north "as safe as the route between Cheyenne and Omaha." None of them, however, seemed anxious to gamble money on a stage line.

While others wavered, two men at the Red Cloud agency, Trader Frank Yates, and his father-in-law, Captain W. H. Brown, sub-contracted the mail to Spotted Tail and launched the *pioneer stage line* to Custer City, by way of the agencies and Red canyon.

The first trip was made by Captain Brown, who left Cheyenne for Red Cloud on january 27, 1876. In the diary of Isaac Bard, under that date, we find:

Mr. Brown came along stoped for dinner (Phillips ranch on Chugwater) first trip of the Black Hill stage line Left 3 horces with Mr. Phillips to be fed hay and grain down mail come along but did not stop

Cheyenne newspapers designated the trip on february 3 as the "initial trip," when the "first coach of the Cheyenne and Black Hills Stage, Mail and Express line, owned by F. D. Yates & Co., stopped in front of the Inter-Ocean hotel at 7 A.M. to pick up passengers." J. W. "Doc" Howard was holding the lines on this stage which left Cheyenne with seven passengers. [16]

It was from this same Inter-Ocean hotel and also in the month of february, eleven years later, that the last

[16] Howard, J. W. *"Doc" Howard's Memoirs* (Denver, 1931) p. 21.

stagecoach to leave Cheyenne for the Black Hills, rolled northward.

Headquarters of Yates & Company was at Joseph Mason's stables, 16th street near Ferguson (now Carey avenue). Tickets were on sale at the Inter-Ocean hotel and at Luke Murrin's saloon.

The first coach out was scheduled to make the trip to Custer, Dakota territory via Red Cloud agency and Spotted Tail, in five days. It was announced that for the first two weeks, the run would be made semi-weekly. After that, a daily stage would travel night and day. It was contemplated that four-horse coaches would be put on, with an extra team on the heavy sections of the route. A fixed amount of fare was not set at first, as it was felt it should be governed by the amount of travel.

Since Yates & Company had to carry mail to Red Cloud, it was more economical for them to operate the stage by the way of the agencies, rather than direct north from Fort Laramie to Custer valley. On february 5, the mail and stage route was reported to be "in excellent condition with very little snow."

The establishment of a line did not deter others from trying to organize similar enterprises. W. D. Terry, esq., of Terry Brothers, Topeka, Kansas wrote to W. M. Ward in Cheyenne, that he intended to start a stage line early in march. He said he had the harness ready and would purchase horses at once, and proposed to build temporary adobe barns at the stations along the route. He claimed to have completed arrangements with the Kansas Pacific railway relative to the sale of tickets, and wrote that as soon as a contract, "which has already been approved by President Dillon, of the Union

Pacific company is signed by Supt. Clark," he would come to Cheyenne and begin establishing the line.

Cheyenne businessmen beamed as various plans went forward. Competition, they knew, would keep passenger rates low, and increase the volume of traffic.

Within a day or so after Yates started his line, there arrived in Cheyenne from Salt Lake City, Utah, a man named H. E. ("Stuttering") Brown, a business scout for Gilmer, Salisbury and Patrick, widely known stage owners in Utah, Idaho, and Montana. (*see plate* 3.)

John (Jack) T. Gilmer, the senior partner of the firm, was one of the most experienced stage men in the entire west. He had skinned mules and whacked bulls for the great firm of Russell, Majors and Waddell, and as he expressed it, "had turned the first wheel of the Wells, Fargo Coach line across the plains, and the last." He and Salisbury had purchased the stage line from Ogden, Utah to Helena, Montana from Wells, Fargo & Co., in 1869.

During the early part of february, the "Magic City" buzzed with rumors as Brown and various veteran stage men gathered information and made estimates.

On february 12, "Stuttering" Brown, acting for Gilmer, Salisbury and Patrick, bought the Cheyenne and Black Hills Stage, Mail and Express from Yates & Company. Brown announced the next day that until the first of march he would continue to carry passengers, mail and express on the present route via the agencies, leaving Cheyenne on monday and thursday at seven o'clock in the morning.

After march 1, the new management, Brown said, planned to run a daily line of Concord coaches between Cheyenne and Custer City over a direct route north from Fort Laramie, by the way of Hat Creek station on Sage creek. Brown's first headquarters were those used by Yates & Company, at Joseph Mason's stables on Sixteenth street.

A sidelight on Brown's character appears in the following incident related by Alex Toponce, a beef contractor with temporary headquarters at Beartown, when the Union Pacific was under construction. Said Toponce:

> I remember Bates, engineer in charge of construction. The Pacific Lumber company, of which Van Tassel of Cheyenne was manager. Also, Oliver Durant, vice-president of the Union Pacific, who was actively supervising the work and also was supposed to be interested with Stuttering Brown, a contractor, hauling supplies to the camp.
>
> I had the contract to supply the camps from the east head of the big tunnel at Carter's station. . . When my contract was finished on the beef I was in Salt Lake for a few days stopping at the Salt Lake house. In the room next to mine I heard Oliver Durant and Stuttering Brown settling up their accounts.
>
> Durant said, "How is this, Brown? When we first started in you had four mules and I had sixteen, now you claim all the mules. How do you account for that?"
>
> Brown replied, "Bib-bib-bib because I'm a sis-sis-smarter man than you bib-bib-bib-be. That's all." [17]

Less than a week after Brown negotiated for the Yates line, Luke Voorhees, an experienced frontiersman, who had followed the gold rushes in Colorado and was the discoverer of gold on Kootenai river in British Columbia, arrived in Cheyenne as superintendent of the new stage line for Gilmer, Salisbury and Patrick. Brown was made superintendent of the danger-fraught division north of Fort Laramie, under Voorhees.

[17] *Reminiscences of Alexander Toponce* (Salt Lake City, 1923) p. 167.

Seasoned by vicissitudes of pioneering in the West, the new owners and employees moved cautiously in order to be thoroughly ready before launching their line across the Indian-menaced country.

General Crook, who was a guest at the Inter-Ocean hotel when Voorhees arrived in february, was keeping the telegraph wires busy with communications for President Grant, Generals Sherman, Sheridan, and Custer, and the commanders at Forts Laramie, Sanders, Russell, Fetterman, and Lincoln relative to a proposed field campaign. He anticipated an Indian outbreak in early spring.

Cheyenne literally swarmed with editors, reporters, feature writers, and others who had come to gather information about the Black Hills. Added to these were a number of well known writers, who had been assigned as correspondents to accompany Crook in the field.

Among these "hasty historians of the day" were: John (Long) Finerty of the Chicago *Times;* Thomas C. Macmillan of the Chicago *Inter-Ocean;* Burt of the Cincinnati *Commercial;* Colonel Whist, editor of the *Colorado Journal;* J. M. Culver and Robert Strahorn of the Denver *News;* R. S. Dill and A. J. Woodbury, Denver *Times;* C. A. Raymond, Denver *Tribune;* Wheeler, *Evanston (Wyo.) Age;* Charlie Whitehead, for a number of years city editor of the *Kansas City Times;* R. B. Davenport, New York *Herald;* Wasson, New York *Tribune;* and Standish Rood of the Salt Lake *Tribune.*

While waiting for the military to move northward, the correspondents wrote many columns for their home papers about Cheyenne as a gateway to the gold fields.

Cheyenne bristled with excitement when word went around that General Crook had ordered an expedition of about eight hundred men, under the immediate command of Col. J. J. Reynolds, to proceed to the Powder and Tongue rivers on an Indian campaign to bring the "hostiles" back to the reservations. By the last week in february, there were seven companies on the road, headed north from Cheyenne, and going north with the troops was Calamity Jane, a familiar Cheyenne figure. In just what capacity she went we are unable to state but we offer the following evidence as one of the rare source items extant showing that Calamity was with the soldiers. This item taken from the diary of Isaac Bard, who was at the time employed on the "Portugee" Phillips ranch at Chugwater, reads:

Feb. 21, 1876 . . . Tewsday . . . Very pleasant all day. Left town (Cheyenne) 9 A.M. Made a short call at Pole creek there is 6 or 8 B. Hill teams hear. Drove over to Fagans. He is crowded full. Calamity Jane is Hear going up with the troops. I think there is trouble ahead every thing is crowded hear there is 7 companies on the road.

Miners were warned not to go to the Hills in parties of less than ten, and to be well armed and ever on the alert. Governor John Thayer, who had made an extended visit to Washington, to urge the president and others to pursue a vigorous policy in regard to the "hostiles," returned to Cheyenne at this time, convinced that the government would not interfere with the miners now in the Black Hills, or who proposed to go there. The army, he said, would be employed in keeping in check hostile Indians, and eventually in removing all the Sioux, the Cheyennes, and Arapahoes to the Missouri river.

What more could eager ears desire to hear?

As superintendent of the Cheyenne and Black Hills Stage company, Luke Voorhees (*see plate* 4) had full authority to locate the most practical route, to establish necessary stage stations, and to equip the line fully. He also was entrusted with the full responsibility of the safety of passengers, the safe delivery of gold bullion, and the safeguarding of the company's property.

He immediately bought enough horses and mules and wagons to keep a tri-weekly line moving to Red Cloud, while he was lining up equipment for the through line north of Fort Laramie. Whether Voorhees bought Homan's equipment[18] is not known, but it is logical to suppose that he did buy some for immediate use. To facilitate the establishment of the line Voorhees acquired freight wagons, buckboards and spring wagons. In the parlance of stage men anything that carried the mail, express, and passengers was called a "stage," whether it was a buckboard or a "jerky," a "mud wagon" with a canvas top and roller curtains, or a wagon box on runners.

Because Voorhees knew from experience that Concord coaches were fashioned for hard service and would stand up regardless of climatic conditions, he planned ultimately to stock the entire line with them. Concords, with their bodies suspended on leather thoroughbraces, made of many folds of leather straps, were capable of swinging up and down over deep ruts and rocks, without injury to passengers.

Gilmer and Salisbury already owned many of these coaches, built by Abbot and Downing of Concord, New Hampshire. Some of them had been shipped to Omaha

---

18 Homan's son, Henry, did considerable freighting from Sidney, Neb., to Custer in the spring of 1876, and later established a line of stages out of Sidney.

in 1868 with the famous through shipment of thirty Concords, that was consigned to Wells, Fargo and Company. A few of those same coaches and other equipment, plus a carload of horses, reached Cheyenne from Ogden, Utah, upon the order of Voorhees, soon after march 1, 1876. In the meantime, Gilmer, Salisbury and Patrick telegraphed Abbot and Downing to make thirty new Concords and to ship them "with all haste" to Cheyenne.

Voorhees had agents out buying six hundred horses, for which he ordered harness from James R. Hill and Company in Concord, New Hampshire, internationally known harness and saddle makers.

The first shipment of new coaches and harness, including "spare parts" for repairing the coaches, hubs, spokes, and thoroughbraces, reached Cheyenne from New Hampshire within six weeks after ordered.

The running gears of each coach were painted yellow and the body, a rich red. Ornamental paintings on the doors and parts of the body (chiefly landscapes, each different), were the work of J. Burghum, a skilled artisan of Abbot and Downing. The intricate scroll work on each coach was done by Charles Knowlton. Each coach bore a name, such as, "The Deadwood."

Inside of each coach were three cushioned seats, capable of accommodating nine passengers. There was room on the front "boot" for two more, in addition to the driver. On the top were two seats that would hold from six to nine more passengers. The front one on top was called the "dickey seat." The rear top was the "China seat," so-called because to it were assigned the pig-tailed Orientals.

Almost fourteen steer hides were required in the making of thoroughbraces and the two "boots" on each coach. These boots, triangular cargo holds, one at the rear and one under the driver's seat, accommodated mail bags, express, and baggage. Heavy trunks were strapped to the rear boot, or carried on top. On the Cheyenne-Black Hills line the driver's seat was commonly referred to as "the boot," rather than "the box."

In a Concord coach a superior quality of white ash was used for body frame, felloes, pole, perches, and axle beds; bass wood for panels and roof; white oak for spokes; and elm or black cherry for hubs. The hand-hewn spokes were fitted into the rim with master joinery and thus were durable and capable of standing up under very hard wear.

Because of the weight involved, very little iron was used in the making of a Concord coach, but that which was necessary was of the best Norway stock obtainable, and was much stronger than the metal ordinarily used in coach making.

It is estimated that about three thousand stage coaches were built in Concord, New Hampshire, and were sent all over the world. The coach was never duplicated by other manufacturers.[19]

Voorhees fitted up "jerkies" of Concord design, for his blacksmiths, with tools, so that they could drive up and down the line to make repairs and shoe horses in their assigned division.

The horses used by the Cheyenne and Black Hills line, mostly were eastern and southern bred, purchased

---

[19] Each coach bore a number either on the body frame under the driver's seat or under the middle seat of the body, and on each axle end. Often the blacksmith's name was stamped in the iron over the end of the pole in front of the axle bed. A record was kept by Abbot and Downing of the sale of each coach. Hence, many years after the Concords ceased to roll over western stage lines and were abandoned in old ranch yards or were kept in some rickety shed, their histories could be unraveled to some extent by the identification numbers. (See Appendix B.)

at the horse markets in St. Louis, Missouri. A "team" usually consisted of six horses, though it might be four, or two. Each pair was well matched as to color and size. In a six-horse hitch the head team or "leaders" usually were smaller than the other horses; next came the "swing team," slightly larger; and lastly, the "wheelers," a fine, sturdy pair, weighing usually around twelve hundred pounds each.

Each team had its own particular set of harness which was kept spick-and-span as it was cleaned by the stock tender after each run. The old Black Hills drivers scorned adornments for the harness such as silver trimmings, colored tassels or hame balls. Sometimes the martingales of a six-horse outfit were fitted with white rings, including a number of solid ivory rings.

Horses were shod at least once a month, or oftener as needed. The hoofs grew and if the shoes were not changed the horse would stumble. Good drivers kept the horses looking sleek and "filled out," not just because they saw to it that they were fed well, but because they knew how to handle the animals on the road and how to keep them properly harnessed. A loosely hitched six-horse team would permit the driver to have free play with the reins. With such an arrangement he could get the best pulling power with the least amount of strain on the animals. A poor driver soon had the horses "dead on their feet." Luke Voorhees kept a poor driver no longer than was absolutely necessary.

Each stage driver's "drive" or "run," was from forty to sixty miles in length. Horses were changed several times during a "run" depending upon the character of the country. The coaches usually went through to the end of a run where they were checked for repairs.

The stage driver's whip was his most cherished possession. These whips varied in length from five to six-foot hickory stocks, with from 18-to-20 foot lashes. One driver, George Lathrop, had a whip stock covered for about two feet with solid silver ferrules. With its long lash it was valued at around $50. The longest six-horse whips had stocks that tapered to about three-sixteenths of an inch.

The Black Hills drivers usually held their whips horizontal to the lines, convenient for urging the wheelers up a bit. Good drivers did not whip the horses, but drove them with the sound of the lash, which, when handled by an expert, cracked like a gun. In the hands of an amateur one of those long whips was a dangerous thing.

The various pieces of equipment that could be adjusted or used, depending upon whether four or six horses were in the harness included lead bars for the leaders and for the swing team, a swing pole to be coupled on to the under goose neck for a six-horse hitch, and a v-crotch under the end of the tongue to keep the tongue from springing out of shape when not in use. The fixed tongue was referred to as the "pole."

The brake was an integral part of driving and a real reinsman could perform on the brake with a rhythm similar to an organist manipulating pipe-organ pedals.

Axle grease, often "Frazer's," was essential in the western stage business, as the axles had to be "doped" with the grease in order to keep the wheels running smoothly and to prevent a "hot box." The grease also was used for treating sores or wounds on man and beast.

A "way pocket," a loose leather sack, was carried by the Black Hills drivers for waybills and important messages, and to accommodate ranchmen and others along the route, who did not have regular postal service.

Buffalo robes were used in coaches to keep the passengers warm and sometimes in the smaller vehicles, in severe winter weather, hot rocks or hot bricks wrapped in "gunny sacks," made satisfactory footwarmers.

It required great skill to load a Concord coach. One day a man said to Jack Gilmer: "You ought to know A – ; he is a big-headed man."

Whereupon Gilmer replied, "Big heads don't count. A man's head is like a stagecoach. Loaded all in front, you cannot hold it on the down grade; loaded all in the rear, you cannot get stock enough to haul it; loaded all on top, the first pebble you strike, over it goes. You must balance it."

While Voorhees, during his first few weeks in Wyoming, was busy buying equipment, distributing the stock, organizing new stations and trying to select men who would stick on the job in the face of Indian danger, he kept the semi-weekly line from Cheyenne to the Red Cloud agency operating via Fort Laramie.

"Stuttering" Brown was hard at work stocking "upline" stations with hay, grain, horses, and equipment.

In those first hectic weeks of early spring in 1876, travel increased so rapidly that the northbound stage out of Cheyenne to Fort Laramie simply could not accommodate all who wanted to go. Voorhees realized that as soon as he made the announcement that the stage line was in full operation, there would be a mad rush for transportation from every direction.

In Chicago, Major James W. Conkling and S. S. Westfall had been busy organizing the Chicago Mining company. Arrangements had been made for a special train from Chicago to Cheyenne, with rail fare of only twenty-six dollars.

Forty miners had recently been escorted to the depot by two thousand citizens of Scranton, Pennsylvania, with a brass band and had been sent Cheyenneward with flying colors.

Other Pennsylvanians were completing arrangements at Pittsburgh to head for the Hills under the leadership of Captain T. H. Russell.

Echoes of the gold discoveries reverberated along the Bowery in New York City, where C. F. Harvey was enrolling two hundred men, bound for the "country between the north fork of the Cheyenne and the Little Powder river."

Wild Bill Hickok's party, organized in St. Louis, Missouri as a nucleus for what he called the Black Hills and Big Horn expedition, was attracting dozens of smaller parties. It was scheduled to join two hundred men from Springfield, Massachusetts, at Omaha, en route to Cheyenne.

With men arriving from almost every corner of the globe, Gilmer, Salisbury and Patrick, early in march, declared their intention of investing one hundred thousand dollars in their new line and made plans to operate on an extensive scale.

They completed arrangements with the railway companies to sell through tickets from all points in the "states" to Custer City, via Cheyenne, over the Cheyenne and Black Hills stage line.

They notified Superintendent Kimball of the Union Pacific railroad on march 10, 1876 that:

We have now on hand and ready for service ten Concord Overland coaches and sufficient harness to equip the line, with facilities to double the number of stages and equipment on a week's notice, if the travel should require it. In addition to this, we have arranged for wagon trains for the transportation of freight, miners' outfits, supplies, and second and third class passengers in large or small numbers. The time for second class will be four days, and for third class, six days. Eating stations between here and Fort Laramie are already established, and from the Fort to Custer City are now being built, and will be ready to commence operations in about two weeks, so that we shall have the daily line of stages fully inaugurated and running through to Custer City on or before the first day of april.

The running time during the spring months will be three days from Cheyenne to Custer, and after that two days, or less, if deemed necessary.

Rates of fare will be as follows: First class, Cheyenne to Custer City, $20; second class, $15; third class, $10. (These rates apply only to through tickets.)

Following we give the distances from Cheyenne to the Black Hills, the points mentioned being, as will be seen, at convenient distances apart for camping, and having accommodations for travelers.

	Miles
Cheyenne to Lodge Pole creek	18
Lodge Pole creek to Horse creek	10
Horse creek to Bear springs	10
Bear springs to Chugwater	13
Chugwater to Hunton's ranch	12.5
Hunton's ranch to Eagle's Nest	9
Eagle's Nest to Fort Laramie	17.5
Fort Laramie to Spring Branch	12
Spring Branch to Raw Hide	12
Raw Hide to Niobrara river	15
Niobrara to Old Woman's fork	12
Old Woman's fork to 2nd Camp	15
2nd Camp to South Beaver	10
S. Beaver to Big Cheyenne forks	12.5

Total 178.5

These distances are by the road soon to be built by the citizens of Cheyenne. By the road now traveled the distance from Cheyenne to Custer City is 246 miles.

Our forwarding houses can furnish transportation for 2,000,000 pounds at a shipment. Freight charges, Cheyenne to Custer, range from 3½ to 6 cents per pound, according to the kind of animals employed and time consumed on the road.

Although the original plan of the stage company had been to run the stages down Beaver to Big Cheyenne forks, instead of through Red canyon, the construction of the short-cut road was delayed almost a year.

Where The Wagons Stopped

SOUTHERN DIVISION

From Cheyenne to Fort Laramie, the earliest stage route, which later extended into the Black Hills, left the "Magic City" by way of County Road number 1, which paralleled the Union Pacific railroad's spur northwestward almost two miles to Camp Carlin (Cheyenne depot), the largest army supply depot in the West.[20] A mile farther on it reached Fort D. A. Russell [21] and then swung north across treeless hills.

Later the trail ran slightly northwestward out of Cheyenne along the course of Ferguson street (now Carey avenue), then north between Second and Third Lakes and merged with the earlier route north of Round Top. From there it continued northward across rolling plains and grassy hills. Not a house appeared until Dry Ravine, where was situated the road ranch called NINE MILE.

This ranch, opened in december 1876, by Leander

[20] Camp Carlin, named for Col. E. B. Carling, was established 1867. It supplied army posts in the department of the Platte as far away as Fort Hall, Idaho, Fort Duchesne, Utah and Sidney, Neb. It comprised many large warehouses, blacksmith shops, wheelwright shops, carpenter shops, saddle and harness shops, sales stores, cook and bunk houses, wagon sheds, stables, huge corrals, and military quarters.

[21] Fort D. A. Russell, designed to accommodate twelve companies, six each of infantry and cavalry, was renamed Ft. Francis E. Warren by congress on january 1, 1930.

Davis, a Horse creek ranchman, was not a regular stagecoach stop but was a popular camp of the freighters. Coaches stopped on necessity. Davis assured the public that he had a fine, deep well with good water and could supply nutritious hay for teams. He later sold the ranch to "Madame" W. Selig, who built a two-story structure with a large dance hall on the ground floor, and sleeping rooms upstairs.

Passing the Nine Mile and traversing a series of gently rolling hills, the road dropped down a steep slope into a valley to the crossing of Lodge Pole creek, eighteen miles from Cheyenne. There POLE CREEK RANCH was the first regular stop of the Cheyenne and Black Hills stage. Fred W. Schwartze, who had ranched here since 1871, owned several hundred head of cattle and horses, and had an excellent meadow, from which he cut one hundred tons of hay. He also raised fine vegetables, including everything from potatoes to artichokes.

Schwartze had a large, round frame barn close to his house. Cowsheds and corrals were on the opposite side of the stage road. He often took visitors for a climb up to the platform on his large windmill from which there was a fine view of Pole Creek valley, including Post's PO Percheron horse ranch, four miles down the creek, and Tim Dyer's sheep ranch, an equal distance upstream.

The Pole Creek ranch was a favorite stopping and camping place for Black Hillers. In may 1876, Schwartze constructed a fine two-story "hotel," in which he furnished sleeping accommodations and "meals at all hours" to the traveling public, – "terms reasonable." He could stable fifty head of stock and here the horses of the stage line were changed.

From this little wind-swept Wyoming ranch came one of the handsomest chorus girls in the original company which played "The Prince of Pilsen." She was Minna Schwartze, daughter of Fred. A young newspaper reporter, who saw the show in Chicago, became enamoured of the striking young actress and married her. His name was Franklin P. Adams, and today he is "F.P.A.", well-known newspaper columnist and radio performer.

Minna Schwartze Adams tells a story about a cowboy fracas at the ranch when she was very small. The memory of the affair has remained vivid with her through the years. She says a storm was brewing that late autumn day and every man on the ranch, including the bartender, had been pulled into service to help with the haying. Mrs. Isaac Bard, from a neighboring ranch, arrived with some friends for a little visit with Mrs. Schwartze. While the latter was preparing some coffee in the big dining room, there suddenly was shooting in the barroom adjoining. The guests and two Swedish "hired girls" ran down the long porch from the kitchen, headed for the willows along the "crick." Mrs. Schwartze, being large with child, moved more slowly. She lifted Minna, then about three years old, to her shoulder and started to follow the others. Then came a shot through the dining room door, which hit the china door knob. The bullet was deflected across the room (*see plate 5*).

"A six-foot Texan with a cocked gun came into the room, very drunk and me looking straight into his gun!" reports Mrs. Adams. "Mama whirled around and said to him, 'What do you want?' 'We want liquor,' he said. 'Well, go out to the bar and get it,' my mother told him. All the while shooting was going on in the barroom. The man was very drunk and lurched toward my mother. She took him by the collar and marched him through the door. I can still see that face leering at me with the gun a few inches from my face."

Mrs. Schwartze with Minna, followed the other women to the willows where they remained until the stage came in. That night Mrs. Schwartze was taken very ill. Her child was born dead. Efforts to track down and arrest the miscreants were fruitless.

The following version of the affair appeared in the New York *Police Gazette* in 1882:

ROLLICKING RIOTERS

The "bad man from Bitter Creek" has been disporting himself with a looseness, of late, in and about Cheyenne, Wyoming. The recent lynching of Henry Mosier for the Wentz murder near that place has not wholly quieted the lawless spirit of the turbulent rustlers. They are, indeed, "wild and wooly and hard to curry." On sunday, the 21st ult., a large party gathered at a road ranch kept by Fred Schwartze, on the Fort Laramie road, about eighteen miles north of Cheyenne, intending to take dinner there. Among the party were about a dozen cowboys, who had been drinking heavily, and were consequently ripe for any kind of riot or rollicking. The boys were employed by different firms. Some are reported belonging to the outfits of Lem Smith, Benjamin Weaver & Co., and Hanna, Anderson & Co. Two cowboys, just over the trail from Texas, were with them, and seemed anxious to show the crowd that they were "bad men," and took the lead. The other boys seemed to have joined in more from a desire to have some fun than anything else. After considerable horse-racing, swearing and shooting, one of the men rode up to the ranch, dismounted from his horse, and placing the muzzle of his revolver against the house discharged it. This was the signal for a general outbreak, and the real fun commenced at once, all hands opening fire, with no intent to take life, but to do as much damage to property as possible. Some fifty rounds of ammunition were discharged, and the house was shot full of holes. Entering the bar-room, they made targets of the bottles on the shelves and one by one the labels fell until not a bottle was left. Then they turned upon a barrel filled with whisky, and, like some of the eastern temperance brigades (only in a different manner), they shot it full of holes and let its contents run out upon the floor. If they had been satisfied with this it might have been settled with dollars and cents, but one of the ruffians, inflamed by whiskey and the smell of powder forced his way into the room where Mrs. Schwartze was, placed a cocked revolver at her breast, and demanded of her to "bring on her women." Mrs. Schwartze, who is in a delicate state of health, was naturally much alarmed, but escaped from her assailant and reached her room in safety. Mrs. Bard, who had stopped there on her way to town for dinner, ran out at the back door at the first alarm, but stumbling over some obstacle fell, and was afraid to rise for fear of being shot. She crawled about twenty yards on her hands and knees to a clump of brush on the banks of the creek, where she remained concealed until the melee was over.

There were half a dozen men present besides the cowboys, but none of them was armed, and as no arms could be found about the ranch, nothing could be done until the cowboys had satisfied their appetites for whiskey and fun. Mr. Schwartze was himself absent from home. When the stage from Fort Laramie came in, a cowboy drew his gun and threatened to shoot the driver, but was prevented by a woman who was with the gang, who threw her arms around him, holding his arms down by his side. At one time the cowboys withdrew to their camp for a fresh supply of ammunition, and while absent all the peaceful travellers left the ranch, and the doors of the building were locked. These the cowboys broke open upon their return, so that they are liable to be prosecuted for breaking and entering the building, for which there is a severe penalty. As soon as possible those who were bound for Cheyenne came in and notified the authorities of what had occurred. A posse of officers was at once started in pursuit. . .

North of Pole creek, the Black Hills trail, for the next ten or eleven miles, lay over rolling hills, which according to one passenger resembled great pillows laid side by side and very close together.

About twenty-eight miles from Cheyenne, the second

scheduled stop of the stage, was the HORSE CREEK RANCH, a meal station, at the crossing of the west branch of Horse creek. It usually was referred to as FAGAN'S RANCHE. Here Michael F. Fagan, in the spring of 1876, completed a very large, solid structure, containing nine rooms and "ladies' parlor." Fagan furnished meals at fifty cents each, and had stabling accommodations for seventy head of stock. He owned about one hundred and fifty head of cattle and prided himself on raising fine watermelons, tomatoes, cabbages, and other vegetables.

During two days in the big snowstorm in march 1876, approximately two hundred and fifty travelers slept in the Fagan ranch kitchen, stables, and outbuildings in addition to the regular rooms.

Ill health forced Fagan to sell the ranch early in 1877, shortly before his death, to a man named Moore. Three years later the new owner sold to Oliver P. Goodwin, who had had wide experience in the west as a fur-trader, soldier, miner, freighter, master of a government transport, and station keeper.

The ranch was treeless. Buildings included a house, saloon, and stage station stables. For a time the post office here was discontinued, but later was reestablished with Goodwin as postmaster.

From Horse creek to Fort Laramie the elevation constantly leveled off, dropping two thousand feet in about sixty-five miles.

Three miles on up the road from Horse Creek station, Isaac Bard, on may 4, 1876, opened a road ranch on Little Bear. Bard, who had been working for John (Portugee) Phillips at Chugwater, realized that the migration of Black Hillers was going to be large, so filed on one hundred and sixty acres of land as a soldier's homestead. In his diary of april 5, 1876, Bard made the following notation:

I will now try keeping a public ranch for a year if the Good Lord is willing and the Indians will let me alone

With the help of his wife, Rose, Bard developed the little homestead into one of the best ranches in the area. Although in the earliest days it was not a scheduled stage stop, stages usually paused there. After the Horse Creek post office was moved to the Bard ranch in may 1877, the place became a regular stage station called LITTLE BEAR. Bard was the postmaster. In the old ledger which he kept, appear the names of many employees of the Cheyenne and Black Hills stage company and of various well-known pioneers.

On july 18, 1876, Bard noted:

Clear but windy the Noted Indian Chief Spotted Taile called on his way to the Agency I drank a glass of beare with him he is a fine large well built man has been on a visit to the whites in Cheyenne

About thirty-eight miles north from Cheyenne, along the Black Hills trail, lay a narrow valley, watered by splendid natural springs that gushed up through the sandy bed of Bear Springs creek.

There in 1875, Joseph (José) Armijo opened the BEAR SPRINGS road ranch, which he advertised as a "first class ranch, plenty of stable room, hay and grain. The bar supplied with the best of liquors, meals at all hours."

Later he sold the ranch to his brother, Miguel Armijo, who evidently was lax in meeting payments. On february 13, 1877, José rode to the ranch to discuss money matters. After a long drinking bout, the brothers quarreled and Miguel shot José to death.

From Bear Springs the road continued over open hills and plains to the comparatively well-timbered, well-sheltered, and generally picturesque Chugwater valley. Perpendicular bluffs, in almost unbroken lines, overlooked the valley on either side. Under the lea of these, on the edge of broad meadows fringed with groves of cottonwood, willow, and boxelder, thrifty ranchmen built a number of substantial cabins. Here were the ranches of John (Portugee)[22] Phillips, Hi Kelly, and Dick Whalen, all engaged in the livestock business.

Early in march 1876, Phillips hung up a sign at his ranch which read:

> Chug Water Ranch
> John Phillips
> Hay Grain and Stabling
> 52 Miles to Cheyenne   45 to Fort Laramie

The discrepancy in the distances between places is typical of that early day, as at that time official surveys

[22] Phillips was nicknamed "Portugee" because he was born on Fayal, one of the Azores islands, of Portuguese parents. He came into the Rocky mountains with prospectors and was at Fort Phil Kearny as a civilian employe when the Fetterman massacre occurred in december 1866. Phillips volunteered to ride to Fort Laramie to bring aid to the beleaguered post. His ride of more than 236 miles through a bleak, unmarked, Indian-infested country, with a blizzard raging and the thermometer at twenty-five degrees below zero, has gone down in the annals of Wyoming as one of the most heroic deeds in the state's history. Bronze plaques and monuments have been erected by the Wyoming landmark commission to commemorate the ride, at the site of old Fort Phil Kearny in Johnson county; in Lakeview cemetery, Cheyenne; and opposite Old Bedlam at Fort Laramie. In 1916, congress gave to the widow of Phillips, $5,000 as payment on livestock stolen by the Indians in 1872, and in recognition of the ride which Phillips made, House Report no. 1912 said: "In all the annals of heroism in the face of unusual dangers and difficulties on the American frontier, or in the world there are few that can excel in gallantry, in heroism, in devotion, in self-sacrifice and patriotism the ride made by Phillips."

had not been completed and too, roads were constantly changing. Most distances were "estimated."

Phillips kept a well-stocked bar, served good meals, and had stalls to accommodate fifty head of stock.

For a time Phillips was postmaster at Chugwater, owned a small herd of cattle, and ran the Chug-Water hotel. He sold his holdings in 1879 to Hambleton & Company of Baltimore for sixteen thousand dollars. Stephen D. Hovey then became proprietor of the hotel. Phillips died on november 18, 1883. Superintendent Voorhees said that Portugee Phillips always could be depended upon when needed to help in the round up of road agents or outlaws.

Near the Phillips ranch was the stage station (*see plate* 6) kept by H. B. Kelly, who had settled on the Chug in the early 'seventies, and who owned one of the best improved ranches in Wyoming. Kelly used irrigation extensively, had two hundred acres of meadow under fence, and raised many varieties of vegetables. With his herd of fifteen hundred cattle he kept five three-fourths blood Shorthorn bulls, valued at more than six hundred dollars each.

Kelly, who had married a woman of Sioux blood, was known as a "Man of the country." Mrs. Kelly, a daughter of John Richards (Reshaw, Reichard), was handsome and was said to perform her domestic duties in a manner that "would reflect credit upon a New England housewife."

According to a reporter who visited the ranch:

There are more trees about Kelly's ranch than there are in all Cheyenne. Larger ones are boxelder and have stout, crooked trunks and gnarled limbs. Also willows and cottonwood and a great deal of thicket brush grow along the Chug. Instead of the usual prospect about a stage station on the plains, Kelly's has the appearance of the home of a wealthy farmer. The houses are of frame, being quite handsome in design, as to the exterior, and as well furnished as some of the best houses in Cheyenne. The hotel stable is as large, complete and clean a structure as you could expect to see out of town.

We have often read of Bill Sharon's wood pile in Nevada, and Jim Ralston's boom of logs, but we never saw anything that approached those in magnitude until we saw Mr. Kelly's fence. We struck it at a point about six miles below his residence. It occurred to us there were a great many miles of real estate under fence, so we made some inquiries about the same. It transpired that Mr. Kelly didn't know how many square miles there were contained in his range, but that he had about sixty miles of fence built. Kelly's home residence is situated about half a mile above the hotel and store. It is a large brick structure of splendid design and beautifully situated among the trees that fringe the Chug. Swan's range, which adjoins Kelly's is also a very fine one.

For a time in 1876, a company of cavalry headquartered at the Kelly ranch while patrolling the valley against Indian forays. The next year, through Kelly's efforts, a small school house was built on his ranch.

Kelly's brother-in-law, Maxwell, ran the stage station for him. Maxwell's two daughters helped with the work and kept the rooms of the station in order. Sometimes they served the table. In telling of her first arrival at Chugwater valley, one daughter, Anna [23] said

We drove to the ranch of a friend of my father, where there were adobe buildings and one log building of two rooms. . . The friend had a wife of some Indian blood and two sons and one daughter. His wife's mother was one of the family also. This wife's grandfather, a full blooded Sioux, lived in a tepee. . . He was called "Christ."

[23] Anna Maxwell attended Colorado Agricultural college and married A. W. Scott, pioneer druggist of Fort Collins, Colorado. She related many incidents of her days at Chugwater to the author. After Mr. Maxwell's death, Anna's mother married Abner Loomis, a livestock man of Fort Collins, Colo. Loomis ranged one of the first cattle herds in Wyoming.

He wore beautiful blankets, with his hair in long braids with silver ornaments hanging from the braids. I found out he had several government medals for kind deeds rendered. We children cut willow of red bark growing on the stream called Kinnikinick and scraped the bark from it. After drying it in the sun, Christ crushed it and smoked it in his peace pipe. After his death his medals and all valuable things were buried with him, as that is the Indian's custom.

In the wooded valley of Kelly's ranch there were hundreds of birds: robins, doves, bobolinks, meadowlarks, snipe, and others. Hawks were often seen on the fence posts and occasionally an eagle wheeled overhead.

Hi Kelly, in 1884, sold his ranch on the Chug, together with his cattle, brands, and equipment to the Swan Land and Cattle company for an estimated half million dollars.

Swinging around the arc of Chugwater past the Point of Rocks, the stage route went down the river valley for some ten miles to the Chimney Rock post office where John McFarlane and his partner, Dan McUlvan had a ranch. Chimney Rock was almost round in shape and rose to a considerable height from a perpendicular bluff.

Four miles from there, at the junction of what later was called Hunton's creek and Chugwater creek, was Hunton's ranch, BORDEAUX.

Early in 1870, John Hunton, who had been handling wood and hay cutting contracts for the government, in the vicinity of Fort Laramie, bought the place from Bordeaux, an Indian trader.

Hunton induced the government to erect quarters and a stable on his place for a detachment of soldiers, and in june 1876, the stage company moved its station from Owens's ranch at Chug springs, to Hunton's and made Bordeaux a relay station.

Being in a key position where the road branched to Fort Fetterman on the old Bozeman road, Bordeaux became a mail distributing station for nearly all of the ranchmen westward, including those on La Bonte, Horseshoe, Cottonwood, North Laramie, and the Sybille. Thomas Hunton, a brother of John, became postmaster when the office was established in 1877.

All through the 'seventies the Hunton ranch had antelope meat on hand, except during the breeding season. Antelope grazed on the benchlands and plains nearby. On some occasions as many as a hundred carcasses were hanging on the shady sides of the house and picket corral. A carcass retailed at one dollar.

In 1881, Hunton built a concrete residence, which "shone white" in the valley. Branching out in the cattle business with Colonel W. G. Bullock, he gradually extended his holdings until he had a good four-wire fence around fourteen thousand acres of government land. When the government ordered fences taken down, he abandoned his. Homesteaders "appropriated" his wire and posts.

In the summer of 1887, as the Cheyenne and Northern railroad approached Bordeaux, Hunton completed the building of a two-story, eleven room hotel, a barn, and an office. He moved to Fort Laramie as post trader in 1888. Two years later when the fort was abandoned, he bought it and lived there for many years.

After passing the Bordeaux stage station, the Black Hills trail crossed hills into bottomlands, which became narrow and not particularly inviting.

CHUG SPRINGS, about four miles northeast, was a very early stopping place on the trail that ran southwest from Fort Laramie into Colorado by the way of

Camp Walbach. Although this trail, in the beginning, was used chiefly by Indians, some white men's wagons traveled it. Robert Campbell, the trader, told John Hunton that he spent the winter of 1834 at the Springs.

In 1871, a man named Patton built a small log road house there as the Fort D. A. Russell to Fort Laramie road passed it. Later, Chug Springs became the property of Johnny Owens, a professional gambler, skilled gunman, and famous early day sheriff.

C. P. (Dub) Meek, one of the first freighters into the Black Hills, claimed that he saw Johnny Owens win the station in a poker game.

Owens later ran the "Hog ranch" at the Three Mile near Fort Laramie, where sporting women lived. Despite his profession as a dance hall proprietor, Owens became known as one of the most respected and honest, straightforward men in Wyoming. He was quiet and reserved, yet was friendly and a good mixer. A slender, handsome man, he was always meticulously groomed and tailored. His hobbies were good clothes and good horses.[24]

Although Owens gambled, he neither drank nor smoked. Officers and men at Fort Laramie used to entrust their wives and daughters to his care on their trips over the Black Hills stage line to and from Cheyenne. He always carried two guns, one "for re-

---

[24] When the railway reached Lusk, Owens opened a dance hall and saloon there. From there he moved to Newcastle, Wyoming where for years he owned the Castle theatre and ran "The House of Blazes," a large gambling and sporting establishment, so called because the guns often blazed behind its scarred walls. He kept a fine stable of racing horses. He was always prosperous and spent his money freely. He served fourteen years as sheriff of Weston county and was instrumental in bringing the Truax gang from New Mexico to justice. He just about wiped out cattle rustling in eastern Wyoming. Owens died in 1927.

serve." It was said that he never aimed in his life. Those who knew him claimed that, as a gunman, he was far superior to Wild Bill Hickok. His twenty killings were made in self-defense, chiefly as an officer of the law.

Seven miles north of Chug Springs, the Deadwood route skirted a fifty-foot high sandstone cliff called Eagle's Nest. The face of the cliff bore many inscribed names and dates, ranging as far back as 1834. The trail which led through Eagle's Nest canyon was a famous old-time cut-off, used by emigrants who branched from the Oregon trail at Fort Laramie to avoid the canyon of the North Platte. Eagle's Nest gap faced Laramie peak, the 11,000-foot mountain, which Jim Bridger claimed was a "hole in the ground" at the time he first visited the area.

EAGLE'S NEST stage station, about a mile from the mouth of the canyon, was kept at various times by Remeyer, Tom Hawk, and others.

SIX MILE RANCH, a relay station, ten miles beyond Eagle's Nest and six miles south of Fort Laramie, was the scene of several violent episodes. Said John Hunton:

The Six Mile ranch, on Baptiste fork, was a favorite place for killing. The first man killed there was John Hunter, the original owner, who was shot by "Bud" Thomason in october 1868. The next two were John Lowry and James McClosky, shot by Boyer in october 1870. Next was Perry Abner, a wood chopper, assassinated by a man whose name I have forgotten, sometime in 1872 or 1873. Then followed two men at different times during the Black Hills excitement, prior to 1877. The last one was Adolph Cuny, killed by Clark Pelton in july 1877.

Most of the women who lived at the "Hog ranch"

WHERE THE WAGONS STOPPED

at the Six Mile, went about in soldier clothes. It was said that there was considerable resentment on their part when Al Swearengen and his three wagons loaded with bar fixtures, roulette wheels, liquor, and befrilled and beruffled *filles de joie,* stopped there en route to the Black Hills in 1876.

In march 1876, John Thornmahlen & Co., bought the old Six Mile ranch from Bottlejohn and stocked it with hay and feed for the accommodation of Black Hills pilgrims. Two months later, Hank Steward, who was running the place, closed out his interests because of the falling off of the Black Hills travel as the result of the Indian troubles.

In june, however, the Cheyenne and Black Hills Stage company established a relay station here with George Hawk in charge.

In 1877, Jack Bowman, said to be in no way related to the man by the same name who ran the Hat Creek station, had charge of the Six Mile. It was rumored that he sheltered road agents. Later, Curley Coleman took the place over.

Three miles down the Laramie river, just off the Fort Laramie reservation, on the site formerly occupied by the Ben Mills cabin, on the north bank of the river, was the THREE MILE, where Adolph Cuny and Jules Coffey erected a large store and many buildings, including a concrete dwelling, store-house, bunk house, ice house, blacksmith shop, billiard hall, and a sod corral one hundred feet square and twelve feet high.

Coffey and Cuny started the place as a general road ranch in 1873, but when business became slack the next year, they decided to add new attractions and for that purpose constructed eight two-room cottages to be occupied by women.

According to John Hunton:

They sent to Omaha and Kansas City and other places and in a short time had their houses occupied by ten or more young women, all of whom were known as sporting characters. Among this bunch was Calamity Jane, who was not the type generally given her by magazine writers and newspaper correspondents. . . Her achievements have been greatly magnified by every writer. . . After being sent back from Colonel Dodge's expedition, Jane returned and resumed her old life at the Coffey and Cuny ranch and other places of similar character at Fort Laramie and Fort Fetterman, until the organization of General Crook's army in may 1876, when she and three other women of the same character were smuggled out with the command and remained until found out and ordered back. After the battle of Rose Bud in june 1876, Crook ordered his extra wagon trains to be sent to Fort Fetterman with the sick and wounded and I know Calamity Jane was with it for I saw her on her way up to John Brown's ranch, the same day the train arrived at Fetterman.

Many prospectors who had evaded the military and gone into the Hills, came back to the Three Mile for supplies. Gold dust began to be plentiful at the place and in november 1875, Coffey and Cuny sent three flasks full of gold, about one hundred and twenty-five dollars worth, to the editor of the Cheyenne *Leader*.

A sign above the door of the store at the Three Mile, said to have been printed by a drunken soldier, read:

"Pay Today and Trust Tomorrow"

In 1876 the Three Mile was a regular meal station on the stage route. Good meals were served at fifty cents each.

Jules Coffey died on november 26, 1876, as the result

of injuries inflicted by a man named Stonewall, who had attacked him some three months previous. His funeral was held at Dyer's hotel in Cheyenne, and burial was in the Cheyenne cemetery.[25]

Adolph Cuny, 42, was killed on july 22, 1877 by Clark Pelton, alias Billy Webster, a road agent. Cuny was buried in the citizens' cemetery at Fort Laramie. He was said, at the time, to be "one of the oldest pioneers in Wyoming." Cuny hills in Platte county bear his name.

For a time Andy Ryan of Cheyenne, was a partner in the Three Mile ranch, but he sold his interest early in 1878. Bob Osborne, former post butcher at Fort Laramie, bought the place in september 1881.

FORT LARAMIE (see plates 1, 7) estimated around ninety-two to ninety-eight miles north of Cheyenne, was perhaps the most important station on the Cheyenne and Deadwood route, because at the time the through stage line was inaugurated it was the base of military operations against the Sioux in their last stand against the white man's invasion of the Indian country.

Originally established as a trading post in 1834, Fort Laramie was purchased by the United States government in 1849, was garrisoned, and became one of the most substantial points on the old Oregon trail.

[25] Although the newspapers often spelled the name "Jules Ecoffey," the burial record of the sexton of city cemeteries in Cheyenne, gives: "Jules Coffey." In *The Indian War of 1864*, p. 276 Eugene F. Ware, who was post adjutant at Fort Laramie in 1864, says: "There was at the post, all the time I was there, Major Bridger, the celebrated scout and guide; also a hunter, trapper and guide named Jules Coffey. At least, that is the way they pronounced his name, although I imagine it might have been the French name of Ecoffe, because I heard one of them pronounce it Acoffay. He seemed to be very prosperous, and to have a great deal of money, and he loved to play poker wonderfully. . ." There also was in the Fort Laramie vicinity, Frank Ecoffey and Charles Coffee – to add to the name confusion.

For many years Fort Laramie was the rallying spot for trappers, traders, soldiers, and emigrants but the treaty of 1868 with the Sioux, marked the close of the Indian trading period, of the fort.

When the gold rush began in the mid-'seventies, Fort Laramie was the "jumping off" place for the vast, unsettled country to the north of the Platte. It became a focal point for prospectors. It also soon became the center of one of the best livestock ranges of the entire west.

Picturesquely situated in the large delta formed by the junction of the Laramie and North Platte rivers, and watered by Deer creek, the frontier post with its wide meadows of native hay, marshes, brush, and heavy woodlands was a mecca to the weary miners who had plodded over the plains and rolling hills, sometimes knee deep in mud or snow, on their northward trek. The weather here usually was much milder and the wind much less than in the "Magic City of the Plains," whose altitude (6,062 feet), was almost two thousand feet higher. Low broken hills surrounded the fort and on the west sloped up to Laramie peak, some forty miles away. The buildings of Fort Laramie[26] which, in 1876, were principally of adobe and stone, called grout, and were neatly painted, were said to be much better than those usually found at frontier posts.

---

[26] A Denver newspaper reporter who visited the fort in 1876 described it as: Quarters for eight companies, two frame and one adobe building, with porches, stone foundations and shingle roofs, and two new barracks, built of concrete, each 23 x 133 feet, two stories high; officers' quarters, eleven buildings, six frame, four adobe, and one concrete; new hospital, built of concrete; guard houses, two buildings, one stone and one adobe; six store houses, frame buildings, capacity 313,000 cubic feet; stables, frame, for one hundred and forty-four horses; magazine, built of stone; laundress's quarters, three adobe buildings; adjutant's office, school house, post office, bakery, workshops, etc., adobe and frame buildings.

As soon as the rush to the Hills was assured, John S. Collins, who had been appointed post trader[27] in december 1872 and had accepted on january 3, 1873, erected a hotel called the RUSTIC, which was opened on march 15, 1876, as headquarters for the Cheyenne and Black Hills stage company, under the managership of J. H. C. Brown. The stage barns and corrals under the hill, close to the Rustic hotel, were near the Cheyenne approach to the fort. Collins and his brother, G. H. Collins, ran a harness and saddlery store in Cheyenne, and were active in public affairs. Their father at one time had been in the tanning business with General U. S. Grant in Illinois. J. S. Collins was appointed secretary of the Sioux commission in 1875, to deal with the Indians relative to the relinquishment of the Hills.

Collins had his store in a building, part of which was said to have been erected in 1849 or 1850. For years it was called the "sutler's store." During the gold rush days his stock comprised everything from flour, bacon,

[27] Previous to 1867, the civilians appointed by the Secretary of War to sell to officers and enlisted men, at fixed reasonable prices, certain articles necessary to their comfort and convenience, which were not furnished gratuitously, were known as sutlers. By Congressional act of july 28, 1866, the office of sutler was abolished and the Commissary department of the Army was required to furnish for sale to officers and soldiers such articles heretofore supplied by sutlers. In view of the failure of Congress to make a special appropriation to carry the new act into effect, however, the Secretary of War directed "That the sutlers at military posts on the frontier, not in the vicinity of any city or town, and situated between the one hundredth meridian of longitude west from Greenwich, and the eastern boundary of the state of California, shall, after the 1st of july, 1867, be retained until further orders as traders at such military posts, under the resolution of Congress approved march 30, 1867, authorizing the Commanding General of the Army to permit traders to remain at certain military posts." (Information pertaining to the various appointments of post traders at Fort Laramie and copies of General orders no. 54 and no. 58 were received from Adjutant General's office, War department, Washington, D.C.)

tobacco, whisky, wolf poison, and family soap to powder for the complexion and carpet bags. In this same store building Jim Bridger, John Hunton, and others had shared sleeping quarters during the winter of 1867-68.

Collins's appointment as post trader was revoked on september 20, 1877, and he was succeeded by G. H. Collins, who died in 1880. John London then became the trader and served until august 28, 1888. For the next two years, John Hunton was the official post trader, serving until march 2, 1890.

During the hey day of the Cheyenne and Black Hills stage line, many stage employees were stationed at Fort Laramie. The first agent was J. M. Ford. John Morrison, Jim Hogle, George Hawk, and Tom Hawk ran the Rustic hotel at various times. Others who worked there for the company were: Green, Joe Wilde, Race Newcomb, Billie Bristol, and George Breckenridge. B. A. Hart, chief clerk of the trader's store, was closely associated with the stage line.

The stone Guard house, on the banks of the Laramie river, often housed road agents and desperadoes who were arrested on the stage route. Medical aid, on occasion, was summoned from the post for those injured in attacks on stagecoach passengers, or stage-wagon drivers.

NORTHERN DIVISION

Through a winding tangle of hoof and wheel tracks the Cheyenne to Custer and Deadwood trail led out of the fort to the new iron bridge over the North Platte river, thence went north across the undulating hills and prairies.

So many changes were made in the "Northern division" of the stage line during the first three years of its existence, that it is difficult to present a clear picture of where the wagons stopped by giving them in chronological order. It is deemed less confusing to describe these stations in geographical order, in so far as possible.

To establish a route across some of the country north of Fort Laramie, especially down Old Woman's fork, demanded utmost skill in plainscraft. According to General R. I. Dodge, who had escorted the Jenney expedition, in the spring of 1875, "Nowhere do the rains cut more deeply, nowhere do frosts split more perpendicular faces. The beds of most of the streams are quagmires, or the more tenacious quicksand. Banks are to be cut down, narrow sharp ridges to be leveled off. . ."

This northbound road had been traced first by the buffalo, then by the Indians' travois. Next it was pressed deeper by the hoofs of the pack beasts of trappers and traders, and then by a few wobbling wheels of the Red river carts. In time it was worn deep by the many hoofs of the ox and mule freight teams between Fort Laramie and Fort Pierre, and later to the Hills. Now the dust flicked under the quick tattoo of the fleet stage horses, drawing the Concord coaches.

As a coach rocked along over the hills the soft-voiced driver might assure the passengers that Deadwood was "jest over that hill, and across a creek or two." But the never-ending hills continued, one after another, to the various stops where passengers rested and were fed, and the horses were changed.

TEN MILE, a road ranch ten miles north of Fort

Laramie, was owned by a ranchman named McGinnis. Coaches stopped here only on necessity.

At fourteen miles was the old GOVERNMENT FARM site, where a station was built that was run for a time by John Montgomery, then George Hoyt, and later it was owned by W. F. Hamilton. Near the head of Cottonwood creek a tract of land had been selected and a number of log buildings erected by soldiers in the 'sixties. Here experiments were carried on for a time in the raising of grain and vegetables for the troops. Since Cottonwood creek had its beginning in a large slough, surrounded by a marsh, there was sub-irrigation to a considerable area. The so-called "Government Farm" was abandoned prior to 1872.

George Ayres, a Black Hiller, recorded in his diary that there were no buildings at this place in march 1876. By 1879, Government Farm comprised: a dwelling, containing five rooms, a good corral, and a barn capable of holding from thirty to forty head of stock. At that time it had two hundred acres of land fenced and "an elegant spring with sufficient water to run a grist mill."

North of Government Farm the road crossed flats covered with buffalo grass and dotted with cactus and soapweed. Here were innumerable prairie dog towns with an accompaniment of rattlesnakes.

As the route approached Raw Hide Buttes[28] it

[28] As to the origin of the name Raw Hide Buttes, Hi Kelly said: "A young man from Pike county, Missouri, had boasted that he would shoot the first Indian he saw on the plains. The young fellow had forgotten about it for the first month from the Missouri river. Upon his attention being called to his boast one day, about the first of june 1849, near the mouth of Raw Hide creek, he saw a camp of a few Indians on the Platte river and the fool shot one of them. That caused a lot of trouble as the Indians demanded the young man be turned over to them at once, else they would attack the train, con-

passed Nigger Baby spring, where W. C. Field, a hospital steward, had a homestead and served meals to transients.

A mile and a quarter to the north was RAW HIDE BUTTES station on Raw Hide creek, near the foot of Raw Hide Buttes.

Because of the fine grass along the creek and the natural shelter offered by the buttes and the adjoining hills, this locality had for many years been a favorite camping place for both red men and white. Remnants of a fur press, where buffalo hides had been baled, were still visible when the Black Hills stagecoaches pulled up.

J. W. Dear, trader at Red Cloud agency, who early in 1876 built some buildings at Raw Hide Buttes, advertised on May 30, as follows:

WANTED TO RENT OR SELL

A Ranche at Raw Hide Butte, on the road to the Black Hills. . . The House contains 4 rooms – kitchen, dining room, sleeping room, and sitting room. In the sitting room there is a large and comfortable fire place. The remainder of rooms will need stoves. In connection with the house there is a panneled corral, eight feet high and about 100 feet square. The Ranche has a good location and plenty of wood surrounding it, and plenty of good water, with good grazing grounds and fine Farming Lands, etc.

A week later, news reached Cheyenne that the Sioux had burned the ranch house and a wagon in the corral. It was not until august 1877 that a stage station was opened here.

sisting of some thirty wagons of California gold hunters. . . The man was surrendered to the Indians, who, in broad day light, tied and skinned him alive. It seems that while the poor fellow fainted a number of times he lived 'till they had him nearly skinned. That was what originated the name Raw Hide."

C. H. Atkins who homesteaded the place leased it to the Cheyenne and Black Hills stage company. For some time in the early 'eighties, while Luke Voorhees still was superintendent of the stage line, the station at Raw Hide Buttes was run by his sister and her husband, Mr. and Mrs. Amasa Lowrey. Although Lowrey was well to do, having made money in cattle, Mrs. Lowrey, an "austere person," milked from ten to fifteen cows and made butter to sell. Some of her butter reached the table at the officers' mess at Fort Laramie at one dollar a pound. Lowrey, as well as Voorhees, was reputed to have been a member of the Vigilantes who helped rid Montana of its outlaws.

Russell Thorp, sr., purchased the Raw Hide Buttes ranch from Atkins in 1882. After he became owner of the Cheyenne and Black Hills stage line in the spring of 1883, he made it his "home station." (see page 315 and plate 3)

Among those who were employed there by the Cheyenne and Black Hills Stage company at various times were: Steve Utter, D. G. Jenks, Henry Chase, Ed Patrick, Tom O'Haver, Poulton, Tom Black, and Bowen.

Leaving the timbered slopes of the buttes, the Black Hills road passed the SILVER SPRINGS RANCH, owned by O. J. Demmon, who raised horses.

The RAW HIDE SPRINGS, a favorite camping place of early freighters, were near Box Elder grove, about ten miles north of Raw Hide Buttes station.

And next came the stage station called RUNNING WATER (see plate 8) because of its location on the Running Water (L'Eau-qui-Court), also called the Niobrara river. Here J. W. Dear erected a station in the spring of 1876. The Indians immediately burned it.

Later another station was built and was run by Jack Madden. It had a large stone stage barn, 24 x 48 feet, with 8-foot walls, covered with a pole-and-dirt roof. The Cardinal's Chair, an eroded stone formation, on the edge of the meadow near the station, was an early day landmark.

In the early 'eighties when the mining boom struck this area, the Great Western Mining and Milling company operated a mine not far from the stage barn, at what was called Silver Cliff.

Saloon, stores, hotels, and other structures were erected near the station on land owned by Ellis Johnson. When the Wyoming Central railroad attempted to buy the land, Johnson held out for a high price. Frank Lusk, who owned a ranch east of the little townsite, offered his land at what the railway officials considered a more reasonable price, so they bought it. The new town, named Lusk, was laid out about a mile east of the old stage station. It quickly mushroomed into one of the most progressive and thriving towns of the entire territory.

Tom Earnest, Calvin Morse, and Jim Hogle were among the stage employees at the Running Water station. Frank Ketchum had charge of the telegraph office in connection with the station in Lusk.

The railway naturally played a big part in the development of LUSK, but the Cheyenne and Black Hills stage line, which for years made the north and south connections, contributed immeasurably to the growth of the little metropolis of the northern plains.

Three miles beyond Running Water, the Hills road branched. The stage at first took the right hand route, over what was known as Pollock's Cut-off, a trail recommended by Captain Pollock as being the most practicable one over which to reach Custer valley. From Running Water this route crossed Sage creek and Horse Head creek, and entered the Black Hills through Red Creek canyon.

At the crossing of Sage creek was the stage station named HAT CREEK RANCHE (*see plate* 9).[29] It was established in the autumn of 1876 by John (Jack) Bowman, assisted by Joe Walters, after the first building erected by J. W. Dear had been burned. This station, near bluffs and broken country called "breaks," was on the edge of the most dangerous section of the entire Cheyenne to Deadwood stage route in which occurred Indian raids and stagecoach holdups.

The main building at Hat Creek station, a compactly built log structure, had a tunnel underneath, which led to the bank of Sage creek and thus afforded access to water in case of an Indian siege.

Early in 1877, Jack Bowman advertised that he had his "hotel" in perfect running order and that he would "furnish accommodations to the traveling public at reasonable rates."

Attached to his establishment were: telegraph and post office, brewery, bakery, butcher and blacksmith shops. Bowman always kept grain and groceries on hand, as well as plenty of hay. He provided good stabling for horses. Soon after opening his station, Bowman brought his bride, Sallie C. Smith, up to the ranch from Denver.

[29] In 1875, after the Gordon party had been removed from French creek by the military, outposts were established in an effort to keep the white men out of the Black Hills. A detachment of soldiers sent from Fort Laramie to establish an outpost on Hat creek, in Nebraska, camped by mistake on Sage creek thirty miles or more westward. They named their camp Hat Creek and the name clung.

A number of buffalo were killed in the vicinity of Hat Creek ranche, as late as the summer of 1878.

Frequently Jack Bowman was deputized to assist in the arrest of outlaws and was one of the most reliable pioneer station masters along the entire Black Hills route. In september 1879, he sold his holdings to Charles Hecht, the "boss freighter." The price paid for the fine ranch of two hundred acres, under fence, buildings, corral, and four hundred head of American cattle was around ten thousand dollars.[30]

In the 'eighties, John Storrie and Tom Swan erected a large two-story building near the original log Hat Creek station, in which they ran a general store and road house which was popular not only with the stage travelers, but with the cowboys from the surrounding area.

Beyond the Hat Creek station, the Cheyenne and Black Hills trail diverged. In earlier times, when the stage ran to Custer City, the route went by the way of Indian creek, later it ran north along Old Woman's fork to Jenney Stockade on Beaver creek.

INDIAN CREEK ROUTE

Fifteen miles eastward from Hat Creek station on the early route was the HARDING RANCH on Indian creek. Clay bluffs surrounded the place and in one of them Harding excavated a dug-out for a dwelling and covered it with a thatched roof. A clay bank served for one side and the back of the station, while the other

---

[30] Bowman and his wife moved to Gunnison county, Colorado where he was elected sheriff in 1883. He built the Forest Queen hotel in Crested Butte, projected and built the Pioneer toll road, and had interests in many of the mines in the Elk mountain region, Colorado.

side and front were constructed of logs. In the structure were a kitchen, bedroom, and store. From the latter a subterranean passage led to a "dug-out fort," with log roof, and portholes on every side. A handful of men could defend themselves there against a large force, it was claimed. Below the "fort" and close to it, the Cheyenne and Black Hills stage company excavated a commodious and comfortable stable in a clay bank, in which the horses were kept.

Harding's ranch was a regular meal and telegraph station. Here during the summer of 1876, Captain James Egan and his "Grays" had a camp, while on patrol duty along the stage road.

Down Indian creek the road continued for twelve miles through the heart of a country over which numerous parties of Sioux crossed back and forth, on their way from the agencies to their hunting grounds along Powder river and the Big Horn mountains. Thence the road veered six miles to INDIAN SPRINGS, also called PRAIRIE SPRING.

Five miles beyond the spring was the CHEYENNE RIVER RANCHE, a stage station, built originally early in 1876 by J. W. Dear. A telegraph office was maintained here, as well as accommodations for the traveling public. Persimmon Bill Chambers and his brother, alleged leaders of a gang of horse thieves, made this ranch their hangout for a time.

About four miles northeast of the Cheyenne River station, near the entrance to Red canyon was the RED CANYON STATION, or Camp Collier, established by Major W. S. Collier, Company K, 4th Infantry. The station had comfortable quarters and the grounds were ornamented by rows of evergreen, set out by the

soldiers. HARLOW'S EATING HOUSE here was well managed and popular. The fine stockade quarters were
abandoned in june 1877, when the new short-cut route
from Hat creek to Jenney Stockade and Deadwood
was opened.

Red canyon offered one of the most practicable pas-
sageways into the Black Hills proper, but in the earliest
days the trip through the long, narrow gorge, shut in
by precipitous rocky walls, which rose a thousand feet
from the canyon floor, filled many a gold-seeker with
terror. Prospect holes scattered along through the
canyon presaged the approach to the mining country.

Twelve miles north from Red canyon was SPRING-
ON-HILL, and nine miles beyond was SPRING-ON-RIGHT,
stopping places of many Hillers.

Continuing about eight miles the stage route reached
PLEASANT VALLEY, one of the beauty spots in the Black
Hills. There, in 1877 James Fielding kept a dinner
station.

As the swaying coaches wound their way northward
from Pleasant valley, along the last nine miles of the
trip to Custer City, passengers could plainly see shafts
and tunnels on the mountainsides and numerous open
mining claims along French creek.

At CUSTER CITY in 1876, the Concord wheels rolled
to a stop in front of the Occidental hotel, kept by
W. M. Ward, an "old residenter" of Cheyenne, who it
was said, "feeds and lodges all who come, and sends
them away rejoicing." The little new town, with its
streets alive with men, wagons, and animals, nestled in
a valley surrounded by wooded hills.

The original trail from Custer north, went by the
way of Hillyo or Hill City, to Golden City (now

Sheridan), thence over a rough and rocky trail to Camp Crook (Pactola), then across Box Elder creek, Elk creek, over into Bear Butte creek, and then to Two Bit creek. From Two Bit creek it passed near what later was called Mountain ranch and followed the Hills to a very steep gulch called Smith's gulch into Split Tail gulch. From there it went into Montana City on Whitewood creek, near the mouth of Split Tail gulch, thence to Elizabeth Town, Fountain City and down into Deadwood.[31]

Later, in the spring of 1877, the Cheyenne and Black Hills stage from Custer followed a fifty-two mile road through the Hills to Deadwood, that was said to be the "nearest and most practicable route and a good one, with the exception of the last fifteen miles, which at present is very muddy and rough. . . Stations are close together, and good meals can be obtained all along the road."

On this route, north from Custer City was the TWELVE MILE station on Spring creek; next was the LOG CABIN HOUSE, owned and managed by a man named Gillette. Six miles beyond Gillette's was MOUNTAIN CITY (now Deerfield). Three and one-half miles farther was REYNOLDS RANCHE, a road stop.

On Rapid creek, twenty-eight miles from Custer, was the BULLDOG RANCH, owned by Madame Bulldog. For a time this was a stage station. Tim Coleman, one time owner of the ranch, was known as one of the interesting characters of the Hills. It was said that at Troy, New York his name had been Daugherty. Prize fighting had been his vocation. A favorite and oft-

[31] Outlined to author by George V. Ayres, Deadwood, from his diary.

repeated tale is to the effect that Coleman had a daughter who was married at the ranch. During the ceremony when the minister asked if she would promise
"to obey" and the bride answered, "Yes," Coleman
shouted: "That's a damn lie; you never obeyed anyone
in your life."

From the Bulldog ranch the road went to the head
of Whitewood creek and on down Whitewood to Deadwood.

As various changes were made in the route, other
stopping places during those early pioneer days were:
COLD SPRING RANCHE, 36 miles north of Custer; STONE
RANCHE, 40 miles; head of WHITEWOOD, 42 miles;
and Deadwood, estimated at from 52 to 54 miles north
of Custer. In Deadwood, the Cheyenne and Black Hills
stage office was next to The Place, a saloon-restaurant.

JENNEY STOCKADE ROUTE

During june 1877, a new cut-off was opened which
went north from Hat Creek station to Old Woman's
fork, so-named because the ghost of an Indian squaw
was supposed to be seen dancing in the moonlight on
a rimrock nearby. At the station on OLD WOMAN'S
FORK, Sourdough Dick was the stock tender.

The next station, about twenty-eight miles north of
Hat creek, was MAY'S RANCH on Lance creek. Here
Jim May was stock tender and station keeper.

Next came ROBBERS' ROOST station, on the Cheyenne
river, with Jim May's brother, D. Boone May in
charge, when he was not riding as a shotgun messenger
on the treasure coach. The crossing of the river here

with its steep embankments was an ideal place for outlaws and their horses to keep under cover preceding a
holdup.

Holding the ridge slightly northeastward from the
station the trail crossed the Cheyenne river and proceeded to JENNEY STOCKADE, close to Beaver creek,
fifty-six miles south of Deadwood.[82] This station was
operated in the summer and early fall of 1877 by James
Mathewson, who sold out in november to a Mrs. Scott,
one-time proprietress of the Scott house at Deer Lodge,
Montana. Under Mrs. Scott's management the station
was a breakfast and supper stop for stage passengers.
Beginning on april 10, 1877, the stages made night
trips between Jenney Stockade and Hat creek.

North from Jenney Stockade the road traversed a
most beautiful region of well-watered valleys, which
in season were covered with rich grasses and flowers of
almost every hue.

BEAVER STATION, with "Frenchy" as stock tender,
was next north along the trail after leaving Jenney
Stockade. It was also called BEAVER STOCKADE station,
probably because the stream was referred to as Beaver
Stockade.

About nineteen or twenty miles north of Jenney
Stockade, in a lonely spot in thickly timbered hills, was
the CANYON SPRINGS relay station, where William
Miner was stock tender. This was merely a log barn in
which quarters had been built for the tender. Here
occurred the biggest and most daring robbery of the

---

[82] In 1857, Lt. G. K. Warren built a corral on this site while on an exploratory expedition. Eighteen years later, Prof. Walter P. Jenney's expedition erected a substantial log cabin, called Jenney Stockade. In recent years
this was moved to Newcastle, Wyo., as a pioneer museum.

treasure coach, in the history of the Cheyenne and Black Hills stage line.

Because of its proximity to Cold Spring ranche, which was some two miles down the gulch, the robbery is often referred to as the "Cold Springs robbery."

Charles L. Snow was keeper of the COLD SPRING RANCHE, which was at the junction of the new cut-off road from Custer City and the Black Hills stage trail running north from Jenney Stockade.

A new and shorter route was opened in the fall of 1877, which crossed Spearfish river, nine miles north of Cold spring, and ran through Icebox canyon, past Valley station, kept by Henry Fosha, and Cheyenne Crossing. Thence the road passed Little Meadow, Divide, Ten Mile, Whitetail, Poorman's gulch, went through Central City, and down through Gayville into Deadwood.

Later, when the mail was diverted from Raw Hide Buttes by the way of Horse Head junction to connect with the Sidney-Deadwood line, the stage company established several new relay stations, including HILL or BLUFF STATION.

A still later mail contract took the Black Hills stages from Hat creek to Jenney Stockade, then northwestward by the way of Inyan Kara, along the western base of the Black Hills to SUNDANCE, Wyoming, and thence to SPEARFISH and Deadwood.

Crude as were these frontier stage stations at the side of the road, where the wagons stopped, they were havens to travel-weary men, women, children, and beasts.

Around their cheerful fires many a frontier tale was

unfolded and history was made. News of the day which was discussed over the stage station dinner tables, often was colored by recountings of holdups, shootings, hangings, and similar tragedies.

It always was an event when the spinning, squeaking, or mudcaked wheels of the stagecoaches and freight wagons rolled to a stop in front of the station's door. Those wheels were the links with the outside world.

The White Man's Road

During march 1876, hundreds of wheels on vehicles of various descriptions, often hub deep in mud, strained northward from Cheyenne for the Cheyenne and Black Hills Stage company. Voorhees and Brown vigorously pushed arrangements for the new stage line. In addition to using their own equipment they hired many freighting outfits to carry passengers, as well as freight and stage supplies. Chief among these freighters were: Small, Ames and Apel, A. H. (Heck) Reel, Charley E. Clay, Charles Hecht, Dick Dunne, Frank Whitney, and C. J. Todd. George Spain, for whom Calamity Jane is said to have whacked bulls that year, no doubt carried some of the stage freight.

Additional teams and outfits were obtained by Superintendent Voorhees, when necessity demanded, from the following feed and livery men: Mason & Kent, J. C. Abney, Terry and Hunter, H. S. Tracy, J. S. Tracy, and J. D. May.[33]

Terry and Hunter, owners of one of the popular stables of Cheyenne, were easily located by the stuffed horse that stood on the roof of their IXL stable. Newcomers who did not know that Frank Hunter, one of the partners, had given his horses most unusual names,

[33] In march 1876, these men signed an agreement to the following feed prices: single horse, per day to hay, 75 cents; span, $1.50 per day. Single horse, hay and grain per day, $1; span, $2 per day. Each man agreed to pay a forfeit of $50 for violation of the agreement.

often were amazed to hear him say: "Old Nero has been kicking Susan B. Anthony into the middle of next week. Olive Logan's all lamed up, and Archimedes, Sir Isaac Newton, and Dr. Mary Walker have been engaged to go to the spelling school tonight. I've sent Anna Dickinson over to be shod, and William Penn ought to have his teeth filled."

Draper and Hammond, Whipple and Hay, E. Nagle, Will Foglesong, Leibey and Nichols, Pease and Taylor, B. Hellman and F. Schweickert furnished everything for the stage stations from beds to pitchforks and saleratus.

In the winter preceding the purchase of the Black Hills stage line by Gilmer, Salisbury and Patrick, General George A. Custer said in a New York interview that he thought the Indians would "wait until the grass is plenty next spring. They will probably raise a trouble then." And "raise a trouble" they did!

As the snowdrifts disappeared from the gullies, the red men began to run off the stock and to attack the trains of miners and freighters going into the Hills. They centered their activities near Red canyon south of Custer valley, and along the Cheyenne river, the area through which the first stage wagons were moving and which soon was to be traversed by the Concord stages.

Added to the threat from Indians was the menace of a gang of outlaws, led by William (Persimmon Bill) Chambers.

The stage men constantly were on the alert, as they realized that their fine horses and equipment would make prized plunder for both the red warriors and the outlaws.

With only about a week to go before launching the

through-line, with its complete equipment, Voorhees received warning from Fort Laramie that the Sioux, who had recently been fighting with General Crook and his men in the Powder river country, would be crossing the stage road on their return to the Red Cloud agency.

The stage superintendent telegraphed to Fort Fetterman for information regarding the exact movement of the Indians. In reply, General Crook sent Voorhees a copy of the message which he had just sent to Lieutenant General Phil Sheridan. It read:

> Fort Reno via Fort Fetterman, march 23, 1876
> Lieut. General Phillip Sheridan, Fort Laramie, Wyo.
> We arrived here today after one of the hardest campaigns I ever experienced in the West. We succeeded in breaking up Crazy Horse's band of Cheyenne and Minneconjous, killing more than one hundred Indians and burning their village on Little Powder river. An immense quantity of ammunition, arms and dried meats were stored in their lodges, all of which we destroyed. Our loss was four men killed and eight wounded. Snow has fallen every day during the campaign, the weather being intensely cold. I cut loose from the wagon train on the 17th and scouted Tongue and Rosebud rivers. General Reynolds with a part of the Command was pushed forward on a trail leading to the Village of Crazy Horse at the mouth of the Little Powder. This he attacked and destroyed. Crazy Horse had with him in all about one-half of the Indians of the Reservation. I would again urgently recommend the transfer of these Indians to the Agencies on the Missouri river. I am satisfied that if Sitting Bull is on this side of the Yellowstone that he is camped at the mouth of Powder River. (Signed) George Crook, Brigadier General

Coincident with the receipt of this message, Voorhees received word that the body of Jake Harker, one of his mail carriers between Hat creek and Camp Robinson, had been found on the road scalped. The mail sacks were torn open and the contents scattered.

Voorhees knew that troops were needed badly for the Indian campaigns in the Big Horn area, but he nevertheless hoped for some help along the Black Hills route and at once appealed to the government for military protection. For, as he said, should the Indians cross the road at a time "when any of our stages are in sight or near a station they will clean up the outfit."

At this time, Scott Davis of Denver, Colorado, who later became captain of the "shotgun messengers" who guarded the treasure shipments of Gilmer, Salisbury and Patrick, was employed by Voorhees to take large freight trains through to Deadwood with forage and supplies for the stage company.

Voorhees opened the main stage office in Cheyenne, just west of the new Inter-Ocean hotel on Sixteenth street, and an office for express, at the Union Pacific depot. The stage barn and corrals, enclosed by a high lumber and log fence, were on the northeast corner of the intersection of 20th and O'Neil streets, with the blacksmith shop extending back to 21st street, on lots 3, 4, 5 and 6 of block 269.

On april 3, the wheels of three fine Concord coaches rolled north out of Cheyenne up the Black Hills trail. The graceful, curving bodies of the coaches, suspended on heavy leather thoroughbraces, were loaded "to the gills," including the China seat. One record gives the number of passengers to a coach as twenty-two; another says eighteen. Jack Gilmer, on the "boot" of the lead coach, was handling the ribbons. The through Cheyenne and Black Hills Stage and Express at long last was a reality!

At Fort Laramie, Gilmer entrusted this first contingent of through passenger coaches into the care of Division Agent "Stuttering" Brown, who took the coaches through to Custer City in safety. Superintendent Luke Voorhees followed close behind to check up on everything and to be on hand, in case of necessity.

The first official advertisement for through Black Hills passenger service, over the new stage line, appeared in the Cheyenne *Leader* of april 11, 1876. The stages now were scheduled to leave each terminus every other day, but the proprietors promised a daily line, just as soon as travel justified.

Scarcely had the dust of these first through stages settled, than Indians attacked a party of Hillers near the Cheyenne river. A few days later, when Superintendent Voorhees started on his return trip from Custer City, he came upon a ghastly scene at Red canyon, about three miles from the Cheyenne river stage station.

According to Voorhees:

The Metz family were all murdered. A colored woman who was with the Metz family was taken prisoner.[84] When I came to where they had camped it was with horror that I saw the beastly, mutilating, scalping and dismembering of the bodies. . . I, with some of my men, gathered up the fragments as best we could and by knocking a wagon box to pieces, did the best we could under the circumstances and excitement to bury them, as we were looking for the Indians to pick us up any moment. . .[85]

[84] The colored woman, Rachel Briggs, also was killed. Her body later was found by a man named Hoskins and his companions. Evidence showed the woman had put up a gallant fight for her life. Her body was full of arrows.

[85] Mr. and Mrs. Charles Metz of Laramie City, had been in Custer City engaged in the bakery business. After making a stake they were returning home. Relatives had their bodies exhumed, taken to Laramie, and on may 14, 1876, a large public funeral was held at the I.O.O.F. Hall. The bodies now lie in Greenview cemetery. A stone marks the grave on which is inscribed: "Killed by Indians in Red Cañon."

Upon his arrival at the Cheyenne river station, Voorhees found that three of the Metz party had escaped, but were badly wounded. In response to his appeal for medical aid, General Bradley sent an ambulance from Fort Laramie, escorted by cavalry.

Before the troops were able to cover the one hundred miles from the fort to the stage station, two of the wounded men, Beergessir of Virginia City, Nevada, and Gresham of Bigelow, Holt county, Missouri, died. The third man, William (California Bill) G. Felton, was removed in the army ambulance to the post hospital, and recovered. Later he worked for the stage company as a stock tender.

Although it was generally accepted that Indians had killed the Metz family, there was some evidence that the crime might have been committed by Persimmon Bill and his gang of renegades.

Voorhees had not been back in Cheyenne long, following the Red canyon tragedy, when he received word that "Stuttering" Brown had been badly wounded, probably fatally, in an attack on the trail north of Hat Creek station. Brown, the message stated, was begging to talk with Voorhees before he died.

Again Voorhees sent a request for medical aid to the commander at Fort Laramie. Then he jumped into the saddle and spurred his horse northward out of Cheyenne. By changing mounts every ten miles, the sturdy stage man reached Fort Laramie in nine hours. Stopping only long enough to obtain a fresh horse, he headed across the Platte river in the direction of Hat Creek station.

About one o'clock in the morning, in the shadow of Raw Hide Buttes, the stage official met a solemn column of cavalry, escorting a blanket-wrapped form. Brown had lived only twenty-four hours, although acting Assistant Surgeon Petteys had done all that he could to save the man's life.

What had Brown wanted to tell Voorhees? Did he surmise that Persimmon Bill had shot him? No one ever knew. Voorhees turned back with the escort. From Fort Laramie he telegraphed for Graves, a Cheyenne embalmer, to bring a coffin up on the stage and take charge of Brown's body.

Charlie Edwards and a man named "Curly," who were with Brown at the time he was shot, told Voorhees that they were making a night trip in one of the company's fast freight wagons. About eighteen miles north of Hat Creek station, a shower of bullets suddenly rattled about the wagon. Brown told his men that he was mortally wounded and urged them to save themselves.

The team ran away, but the men helped Brown mount one of the mules which they had been leading behind the wagon. The men then mounted other mules and rode into the night.

Three men from Hat Creek stage station, who had started north to look for the outfit when it did not arrive at the station as expected, found Brown lying on the prairie the next morning. The mule was standing by his side.

As in the case of the Metz murders, it was generally supposed that Indians had made the attack. George V. Ayres, who was in Custer City at the time, recorded the following in his diary:

Wednesday. apr. 26. . . . Parties coming in from Cheyenne report the shooting of Stuttering Brown by Indians about five miles this side of Indian creek.

A few men were of the opinion that it was not the work of Indians, as the red men seldom attacked late at night.

Investigation showed that Brown had been having a good deal of trouble with thieves who were taking the stage stock. On his way down from Custer City, he discovered that a fine team which he intended to use on the run north through Red canyon, and which he had left at the Hagers ranch on Cheyenne river, had been stolen. Being quick of temper, Brown was incensed at his loss. He accused Persimmon Bill of the theft and threatened to kill Bill if he did not quit the stage road.

Bill went away at once with the remark that he would get even with Brown. Hagers tried to persuade Brown and his men to stay at the ranch all night, but Brown insisted on pushing along. It seems logical to believe that he met his death at the hands of Persimmon Bill.[36]

Brown's wife and daughter and son, aged 13 and 15, came to Cheyenne immediately upon being notified of his death. Accompanied by Colonel M. T. Patrick, one of the owners of the stage line, they took the body to

[36] A little more than a month before Brown's death, Persimmon Bill shot and killed Sergeant Sullivan near Fort Fetterman, when the sergeant was trying to retrieve stolen Indian ponies. Next, Bill joined a party to the Black Hills and bragged that he was the leading spirit of a regularly organized chain of horse thieves which stretched from far distant diggings to railway points in every direction. Some of its members, he said, were stationed at different points between the Hills and the San Juan and southwestern Colorado. Evidence pointed to Bill and his confederates as the ones who had recently stolen 100 mules and a team of horses from Charles Sasse who was freighting a $10,000 cargo of "Early Times" whisky into the Hills. That robbery occurred near Red canyon.

Omaha for interment. Brown left an estate of twenty-five thousand dollars.

Said the Cheyenne *Leader:*

Cheyenne owes H. E. Brown a heavy debt of gratitude. He has worked night and day for the past two or three months in getting a stage line established from this city to the Black Hills, and by so doing aided inestimably in our city's advancement. His personal friendship and influence with men of large means, and his willingness to invest his own money in the enterprise, his arduous labors in the establishing of the route, the completion of which was on the eve of attainment at the time of his murder, show that he was deeply interested in the welfare of Cheyenne. . .

Before leaving Fort Laramie, Voorhees telegraphed to Governor John Thayer asking for guns and ammunition for use on the stagecoaches between Fort Laramie and Custer City. Four days later the governor went to Omaha to confer personally with General Crook. He asked for military protection, especially for the stage stations at Red canyon and Hat creek (on Sage creek). He reported that, "The Indians crawl up the sides of the canyon and shoot down or throw rocks upon travelers."

As a result of the governor's trip, General Crook made a hurried visit to Cheyenne and Fort Laramie and immediately ordered a force of cavalry sent from Fort Laramie, under command of Captain James Egan, to protect the Custer route.

The word that Captain "Teddy" Egan and his "Grays," known as the "pick and pride of General Crook's cavalry," were to be placed on the Black Hills road was very welcome in Cheyenne. Egan and his men had recently distinguished themselves in Reynold's command, during an attack on Crazy Horse's village in the Powder river area.

Cheyenne at once boasted that no other route to the Black Hills had such military protection as the Cheyenne route now had! And put on a bold front. In the very month when the stage line had been launched with much misgiving and fear of Indians, when the Metz family had been murdered, and "Stuttering" Brown been killed, the theater goers of Cheyenne complacently enjoyed burlesques, comedies, and farces by the Lovell Family at the Opera house, including "Bombastes Furioso" and the first act of "Richard, the Third."

But Cheyenne's bravado did not convince everyone that the way to the Black Hills was safe. There was a noticeable slackening of northbound travel, except by large trains moving along together.

Toward the last of april, Hank Steward closed the Six Mile ranch, near Fort Laramie, because of the "falling off" of the Black Hills travel. Few teams ventured north of the fort.

Isaac Bard, whose road ranch on Little Bear, had been opened only a few weeks, recorded in his diary on may 1, 1876:

Men are coming out very fast in large parties. Some of their wagons show marks of the Indian bullets.

Many of the men who were "coming out" of the Hills, had gone there with little or no money and scant provisions. Pathetic and forlorn figures many of them were now. They had not been able to pick up the coveted gold nuggets on the streets of Custer City. Many of them were embittered and destitute. Disappointed, disheartened, and disgusted, most of these unfortunates walked back to Cheyenne beside the wheels of freighting outfits.

Around the Cheyenne bars in the wee sma' hours, in that spring of 1876, could be heard the plaintive notes of various versions of a song called "The Dreary Black Hills."

As remembered by one of the "returners," the song went:

> Cheyenne's round-house is filled every night
> With loafers and bummers in all sorts of plight;
> On their backs is no clothes; in their pockets no bills
> Each day they keep starting for the dreary Black Hills.
>
> And when I got there no gold could I find
> I thought of my true love I left behind
> And my old daddy's home that lay in the dell
> And the gold in the Black Hills can go plumb to hell.
>
> Don't go away, stay at home if you can
> Stay away from that city, they call it Cheyenne,
> For old Sitting Bull or Comanche Bills
> Will lift off your hair in the dreary Black Hills.

In contrast to these disillusioned men, hundreds of newly arrived miners were congregating in Cheyenne, restless to be off to the Hills. They inspected the Indian trophies captured in the recent fight with Crazy Horse, which were being displayed by George M. Jones at the Railroad house before being sent to the Centennial exposition in Philadelphia. They took chances on "an elegant pair of carriage horses and a light open wagon and harness" which were raffled off at the Inter-Ocean hotel bar.

Some drifted into McDaniels theatre where Alf

Burnett, favorite humorist, and Martinetti's pantomime troupe were features. Others attended the renowned Georgia Minstrels and the Tennessee Jubilee Singers at the Opera house. It is not of record how many attended the lecture entitled, "Love and Marriage," delivered by Dr. Mary Walker, late surgeon in the U.S. Army, who also appeared at the Opera house.

At the Bella Union the time flew swiftly with clog and bone solos, and the serio-comic songs of Lurline Monteverde, "the favorite of the public." The Lenton troupe of acrobats also proved popular with the miners. Mdlle. Cerito, a fascinating "quick-change artiste" of much grace and beauty, played to Cheyenne audiences for many weeks.

Especially busy during those uncertain spring days were the well known and highly paid, well-dressed gamblers of the "Magic City," who worked in regular shifts and were "gentlemanly in manner." Among these were: The Preacher, Squirrel Tooth, Poker Dan, Wiffletree Jim, Coon Can Kid, and Timberline. The latter was discovered to be the "locater" for the buckfoot gang, which headquartered at Webb City, Missouri. As advance man for the pay-off gang, which framed races, Timberline picked out lucrative locations.

Often seen in front of the Black Hills stage office were the familiar street characters: "Cherokee Bob" and "Old Zip Coon." The former, a plainsman, usually wore only one boot. His garments were tied together and hung loosely on his form. He was famous for stories and the amount of liquor he could hold. "Old Zip Coon" was an artist on the violin.

Cheyenne had a number of Chinese residents and

at least two dens where opium was smoked by both Orientals and Occidentals. And while Red Cloud and Sitting Bull were rampaging in the north country, a small Tong war was being carried on within Cheyenne's own limits.

According to Josh Wong, who had recently arrived from New York, there were in Cheyenne at the time, six Kung Chows and nine Ning Yungs. The latter, he declared, were the "riff raff of China."

One evening, quite oblivious to the Tong war going on in the rear of McDaniels' famous house of entertainment, Chief Spotted Tail of the Brule Sioux, with a retinue of lesser head men, occupied a box in the theater and seemingly enjoyed the performance as much as anyone in the audience.

Despite the restless mobs of men milling up and down the streets and the streams of liquor that passed over the bars, Cheyenne was remarkably orderly except perhaps for the numerous runaway teams on the main streets. Contrary to the "Magic City's" reputation, shootings were more uncommon than common, and although it often was conceded that Cheyenne was comprised of a "mixed people who took their liquor straight," it was no longer the hell-bent, riotous, frontier town of the late 'sixties. And this change had not come about by accident.

A steady, progressive development was the result of the leadership of such men as Joseph M. Carey, Alex Swan, and Francis E. Warren. At an early political meeting, at which Judge Joseph M. Carey presided, he laid two revolvers on the table in front of him with the quiet remark, "Gentlemen, this will be an orderly meeting."

Rival towns never failed to emphasize Cheyenne's failings. For instance, one evening in a Denver theater the villain of the play was advised to "leave the United States and go to Cheyenne."

After the death of "Stuttering" Brown, the stage officials did not attempt to send the regular coaches through to Custer City. Instead, they kept their freight wagons moving with supplies, in large trains, with other freighters and outfitters, and accommodated as many passengers in the wagons as could be cared for.

May 1876 was a month of continual Indian harassment on the stage road between Hat Creek station and Red canyon. When P. A. Gushurst,[37] a passenger, who had purchased a "through" fare, asked for a refund on his ticket between Fort Laramie and Custer, because of the suspension of coach service, Colonel Matt Patrick told Gushurst and his partner, that if they would go in a freight wagon they could take whatever they wanted with them, in lieu of a refund. According to Gushurst, "we took plenty."

Among other passengers carried by the Cheyenne and Black Hills Stage company around may first, was M. V. Boughton, cattleman of Cheyenne, who with five others, went into the hills on a stage freight wagon. Boughton's herders preceded him with the first herd of cattle to reach the vicinity of Custer valley.

A. J. Parshall, of the firm of Ward, Parshall & May, who had taken the second sawmill into the Black Hills in february, arrived in Cheyenne from Custer City on may 6. Parshall had with him five pounds of coarse gold, worth about twelve hundred dollars,

[37] Statement made by P. A. Gushurst to author. Mr. and Mrs. Gushurst, who were married in the first ceremony held in Lead, South Dakota, may 26, 1878, are now (1948) residents of Denver, Colorado.

washed from virgin soil of the Hills. It had been purchased for the Cheyenne and Black Hills Stage company, then buying up all of the gold obtainable. Parshall also carried an order from George B. Moulton,
agent, for some gold scales and a safe for the stage
office in Custer.

Early in 1876, Custer City comprised approximately
four hundred buildings. But almost immediately the
news of richer strikes to the north turned men's eyes
and feet in that direction.

By the time the first through stagecoaches of Gilmer,
Salisbury and Patrick reached their Black Hills terminus, Custer City, in april, a rush was on toward
Deadwood Gulch. Almost over night Custer City became a so-called "deserted village," except for the continual turnover of Hillers, freighters, and others who
stopped en route north.

Judge Kuykendall, who with Peter McKay, had led
a large party of prospectors up to the Hills late in
december 1875, wrote to Cheyenne, early in may 1876,
as follows:

Custer City is a "dead duck"; Indians and white thieves are stealing
all the stock; one or the other got away with my ponies. . . Am on
foot in a strange country; but am not like Richard, for I have no
kingdom to squander on a plug.

Very soon the Judge moved on up to Deadwood,
from which he wrote:

Every miner having a claim is taking out money, running all the way
from five to one hundred and fifty dollars a day to the hand. . . Millions will be made. . . I cannot describe it on paper. . . *Stages,
telegraph,* and a *bank* are needed.

Instead of talking about Harney's peak, Spring and Rapid creeks, men in Cheyenne now talked glibly of Gold Run, Blacktail, Splittail, Hoodoo creek, Stand Off bar and Falsebottom creek. Hillyo or Hill City, fourteen miles north of Custer, mushroomed to two hundred and fifty or more cabins almost over night.

Luke Voorhees realized that the stage company's plans must be expanded to push the stage line on to Deadwood as soon as possible.

The Indians kept up their attacks on the wagon trains. Scott Davis, who was taking a twenty-mule team outfit of supplies into the Hills for the stage company was in a fight on Indian creek. With outfits belonging to May and Parrot and S. R. Gwinn, Davis helped ward off the Indians for more than three hours. One man with Gwinn's party was wounded and fourteen head of stock were killed or wounded. Through the timely arrival of Egan's "Grays," who were summoned from Raw Hide Buttes, many of the freighters retained their scalps.

Shortly afterward, Charles Clark, employed by Voorhees as stage driver and mail carrier from Fort Laramie to Red Cloud, was ambushed and killed about ten miles west of the agency. The murderers, evidently a war party, took the four stage horses and left the dead man, the stage, and the mail on the road. Clark's body was found by a detachment of troops, sent out from Camp Robinson. Clark, one of the best men in the employ of the stage company, who had been tending stock at Fort Laramie, volunteered to make the trip to the agency with the mail, when the regular driver refused to take the run because of Indians. Three days after Clark was killed the service was temporarily suspended.

With additional depredations occurring almost daily, Cheyenne acknowledged the Indian trouble along the Black Hills trail, and complained bitterly that the "starving" Indians from the Red Cloud agency, "having been supplied recently with a surfeit of flour, sugar and coffee, have recovered sufficient strength to go on their annual horse-stealing expeditions."

Spotted Tail replied, in reference to the "free rations," that he saw "white men going to the Black Hills and carrying off our gold. I do not trouble them. So if the white man gives us rations for nothing, he comes and takes away our gold, without our consent, for nothing. We do not feel much in debt."

Less than three weeks before the terrible battle in which General George A. Custer and his men lost their lives in june 1876, Spotted Tail and his son-in-law, a Frenchman named Bousquet (Bushy), were guests at the Inter-Ocean hotel in Cheyenne. Spotted Tail said then that his own people, the Brules, would not go on the war path, but declared that "large numbers have gone from Red Cloud and other agencies on the Missouri river, all concentrating on Powder river for a fight. Their chiefs are haranguing the braves and urging them to stay in camp until the troops come and not to go out in small parties." He reported at that time that more than seventeen hundred lodges were collected up in the north.

Evidently what he said was taken rather lightly in Cheyenne, as the editor of one newspaper referred to the Chief as "Old Spot" and "Variegated Narrative, the noble son-of-a-gun."

As the result of the efforts of Governor Thayer and the business men of Cheyenne, it was announced the last of may, that two troops of cavalry and three companies of infantry would be stationed on the Black Hills route to escort trains from station to station and to skirmish in the vicinity of the route. Additional companies were expected to arrive in june, to bring the total force on patrol duty to about ten troops of cavalry and seven companies of infantry.

It was a great strain on the military just at this time to place the troops on such duty, as the men were needed badly in the northern campaign under General Crook.[38]

Indian depredations in the Red canyon area were so numerous, while troops were getting ready to go on patrol duty, that the line of supply was practically severed between Custer City and Fort Laramie, around the first of june. In desperation, Voorhees assigned Agent Moulton of his Custer City office, the task of organizing an expedition to negotiate a trip with supplies from the fort straight through to the Deadwood mining district. Under escort of Captain Egan's "Grays," reinforced by Captain G. Russell's Company K of the Third Cavalry, Moulton's train of seventy-five teams crossed the treacherous stretch of country early in june, and brought to the miners thousands of pounds of badly needed supplies.

After escorting this outfit to Deadwood, Agent Moulton returned to Custer City and soon went down to Cheyenne, where he reported that approximately ten thousand men were working in Deadwood and Whitewood gulches. Deadwood, he said, was hard to describe, as it was "about three miles long and fifty feet wide."

---

[38] General Crook left Fort Fetterman with 47 officers and about 1,000 men on may 29 for the summer campaign against the "hostile" Indians in the Big Horn area.

Just when it seemed as if Luke Voorhees had almost more than he could handle with his new stage line, Second Assistant Postmaster-General Brady asked if it would be possible for him to investigate the feasibility of the Post Office department establishing a mail route from Livingston, Montana to the Black Hills.

Brady stated that numerous petitions had been sent to the department urging such action and said that because of the reports of Indian troubles he had not been able to get one of his special agents to attempt a trip through the district of the proposed route.

Voorhees went. And in telling of the trip later he said:

I knew very well the safest and quickest way for me was to take one of my best horses, one able to endure a severe and hard ride; that would feed on the grass at the end of a picket rope, as there were no settlements on the trail between Custer City and Livingston, Mont. As I had many streams to cross which compelled me to swim my horse, and which were too dangerous to undertake the fording in the night, I was compelled to travel in daylight, although it was at that period the fiercest part of the Indian war of 1876. I had been informed that General Miles was on the Little Missouri and Big Horn rivers. General Custer, in conjunction with Majors Benteen and Reno, was ordered to strike Sitting Bull's bands on the Little Big Horn, so it was extremely lucky for me that the Indians were farther east than my trail caused me to take, as I did not see either Indian or white man until I had gone far enough to satisfy myself that there could be no practicable road for a mail route from the Northern Pacific railroad to Custer City or Deadwood. I camped with some prospectors who I was lucky to find and get a cup of coffee. I then pulled out at about four o'clock in the morning of june, the 25th.

I almost lost my courage when ready to return, as the reports of Indian depredations caused my friends to insist upon my not making the attempt to return alone. I knew I could make the return in 24 hours if I had no bad luck. I did make the trip to Custer City in twenty-four hours. I then took another fresh saddle horse to ride to Fort Laramie. During my trip from Livingston to the Black Hills was the day of the Custer massacre by Sitting Bull's Indians.

While Voorhees was on the Montana trip, the buildings at J. W. Dear's ranch on Raw Hide creek, which he had erected in anticipation of the new through stage line, were burned by the Indians. Simultaneously two or three of the stage company's new stations between Fort Laramie and Custer, including one near Sage creek, were also burned. A band of Sioux even ventured as far south as the Chugwater stage station. There they swooped down and ran off twenty horses belonging to Hi Kelly.

For a brief time the wagon wheels along the Black Hills trail stood idle, as men hesitated to cross the Indian-infested country.

They Roll Again

While wagon wheels were idling in that late spring of 1876, word reached Cheyenne that one hundred and fifty Montana miners had reached Deadwood and were paying from two thousand to seven thousand dollars each for claims. Nothing, not even the painted, befeathered warriors, could continue to hold back the gold-maddened throng. They demanded immediate transportation into the Black Hills!

Gilmer, Salisbury and Patrick decided to try to open up quick through communication with Deadwood. They loaded a "fast freight train" with grain, flour, and vegetables. In charge of C. A. Skinner, the "train" rolled out of the "Magic City of the Plains" on the morning of june 12, 1876, headed north. Twelve days later it reached Custer City safely and pulled into Deadwood on june 28, having made a remarkably quick trip, in view of the 32-hour lay-over at Hat Creek station, and eighteen hours spent at Custer City.

Close on the tracks of the freight wagons rattled a large passenger wagon belonging to the Cheyenne and Black Hills Stage company, into which were wedged Jack Langrishe, the well known actor, his wife, and twelve troopers. After successfully opening the New Dramatic theatre in Cheyenne early in june, Langrishe had decided to head for the gulches of gold.

Everything along the Black Hills route was in a

state of excitement and hustle. The military was busy establishing permanent camps and sending escorts with the Hillers. Egan and his "Grays" had orders to patrol the road between Fort Laramie and Custer City, at least twice a month.

Calamity Jane, evidently catching the northern fever, made a dash for the "borderland." Said the Cheyenne *Leader,* june 20, 1876:

On sunday, june 10, that notorious female, Calamity Jane, greatly rejoiced over her release from durance vile, procured a horse and buggy from Jas. Abney's stable, ostensibly to drive to Ft. Russell and back. By the time she had reached the Fort, however, indulgence in frequent and liberal potations completely befogged her not very clear brain, and she drove right by the place, never drawing rein until she reached Chug, 50 miles distant. Continuing to imbibe bug-juice at close intervals and in large quantities throughout the night, she woke up the next morning with a vague idea that Fort Russell had been removed, but still being bent on finding it, she drove on, finally sighting Fort Laramie, 90 miles distant. Reaching there she discovered her mistake, but didn't show much disappointment. She turned her horse out to grass, ran the buggy into a corral, and began enjoying life in camp after her usual fashion. When Joe Rankin reached the Fort, several days later she begged of him not to arrest her, and as he had no authority to do so, he merely took charge of the Abney's outfit, which was brought back to this city sunday.

With the distribution of troops along the Hills route, the Concord coaches were soon rocking along again. A weekly coach, scheduled to leave Fort Laramie for Custer City every saturday, went into operation on june 24. The stage company announced that as soon as the roads were "clear of Indians," so that the station keepers and stock on the route would be safe, it would put on a tri-weekly.

The day after the regular run was resumed, there occurred, not far from Wyoming's northern boundary, the disastrous Battle of the Little Big Horn, in which General George A. Custer[39] and 256 men met death. News of the tragedy, however, did not reach the outside world until around the fourth of july.

On july 6, news headlines in Cheyenne were heavily "boxed" and read:

Satanic Sioux. General Custer's Command Slaughtered Like Sheep. Seventeen Commissioned Officers, Including Custer Family, Killed. The Seventh Cavalry Was Cut To Pieces by Sitting Bull's Fiends. The Battle Field A Slaughter Pen. . .

The states nearest the Indian troubles were greatly aroused over the so-called "massacre." Public meetings were held and hundreds of men volunteered to go into the field to fight the "hostiles." There was, however, no legal provision to permit the secretary of war to accept the services of the various hurriedly organized groups. General Sherman explained that the summer campaign was being made at the request of the Indian department and not the War department, and that the purpose was to drive the Indians back to their reservations, not to try to annihilate them.

The eagerness of the volunteers to go after scalps cooled.

Travel resumed its regular flow through Cheyenne. Soon the streets were filled with great trains of freight wagons; merchants worked long hours filling huge

[39] In view of the fact that present day authorities give New Romley, Ohio, as the birthplace of Custer, it is interesting to compare the following paragraph from the Cheyenne *Daily Leader,* july 29, 1876, which reads: "It will be surprising to many to learn that the brave Gen. Custer was of foreign birth. He was born in Ispringen, near Pforsheim, in Baden, Germany, and emigrated when a child with his parents, who settled in New Romley, Harrison county, Ohio. Formerly his name was written 'Custar'; since his return from a trip to Germany, however, he appears to have written 'Custer,' his original family name, however being Kuester."

orders, destined for Custer City and Deadwood; and money circulated freely. The northbound stages were crowded to capacity, and the stage management stressed the fact that it was "taking every pains to make passengers as comfortable and time as fleet as possible."

Within a few weeks, in that summer of 1876, more than half a million dollars worth of Black Hills gold reached Cheyenne, chiefly via stage coach express. In the windows of most of the Cheyenne business houses, gold was displayed in the form of dust, nuggets, bars, or jewelry. Reports told of the Stebbins and Post bank buying gold dust in lots of from two thousand to ten thousand dollars a day. Shipments were made by the local banks to large eastern cities. That was all the people in the east needed to send their enthusiasm for the Hills to high pitch.

A matter of great concern to everyone in the Hills, from the first days of prospecting, had been that of receiving and sending mail.

During the early rush there was no government provision for mail delivery. Letters usually were carried in or out by freighters or individuals as an accommodation.

On january 12, 1876, James W. Allen, recorder of the Jenney mining district, who brought a large letter mail to Cheyenne from Hill City and Custer valley, emphasized the fact that the miners were clamoring for established mail service. It was pointed out then that no government contract could be let while the Sioux claimed title to the land.

A month later, on february 10, sixty letters were carried on horseback from Custer to Red Cloud agency, by Ben Arnold (Connor) at one dollar per letter. This often was referred to as the "first pony express in the Hills."

Late in february 1876, when Judge William Kuykendall reached Cheyenne with hundreds of letters written by Hillers, he carried a petition signed by four hundred "residents" of Custer City and Hill City, who asked for the establishment of a mail route. This petition was forwarded to Washington, D.C.

On his return to the Hills on march 8, Judge Kuykendall carried all letters that were in the Cheyenne post office awaiting delivery in the Hills. He made no charge for his services. Soon afterward, Godfrey Mason, also a good-will letter carrier, reached the camps.

Among the six hundred letters carried early in april, to the Hills by J. W. Lytle, some were not stamped. But the post office officials forwarded them by Lytle to their designated destinations.

About this time, a man named Clippinger established a pony packet line to carry mail and light express matter from Fort Laramie to various points in the Hills. His service, however, was rather intermittent.

In july, Seymour, Utter & Ingalls launched what they called the "Pioneer Pony Express" and advertised that they were fully prepared to deliver express, as well as mail. Their carriers made the trip between Ft. Laramie and Deadwood in forty-eight hours and often carried three thousand to forty-five hundred letters, at a charge of twenty-five cents each.

Two members of this company, "Bloody Dick" Seymour and Charlie (Colorado Charlie) Utter, were friends of Wild Bill Hickok. Utter, who had handled pack trains over Argentine pass and all over the early Colorado mining country from Georgetown to Snake river, some seven years before, maintained a camp at Deadwood during the summer and fall of 1876.

A spectacular 200-mile race was scheduled between Utter's pony express and a rival line, to finish in Deadwood, on august 2, but that was the day Jack McCall shot Wild Bill Hickok.[40] The death of Wild Bill stole the spotlight, and the result of the race received little or no publicity in the newspapers.

Joseph Mason, an experienced liveryman of Cheyenne, went to Deadwood in august, to survey the possibility of establishing a second pony express line from Cheyenne, but abandoned the idea.

Although the company in which Charlie Utter was the prime mover, was "meeting with great favor at the hands of the people," the owners sold out to Clippinger, whose services did not prove so satisfactory.

As the stage wagons began to go through to Deadwood and the regular Concord runs later were established, the local mail and express were entrusted entirely to the stage line and the pony riders sought other trails.

Encouraged by the defeat of Custer and his men,

---

[40] James Butler (Wild Bill) Hickok, soldier, scout, and United States marshal, was well known to the owners of the stage line, as he had been a familiar figure on the streets of Cheyenne. There he had married Agnes Lake, an accomplished equestrienne, a few months previous. Hickok's shooting matches with Major Talbot, a noted marksman, were much talked of events in the "Magic City." Talbot's favorite expression before each match was, "Get out yer eagle eye, Bill."

Wild Bill's remains were taken in charge by Charlie Utter, who paid for burial and placed a headboard on the grave that read: WILD BILL/ J. B. Hickok,/ killed by the assassin/ Jack M'Call,/ in Deadwood, Black Hills,/ Aug. 2d, 1876./ Pard, we will meet again/ In the happy Hunting Ground/ To part no more,/ Good bye,/ Colorado Charlie C. H. Utter.

the Sioux, in the summer of 1876, became bolder than ever. Aided by white renegades from the mining camps they continued their depredations along the Black Hills stage route.

In july, William F. (Buffalo Bill) Cody, as a scout with General Wesley Merritt, for the Fifth Cavalry, had his notorious fight with Chief Yellow Hand at a point where the main Powder river Indian trail intersected the Cheyenne and Black Hills stage road.

Shortly afterward, on august 2, an open attack on the down coach occurred. C. H. Cameron was on the boot, with four passengers aboard. The Indians began the attack on Indian creek and followed the stage for twelve miles. Using long range guns, they shot from every bluff near the road. Soon the one needle gun on the stage, went out of order, and the Indians began to close in.

One of the passengers was shot in the cheek; another had the rim of his hat shot away and his forehead skinned; another was shot through the clothing.

When the red men at last blocked the road in front of the coach, Cameron swung the horses out of the ruts and sent them galloping toward a bluff. There he and the passengers took to some brush. After dark they made their way on foot to the Hat Creek station. A party of soldiers, sent out the next morning to bring in the coach, found that the attackers had cut up the harness, bashed in the top of the coach, opened the mail sacks, and had made off with the horses.

Immediately afterward small bands of Sioux swept down into the Chugwater valley. Like lightning they struck all along the stage route. They ran off stock from the ranches of Johnny Owens at Chug springs and from his neighbor, Ed Carrington. Hi Kelly, the stage station proprietor at Chugwater, who was in Cheyenne on business, rushed north at once with men and ammunition. But the Indians had "vamoosed."

On august 15, congress stipulated in the Indian appropriation act[41] that no money should be paid to any band of Sioux Indians,

"while said band is engaged in hostilities against the white people; and hereafter there shall be no appropriation made for the subsistence of said Indians, unless they shall first agree to relinquish all right and claim to any country outside the boundaries of the permanent reservation established by the treaty of eighteen hundred and sixty-eight for said Indians, and also so much of their said permanent reservation as lies west of the one hundred and third meridian of longitude, and shall also grant right of way over said reservation, to the country thus ceded for wagon or other roads, from convenient and accessible points on the Missouri river, in all not more than three in number. . ."

With this bold stroke, congress forced relinquishment of the Hills and northeastern Wyoming by the Sioux. The transfer of the rights granted under article XVI of the 1868 treaty was now merely a matter of form. Red Cloud, Spotted Tail, and other chiefs signed the treaty late in 1876. Congress ratified it on february 28, 1877. And when the president's signature was affixed, the Black Hills were at last legally opened to prospecting and settlement.

Of extreme importance to the stage line in 1876, was the extension of the telegraph line from Fort Laramie to Deadwood, by the way of Custer. The telegraph wires paralleled the stage road most of the way, and

[41] 44th Congress, 1 sess. Ch. 289. 1876 (u.s. Statutes at large, vol. 19, p. 191, Washington, 1877).

telegraph stations were established at the important stage stops.

Construction work was begun early in july, by W. H. Hibbard, manager of the Cheyenne and Black Hills Telegraph company, but work was slowed down because of the Indian menace and the lack of military escort for the workers. On september 12, the telegraph office at Hat Creek stage station was ready for business. Ten days later the line reached Indian creek. On october 7, messages began to come through to Cheyenne from Major Collier's camp in Red canyon and on october 19, the system was pronounced completed to Custer. The first through messages were not sent from there, however, until october 23, as service was temporarily blocked when Indians tore down the line near Hat Creek station.

On december 1, James Halley, operator at Deadwood, sent a message to Mayor L. R. Bresnahen at Cheyenne, announcing that the through line was completed.

In order to finance the building of the telegraph, Hibbard issued scrip which could be used in sending telegrams, at regular rates, for the face value of the scrip (*see plate* 10). It was purchased by business men of Deadwood, Custer City, and Cheyenne. In 1877 the company built an extension from Hat creek to the Red Cloud agency.

To enumerate all of the passengers who rode the stage coaches in the summer of 1876, would of course, be impossible. There were New York promoters, including one who wore a tall "stovepipe hat." There were Chinese mine laborers and laundrymen, missionaries, tin horn gamblers, millionaires from California,—in fact, those from every stratum of society.

With the development of quartz mining and the founding of Lead City on Gold Run, in august, traffic increased immeasurably over the stage line. Passengers went to Custer City by coach and thence northward by wagons.

A newspaper man, who went over the line had this to say:

While New York is lauding DeLancy Kane and his four-in-hand as a revival of old time coaching, the Black Hills pilgrims mount a sixteen passenger Troy coach at Cheyenne and pull up at Fort Laramie, one hundred miles away, in ten hours. Six-in-hand, if you please, and spankers at that, a cousin of Hank Monk on the box, a good hard gravel road and presto! here I am tonight, one day off the U.P.R.R., and only one hundred and forty miles from Custer City. I shall always swear by the Cheyenne and Black Hills stage line, Luke Voorhees, superintendent, when fast and pleasant staging is the topic.

It was a well known fact that white outlaws from the mining camps had been helping the Indians in their recent deviltry along the Black Hills trail. But it was little wonder that the thieves swarmed to the stage route with the newspapers full of reports of gold, gold, and more gold in transit!

One passenger on the down stagecoach was reported to have had with him a "choice lot of ore specimens, gold dust and nuggets" that he was taking to the Centennial exposition in Philadelphia; another was said to have "brought out with him as a souvenir of the summer's work in the Hills, a handsome pile of dust and nuggets weighing thirty-five pounds and valued at $7,500." One report stated that E. A. Smith and Henry Oakes had just arrived in Cheyenne on horseback with "gold dust in buckskin bags and belts strapped about their waists containing $4,000 each."

Other items regarding stagecoach-transported gold ran:

Fourteen thousand dollars worth of gold was brought in from the Hills by the stage last evening; Colonel C. V. Gardner and other gentlemen who came by the same stage brought $10,000 in dust with them.

But the most exciting report read:

A seedy individual arrived on the coach, having in his possession a dilapidated carpet-bag in which we have since learned was stored $103,000 in gold.

While businessmen and county commissioners were "considering" laying out and building new roads to the Black Hills, Gilmer, Salisbury and Patrick carved their own way through the wilderness as best they could by blasting stumps, digging dugways, constructing trestles and laying corduroys and bridges. At their own expense they laid out a more direct route from Custer to Deadwood than the deeply rutted freighting trail.

Although early in september, only twenty miles of this new stage road had been completed north of Custer, with the rest "only a blazed trail through the timber," the road was completed in time to be used when the first through Concord coach pulled into Deadwood on september 25.

Dave Dickey, skilled reinsman, was on the boot of that first Deadwood stage. He proudly sent his well-matched six-horse outfit rocking down the long narrow gulch that was fringed by gambling rooms, stores, dance halls, and barrooms. And when the wheels ground to a stop in front of the stage office, loud cheers went up from the miners who swarmed around the coach.

E. C. Bent, described as "a young and popular Cheyenne medicine man," who had been appointed stage agent, was on hand to receive the first cargo. He was shortly succeeded by Isaac Gray, who served as stage agent for many months.

The return coach to Cheyenne carried eleven passengers, more than one thousand letters, and a considerable quantity of express, including gold dust. The stage company carried letters out of the Hills without charge, but after october 1, 1876 sold stamped envelopes at Cheyenne at ten cents for upgoing mail.

Additional new coaches and many more horses had been purchased by the stage company in anticipation of a through tri-weekly service. Superintendent Voorhees immediately concentrated upon reducing the time of the stage runs from four days to two and one-half days. During october he was listed many times as a passenger on the stagecoaches in and out of Cheyenne. Voorhees was a splendid executive but he was not much of a reinsman. He could not handle the lines on a four or six-horse hitch. He either rode horseback up and down the line, drove a team hitched to a buckboard or buggy, or sat on the boot next to the coach driver.

In recognition of the almost superhuman task which the owners of the stage company had accomplished in pushing the line through to Deadwood so quickly, the Omaha *Bee* said: "Cheyenne is now the boss at the cue on Black Hills transportation."

In the same month that the first stage went through to Deadwood, stage wagons brought the Wheeler Brothers to Cheyenne, with an escort of fifteen men. They had with them four hundred thousand dollars worth of gold taken from their famous claim, no. 2 on

Deadwood creek. The gold, in the form of coarse flat flakes, was carried in bags packed in stout satchels. One man who saw the treasure reported that there were enough sacks of gold to cover the floor of a hotel room at the Inter-Ocean.

A frequent Concord passenger in the autumn of 1876, was Buffalo Bill,[42] who was a personal friend of Luke Voorhees. They had met nineteen years before when Voorhees was on his first buffalo hunt and had stopped for a meal at the Cody farm on Salt creek in Kansas.

Numerous army officers and soldiers also were passengers on the stage, including General Crook and some of his men, who had reached Deadwood after their ill-fated summer campaign on Powder river. After having subsisted on horse meat for seven days and having suffered almost indescribable hardships, Crook looked upon Deadwood as a Golconda, indeed.

One military group over the stage line comprised General Phil Sheridan and his party, who were escorting M. Notu, commander-in-chief of the royal army of Japan, and two of his best generals, Y. Fukushima and S. Tashoro. These Japanese officers toured the forts nearby and the Indian agencies, and then returned to Cheyenne via coach, to "still further investigate the workings of our military system before returning to their native land."

Not all the cargo, however, pertained to the military and to the pursuit of gold mining. At the ninth annual meeting of the Cheyenne Bible society, held in

---

[42] It was through his friendship with Voorhees that Buffalo Bill, in 1883, obtained one of the old Deadwood Concord coaches, which he took to Europe with his Wild West Show. In it he transported many members of royalty. (See Appendix B.)

late autumn, about sixty dollars was collected and a committee was appointed to distribute copies of the Bible in the Black Hills mining towns. Soon afterward, Reverend J. Y. Cowhick was listed as a passenger on the Black Hills stage. There were Bibles "in the boot."

A card issued by S. M. Booth, proprietor of the Booth's hotel at Custer, D.T., carried one of the first published mileage (estimated) schedules for the Cheyenne and Deadwood route. It read:

CUSTER CITY TO CHEYENNE

	Miles	Total
Pleasant valley	9	
Spring-on-Left	12	21
Spring-on-Hill	14	35
Down Red Canyon	12	47
Cheyenne river	4	51
Prairie spring	18	69
Up Indian creek	12	81
Indian creek	19	100
Hat creek	8	108
Running Water	15	123
Raw Hide Springs	8	131
Raw Hide Buttes	10	141
Government Farm	12	153
Gov'm'nt bridge	12	165
Fort Laramie	2	167
Six Mile ranche	6	173
Eagle's Nest	10	183
Chug springs	7	190
Hunton's ranch	4	194
Chimney Rock P.O.	4	198
Chug Water	10	208
Bear springs	14	222
Horse creek	10	232
Pole creek	10	242
Cheyenne	18	260

The distances from Custer City to Deadwood were "estimated" as:

	Miles	Total
Spring creek	12	
Mountain City	9	21
Reynold's ranch	3½	24½
Rapid creek	3½	28
No. Rapid creek	4	32
Cold Spring ranch	4	36
Stone ranche	4	40
Deadwood	11	51

On november 1, 1876, the Cheyenne and Black Hills Stage company began to operate a weekly pony express line from Fort Laramie to Red Cloud and Spotted Tail agencies, with J. W. Burns as the courier. Later the trips were increased to bi-weekly.

At this time, citizens of Custer City demanded that an official mail contract be let to the Cheyenne and Black Hills stage line. One had been advertised in june 1876, but nothing more had been heard of it.[43]

These Custer citizens said that their mail was being diverted through Sidney, Nebraska and that when a Sidney coach broke down recently their mail was nine days on the road between the railway and Custer City.

Soon after the Custer City complaint was made, members of the United States postal commission passed through Cheyenne in a "special car" on their way to the Pacific coast. Francis E. Warren, M. E. Post, and Mayor Glafcke, representing the "Magic City of the

---

[43] This bid called for no. 37112 "from Fort Laramie by Cheyenne river (N.O.), to Custer City (N.O.), 184 miles and back, once a week. Leave Fort Laramie, wednesday at 8 A.M.; arrive at Rapid Creek, saturday by 6 P.M.; Leave Rapid Creek, monday at 8 P.M.; arrive at Fort Laramie, thursday by 6 P.M. Bond required with bid, $3,000."

Plains," boarded the car and rode as guests of the party to Laramie City. En route over Sherman hill, the three Cheyenne men put the case of the Black Hills mail before the commissioners. It was reported later that Mr. Warren, the "Merchant Prince," formed such a glowing picture of the unlimited resources of the land of gold, that he almost induced his listeners to abandon their journey westward, in favor of seeking their fortunes in the Hills.

As the result of the "special car conference," the mail within a few days, began to arrive in Cheyenne, instead of Sidney, but a formal contract for carrying the mail to Deadwood, was not awarded to the Cheyenne and Black Hills Stage company until in march 1877. And then it was only temporary.

A comparison of conditions in the early months of the Centennial year with later ones, showed almost unbelievable changes in the Hills. On march 1, there had been only about fifty men in the vicinity of Deadwood, who were living on "meat straight" without even salt, and who were undergoing nearly every privation known to man, including constant danger from Indian attack.

With the aid of organized transportation, within six months there were ten to twelve thousand hardy, energetic men in Deadwood, Whitewood, and the neighboring gulches.

Everywhere was the sound of the pick, shovel, rocker, and sledge. Sluice boxes, ditches, and dams were in every direction.

Along the gulches columns of smoke curled up from cluster after cluster of miners' cabins. Rows of houses, stores, places of entertainment, saloons, rooming houses, and hotels edged the long, narrow, winding main street of the town of Deadwood.

With the approach of winter, paper collars were reported to be common on some of the miners, as women began flocking into the Hills. Even an occasional broadcloth coat was seen on the highway. A canary bird in a cage out in the morning sun on Deadwood's main street was reported to have drawn almost as great a crowd as the dog fight a block away.

And while many women were lending stability and dignity to the new gold camp, others were participating in the more "unstable diversions." At this time there were several "female dealers" in the gambling houses, where faro was the principal game, who were said to have an expert manner of handling the cards that "could not be surpassed." There were plenty of chances to hazard a man's dust on rondo, vingt et un, rouge et noir, casino, California Jack, euchre, roulette, keno, or the strap trick.

In describing the Deadwood miners at that time, George Stokes, a correspondent, wrote to the Denver *Tribune:*

The smartest Alecks on all subjects here are men from Montana. The best miners in lean ground are men from California. The men who demand the highest wages, and earn the smallest are from Utah. The men who look you in the eye and ask the most unheard of prices for their claims hail from Nevada. The most persistent prospector, and – tell it not in Goth – the ones most given to contemplating of the cocktail come from Colorado. The weakest kneed, no account growler generally comes from down east. One of these told me last week, in a burst of confidence, that he had actually been compelled to "work for wages" since he came here. . .

And after being in the Hills several weeks, Stokes again wrote:

Where can the miner of olden times have gone? I see no Starbottles, nor John Oakhursts here; not even a Green Russell or a John Gregory, to bring the simile down to Colorado. The miner of today is a bitter disappointment to Bret Harte's readers. Common matter-of-fact fellows; I grieve to say that even the buckskin shirts, long hair and bowie-knives are falling into disuse. One sees no eight-foot neck chains nestling against coarse woolen shirts, no three-ounce nugget breastpins, no betting of oyster cans of gold on the sex of a horse three blocks away. It is true the miner of today loves whisky, cards and women; but as compared with the forty-niner of California or the fifty-niner of Colorado, he is a hollow mockery, and a fraud. He is close and calculating, refuses to be swindled, and as a rule expects his money's worth when out for a lark.

Wild rumors of new discoveries in various places took some of the miners off on a stampede toward Wolf mountains, but most of them returned to Deadwood disillusioned and disgruntled.

So many Cheyenne men had business interests in the mines, stores, freighting outfits, stage line, and saw-mills in the Deadwood vicinity that Reporter Finerty of the Chicago *Times* said, "While walking down the main street of Deadwood I encountered half the population that I met in Cheyenne last may."

And while these rapid and almost unbelievable changes were taking place, the Cheyenne and Black Hills Stage and Express company advanced its service to Deadwood from that of a rough-riding freight wagon to a hand decorated, cushioned Concord made by Abbot and Downing.

From april 1, through november 30, 1876, the Cheyenne and Black Hills Stage company carried 556 passengers from Cheyenne to Fort Laramie in the 72 trips made. This was an average of more than twelve passengers in each coach run. Between Fort Laramie and Deadwood there was an average of approximately eight to a coach, during the same period.

No record is available of the number of passengers who accompanied the stage company's freight and express wagons during the time in the spring and early summer when the regular coach service was disrupted by Indian troubles.

The company carried in the first year of operation about forty million pounds of freight and express matter.

Early in december there were heavy snows and stages were delayed by almost impassable roads, particularly between Fort Laramie and Cheyenne. Later in the month, temperatures dropped to thirty degrees below zero.

Regardless of the weather, the Indians went on several rampages. About Christmas time, they killed Tate, a mail carrier from Hat creek and two couriers, on their way to the Red Cloud agency. In the same week four freight teams were attacked while encamped on Indian creek, six miles north of the Hat Creek station. Three men were murdered, the contents of their wagons were scattered over the prairie, and six horses were driven off.

Superintendent Voorhees kept the coaches moving as fast as possible. In dry weather the average running time was from forty-seven to fifty-two hours between Cheyenne and Deadwood; in bad weather, with muddy roads, it varied from sixty to seventy-two hours, and sometimes longer.

When in the middle of december, the coach brought in thirty thousand dollars worth of gold on one load, the stage owners began to map out plans for guards and special strong boxes to protect future shipments.

Because the Black Hills country not only was rich in gold and precious metals, but was a beautiful and productive country agriculturally, it was apparent that settlers, as well as miners, would be attracted Hillward, as soon as warmer weather approached.

Captain D. B. Akey, of California, a stage passenger in late december, assured Voorhees that California would send ten thousand people to the Hills with the opening of spring. He pronounced the Hills to be the "most charming country" that he had ever seen.

Said the *Black Hills Pioneer* of Deadwood, as the year closed:

Luke Voorhees, of the Cheyenne stage line, is in town this week. He is busy making arrangements for the accommodation of the immense travel that will shortly set toward this country.

Wheelers and Leaders

As soon as the regular stages began to go through, Gilmer, Salisbury and Patrick contracted with freighters for the handling of large consignments of hay and grain (*see plate* 11).

The freighting of supplies for stations was as important and necessary a part of the business of the Cheyenne and Black Hills Stage company, as keeping the Concords themselves rolling.

All during that summer of 1876, the freighting teams congregated at Fort Laramie and then moved north in as large trains as possible. On the down trip the smaller outfits waited at Custer City or Red canyon for others before starting southward.

Freighting had been carried on in the western country since the establishment of the Oregon trail in the late 1830's. Ox teams and mule teams, and a smaller proportion of horse teams, carried hundreds of thousands, yes, millions of tons of supplies across the plains into the mountain country for military and other expeditions, and for emigrants on their way to California, Oregon, or to the Great Salt Lake valley.

With the establishment of Indian agencies in northwestern Nebraska and in Dakota, large freighting trains had carried supplies from Camp Carlin (Cheyenne depot) by the way of Fort Laramie and also through the Goshen Hole. Hence, there were many experienced teamsters and freighting outfits around Cheyenne when the great gold rush to the Black Hills began. In each outfit there were usually units of seven or eight yoke of bulls and two wagons, a lead and a trailer.

Gold seekers eagerly paid the freighters to haul their belongings and supplies and trudged along beside the wagons through snow, mud, and sand, bound for the Hills.

The trains travelled at the rate of from twelve to fourteen miles a day when loaded. George V. Ayres, who later became an outstanding businessman of Deadwood, was one of those who walked to the Hills by the side of a freight outfit. In a daily diary he recorded a vivid picture of the old trail in early 1876.[44]

C. P. (Dub) Meek, one of the first to take freight into the Hills from Cheyenne said:

It generally took from thirty to forty days to make the trip from Cheyenne to the Black Hills. When the outfit went into camp the wagons were corralled in two half-moons, about two rods at each end being left open. A day's drive was made according to where water could be found. Sometimes we went into camp at 9 o'clock in the evening, sometimes at twelve midnight. The herder always brought in the cattle in the morning, just as soon as it was light enough to see to yoke them. In the summer it was usually about three o'clock when the oxen were brought in. Every outfit had a night herder. One or two of the oxen wore bells so the herder could tell more easily if they were wandering off or were disturbed.

Bill Hooker, who night herded several months for Charley Clay, one of the bull train "magnates," said that very often "there were moonless and starless nights on ranges that were full of washouts, precipices, etc.,

44 See Appendix c.

to fall into if one was not careful, and most of the time we had to close herd the stock and keep awake and on the alert for Indians. One man usually herded, although when Indians were known to be about there would be two or three on the job."

As soon as the cattle were brought into the "corral" in the morning, the bows were placed on the two wheel oxen and they were led to their places near the tongue and each yoke pin was fastened securely. Then the ring of the yoke was fastened to a piece of curved iron on the end of the wagon pole called the "goose neck." After the wheel oxen were in place, the rest of the team were hitched to the wagon by a stout swing chain fastened to the "goose neck."

The first pair ahead of the wheelers was called "first pointers," the next two or three were called the first, second, and third "swings."[45] The oxen in the swings were changed about after long drives, with one swing pulling the lead in the morning and another, in the afternoon.

No lines or harness were used with oxen and the bullwhacker walked beside the team and drove with his whip, which he handled with great skill. He shouted "Gee," when he wanted the oxen to turn to the right, and "Haw," when he wanted them to turn to the left.

A bullwhacker's whip was said to be more precious to him than any other article he possessed. No bull whip was ever reported to have been found in a pawn-shop.

The Black Hills bullwhacker of 1876 carried three whips: one, a heavy and crude whip which he used

---

[45] Jesse Brown and A. M. Willard in their *Black Hills Trails* (Rapid City, 1924) call these "wings"; but "swings" seems to have been more commonly used.

for rough work; the second, made of hemp or other material that water wouldn't harm when used in wet and foggy weather; the third, his best or sunday whip, a prized possession for show occasions. With his whip he "could easily lift an inadvertent Chinaman who crossed the street in front of his team, from his feet."

Freighters' whips ranged from sixteen to twenty-four feet in length and were all handmade. Cracking a 20-foot whip wasn't a very safe pastime for an amateur, as there was too much danger of severing an ear or wrapping the whip around the neck.

Good bullwhackers never brought blood on the animals with the whip. The noise of the popping of the whip lash was supposed to have as much effect as a cut with the lash on the hide.

Many freighters, driving mules or horses, used the jerk-line method of handling their teams. Seated on the nigh wheel animal, the skinner jerked the line to turn his team to the right and gave a steady pull if he wanted to head left. There always was a well broken leader on the near (left) side, with the jockey stick snapped on to the lower part of the collar over to the bridle bit of the off (right) leader. Many outfits used "hame bells," supported by a metal bow, which was riveted to the harness hames. Harness so equipped often was used on the lead pair of horses or mules of a string team. As the leaders moved along, the bells jingled and supposedly encouraged the following team to lean harder in the collar.

When the road was very crooked, winding around projecting rocks, the whacker or skinner often could not see the leader. In such cases the wagon boss or his assistant, or perhaps another driver would be stationed at the proper place to prevent a unit from going over a cliff.

When the ground was soft or there was sand in abundance, a driver would make a new trail to the left or the right of the old trail in order to strike sod, or heavy, hard hillside. Such maneuvers might take the outfit anywhere from a half-mile to two or three miles off the main trail, and sometimes when the discovery was made that the new route was better than the old one, it would be used by every outfit that followed, until it, too, was badly cut to pieces. Then all outfits would either return to the original trail or seek a new one. These changes frequently were made at the approaches to streams where it was necessary to ford.

Sometimes bull teams took a long midday rest from nine or ten in the morning until three or four in the afternoon and then, if the night were clear, would keep going until long after dark. In the first days of the gold rush there was plenty of grass near the road on the rolling hills. Oxen depended upon buffalo grass for food.

As the number of teams on the road increased and feed near at hand became scarce, many of the freighters were forced to carry hay and grain for their stock. In the winter time it was necessary to put the stock up at feed stables along the way. Oxen were used chiefly in late spring and summer and early fall, when the mud was less and grass was plentiful.

When it was necessary to make dry camps, that is, camps away from water, the freighters carried barrels of water from the last spring or creek for cooking purposes and drove the work stock ahead to the next water.

The regular "stops" for the bull teams were: Cheyenne – along Crow creek, Nine Mile or "Dry ravine,"

Fred Schwartze's ranch on Pole creek, Horse creek, Bear springs, Chugwater, McFarlane's, Chimney Rock (Clay's), Jack Hunton's, Chug springs, Eagle's Nest, Six Mile ranch, Fort Laramie and on to Custer City and Deadwood, with many dry camps in between.

The larger freighting outfits used the Murphy or Kern wagons made in St. Louis, and later, the Schuttler from Chicago, the Studebaker, or the Bain.

In Cheyenne, John Nealon handled the Studebaker, while Herman Haas dealt in Bain wagons, Cayuga Chief, and iron, hardwood of all kinds, ox yokes, bows, chains, and the like. The Bain wagon which Haas sold was equipped with improved California brake and was made especially for the Wyoming and Black Hills trade. Haas, a native of Prussia, who was one of the most skilled blacksmiths and wagon-makers of the western plains country, advertised early in 1876 that his wagons had "felloes boiled in oil; timber lies in stock years before being used; no tire can come loose in any climate. Every wagon is warranted to be no. One in every respect." He also carried a full line of express and freight wagons with all kinds of repairs for them.

One type of wagon, used for long hauls in the mountainous country, had a linch pin dropped through the groove in the outer rim of the hub into a rectangular hole in the spindle. The wheel was kept in place in this way by the turning of the wheel, which kept the pin head from working out.

Most of the teamsters carried heavy chains called "rough locks," to lock the wheels on steep mountain descents. Some used wagon shoes, made of stout clevises with sharp steel calks hung from a chain and pinned to the uphill hind wheel to keep the wagon from skidding and perhaps dragging the team over an icy ledge.

During the Indian troubles, the freight trains had "out riders," men on horseback both in the lead and at the rear of the train, acting as scouts, always on the alert for the flash of a mirror from a hilltop, a small puff of smoke, or a swift moving cloud of dust on a distant horizon.

The usual load for a team of five or six yoke of oxen was about three tons. The seven team outfits often carried as high as eight thousand pounds (*see plate* 12). These freight trains carried everything from flour, bacon, calomel, overalls, engineer's transits, guns and ammunition, to whiskey and mouth organs.

The following tale was often repeated in the early days. It was said that when unloading a freight wagon containing twenty barrels of whiskey and one sack of flour, a bystander asked:

"What do they want of all that flour?"

Freight charges from Cheyenne to Custer City ranged from three and a half cents to six cents per pound, according to the kind of animals employed and the time consumed on the road. The quartermaster's department offered on its contract for transportation service between Cheyenne depot, W.T., and Fort Laramie, november 1876 to may 1, 1877, twenty-five per cent less for "ox transportation" than for mule or horse drawn freight.

The food carried by the freighters was simple, but nourishing. It consisted chiefly of sides of fat bacon, three to four inches thick; Arbuckle's coffee, which then cost twelve and a half cents a pound; beans, prunes, dried apples, sugar, blackstrap molasses, and hard tack bread, which came in squares, about six by six inches and about a half inch thick. There seldom was an extra man to do the cooking on the Black Hills hauls. Two whackers would cook for a week while two would herd the cattle at noon and in the evenings until the night herder came to take over. Then they changed off.

They did most of the cooking in Dutch ovens, six to eight inches deep and twelve to twenty inches wide. These ovens had thick lids and rested on the coals of the campfire. Bread was baked in them, if there was time, and if sufficient wood could be had to make coals. While the bread or biscuits were baking in one oven, meat would be frying in the others. The grease from the fat bacon was used on the bread as a substitute for butter. The huge coffee pot held about two gallons and together with the bean kettle was hung on an iron rod laid across two iron stakes over the fire.

The freighters did not carry tents, but rolled up in heavy tarpaulins called "tarps," that were supposed to keep water from their beds.

Vermin was one of the worst things the freighters had to contend with. One old time bullwhacker said:

It is an absolute fact that I was lousy with but an intermission of about 24 hours, for about six years, so was everyone else. I once went into Cheyenne with a roll of several hundred dollars in bank notes, and it was full of lice and nits. I spent several hours stark naked, on the banks of Crow creek, with soap and water, had a new suit of clothes which I carried there on the end of a long stick; also I had a couple of towels and a large can of anquintum (blue ointment), which I put on my body after being thoroughly dried; also I filled the seams of my new garments with it. But in a few hours I was as lousy as ever.

Sometimes the men, in desperation, threw their

undergarments on ant hills and let the red ants destroy the vermin.

One of the most popular early freighters on the Cheyenne to Black Hills route was Curly (Silvin Bishop) Ayres, a brother of George V. Ayres of Deadwood, and of Alva Ayres, for whom the Natural bridge near Douglas, Wyoming is named.

Curly Ayres was always the wit of the train and was a practical prankster. One winter day while encamped on the west bank of Crow creek, in the "suburbs" of Cheyenne, Curly tried to get close to the campfire but found that the men were packed so thickly around it that he could not get within warming distance. He reached in his overcoat pocket and gathered a handful of Spencer cartridges, 50 caliber, and tossed them into the log fire. Within a few minutes, Curly had plenty of room, as few of the fire circlers realized that there was little danger from the explosion which followed. If, however, the butt of a cartridge had happened to lodge against a log the result, it is said, might have been serious. Another time when Curly was late in reaching camp for supper, he tipped over eight plates that were filled with food and in the hands of hungry drivers. He was looking for a plate with his name on it.

According to Harry Williams of Basin, Wyoming, pioneer Hiller, on one occasion the freighters went on a strike and took the bolts off of the hubs of the wagons and sat with their oxen at Deadwood, until their demands for better pay were met.

Small freighters, who were working for themselves, often were robbed of valuable freight or money or sometimes were murdered by bands of renegade Indians or white outlaws.

One old timer who sold his outfit for two thousand dollars and was paid in twenty-dollar gold pieces, kept on driving the teams for their new owners. Not being near a town where he could deposit the money, he kept it in the jockey box covered with dirt and muleshoes for six months.

"My life would not have been worth much if some of the tough characters on the road had known the whereabouts of this money," he laughed.

The freighters referred to Buffalo Bill Cody as "See Me Bill," because they said he was always seeking notoriety and lived a life as different from their daily grind, as could be imagined.

The following conversation is said to have taken place in Cheyenne between a bullwhacker, who had just arrived, and a bystander on a sidewalk. Observing a particularly scrawny looking bull in the team, the bystander remarked:

"Old man, you work that ox too hard, don't you? He's a perfect walking skeleton."

"No, pard, he don't pull a cussed pound an' I only use him to hold up that end o' the yoke. He use ter be a rattler to pull, an' would tackle a mountain ef ye'd hitch him to it, an' thet dam rushin' nater o' his is jes' what ruined him. Goin' up to Deadwood las' trip, I got stuck on Hat creek an' the critters couldn't budge the load. I'd about give up, an' war goin' ter wait fur some other teams ter come up an' help me out, when I thought I'd try jes once more. I got beside old Bruiser, thar, an' when all was ready, gin a yell an' ye jes' ought to a seen thet cuss straighten out. He stood out ez straight ez thet whip-stock, an' his eyes hung clar down to his nose. All to once I heered a kind o' a tear-r-r an' so help me, pard, thet cuss went right through the yoke, leavin' his hide layin' quiverin' beside the tongue o' the wagon an' he stood thar without hair or hide on him ahind o' whar the yoke sot. I got the skin open and backed him inter it, but he hasn't been the same steer since, an' don't seem tuh thrive wuth a cuss. It's a fact, pard, an' I kin prove it by every other steer in the team. Wo-haw, git up, January, whoo-boy."

And the team moved off to an outfitting house.

The wheels of the freighters continued to rumble along over the deeply worn Deadwood trail, as the daily, through-stage became a reality during those first gold rush days. The life blood of the stage line flowed through the freighting channels.

The Mail Goes Through

As if to inaugurate a year of transportation, Governor John M. Thayer celebrated new year's day, 1877, by riding through the streets of Cheyenne in a carriage drawn by four milk white oxen in harness, driven by one Dexter.

With assurance of the legal opening of the Black Hills in the immediate future, there came an unprecedented material development and a resultant influx of thousands of persons into Wyoming and Dakota. Henceforth for a decade there was an incessant rumble of stage and freight wheels in and out of the "Magic City of the Plains."

The tomahawk and arrow gave way to the rim fire Henry, Winchester, Sharps, and Colt. The war whoop soon was replaced by the clipped command of "Hands Up!"

And because the Cheyenne and Black Hills Stage and Express line endeavored to carry so much material wealth across a stretch of unsettled country, it was harassed for the next two years by bands of as brazen and daring road agents as ever infested a new gold rush region.

Those months and years of the late 'seventies, taxed the courage and skill of the stagefaring men and called for a display of stamina such as only pioneers of their caliber possessed.

It was little wonder though that palms itched with greed, as reports were sent broadcast concerning the gold in the Hills. In glowing terms the press described the marvelous strikes being made, the fabulous prices being paid for claims, and recited in detail the amounts of various shipments of bullion and dust as they reached Cheyenne over the stage line.

Billie Gay, a passenger, owner of some of the richest placer mines in the Black Hills, was said to be wearing a "watch chain about two feet long composed entirely of gold nuggets from the size of a pea up to the size of a hickory nut, with two or three larger ones for pendants."

One gold bullion button carried by stage from Nichols & Haven, owners of the Father De Smet mine and mill at Golden Gate, near Deadwood, to Stebbins, Post and Company in Cheyenne, was reported to "weigh one hundred and fifty-six ounces and to be valued at three thousand dollars."

The treasure box of the Cheyenne and Black Hills coach, which reached Cheyenne on january 21 was said to contain "thirty thousand dollars in gold dust." On january 26, it had twenty-five thousand dollars in Deadwood gold.

During the entire month of january 1877, Superintendent Luke Voorhees was out over the line inspecting equipment and livestock, establishing new stations, and checking the roads.

Under his supervision at that time, the stages between Custer and Deadwood were routed over a new toll road by the way of Mountain City, instead of over

the old road through Golden. This new route was
given as follows:

From Cheyenne	*Miles*
to Nine Mile ranch (Davis)	9
" Pole Creek ranch (Schwartze)	9
" Horse Creek ranch (Moore)	10
" Bear Springs ranch (Armijo)	10
" Chugwater ranch (Phillips)*	14
" Hunton's ranch (Hunton)*	14
" Eagle's Nest	12
" Fort Laramie (Breckenridge)	16
" Government Farm (Montgomery)	12
" Raw Hide Buttes	12
" Running Water	16
" Hat creek (Jack Bowman)*	14
" Indian Creek*	15
" Alum springs	17
" Red canyon	16
" Spring-on-Hill	12
" Spring-on-Right	19
" Pleasant valley	10
" Custer City	9
" Twelve-Mile station	12
" Mountain City	10
" Rapid creek	10
" Head of Whitewood	10
" Deadwood	12
*Meal stations Total	290

This route, for the most part, followed the old stage
road.

Although scheduled to leave Cheyenne every other
day, the six-horse stages left for Custer City semi-
weekly until february 12, 1877, when a tri-weekly
schedule was put into effect.

At this time, the stage company decided to patronize home industry and ordered a set of harness from G. H. & J. S. Collins of Cheyenne. The "six-horse harness, with elegant nickle-plate trimmings," made by the local firm, was said to be the "finest set of harness ever manufactured west of the Mississippi river." It was used on the run between Cheyenne and Pole Creek station.

During the early months of 1877, Cheyenne's hotels: The Inter-Ocean, Railroad house, Delmonico, Western, Simmons, Dyer's, Lone Star and others, were crowded to overflowing with military men attending the court martial at Fort D. A. Russell, which was held as a result of the disregard of General Crook's orders in the recent Indian campaign. Too, the lobbies were thronged with freighters, ranchmen, settlers, a never ceasing stream of gold-seekers, and surveying parties. General J. A. Evans arrived with a party to begin a preliminary survey of a proposed railway from Cheyenne to the Black Hills.

This steady tide of newcomers to the "Magic City" meant increasing business to the Cheyenne and Black Hills stage company, as many of the visitors went north.

Organized society had not been able to keep up with the flood of Hills immigration. Much lawlessness prevailed. Marauding bands of young Sioux kept up continual attacks on cattle trains, ran off horses, and killed cattle belonging to ranchmen. In february and march, these forays were particularly numerous in the Deadwood vicinity.

Evidence often pointed to the fact that *white* banditti were committing many of the crimes for which the red men were being blamed. For instance, after two mail carriers were killed and scalped on the road between Fort Laramie and Red Cloud, it was found that only the registered mail had been pilfered from the mail sacks. And when a band of horses was stampeded from a corral on the stage road between Cheyenne and Fort Laramie, a telegraph operator at the stage station, called General Crook's attention to the fact that the thieves had, by means of a duplicate key, unlocked the gates of the corral! Heap smart Injuns!

Various meetings of citizens were held in the Hills to discuss the organization of home guards. A facetious correspondent in describing some of the conditions then existing in Deadwood said:

Feb. 10, 1877. There is no regularity about anything. A man opens a place of business and makes lots of money, then he gets the prospecting fever, starts for the gulches and shuts up his shebang. When a place is closed up it means the owner is in a fight or off on a spree. . . Every once in a while the boys call a mass meeting, draw up resolutions, etc., and decide to incorporate the town and have a board of aldermen, but at the end of the week nobody knows what in h--l has become of the resolutions of the aldermen.

In february, Monroe Salisbury and Jack Gilmer, who went north on the stagecoach with Luke Voorhees to inspect the line and its equipment, remained in Deadwood to examine various mining properties with a view to investment. While there they bought three claims: nos. 11, 12, and three-fourths of no. 13, considered by experts to be among the "best in the locality." Salisbury was experienced in mining, having been engaged in various enterprises in Nevada, Utah, and Montana. Gilmer and Voorhees also had previously been connected with mining. Within a short time they were working day and night shifts in no. 12 below "Discovery."

While his partners were in Deadwood, Colonel Matt T. Patrick went to Washington, D.C., to perfect mail contracts. He also visited Concord, New Hampshire, where he purchased a number of new stagecoaches from Abbot and Downing and a new supply of harness from Hill. On his return westward, Patrick negotiated for two carloads of fine stage horses at St. Louis, Missouri.

One of the first most important responsibilities of the stage company in 1877, was the transportation of the spring "cleanup" from the Hills, which approximated two hundred thousand dollars in gold. Among the special shotgun messengers who brought the shipment through to Cheyenne, without mishap, was the gun-handy ex-marshal, Wyatt B. Earp, who was on his way back to Kansas.

Always did the stage company have obstacles to overcome. Wagons would break down, harness had to be repaired, horses played out or became sick, and then there were blizzards, cloudbursts, hailstorms, and wind storms to be reckoned with, to say nothing of delays caused by road agents. And in addition to all of these things, the increase in travel during the spring, as Voorhees had anticipated, was almost overwhelming.

Cheyenne became the great rallying point for the bulk of the Black Hills travel in those early months of 1877. Black Hillers seemed to spring up like newborn grasshoppers. Parties, both large and small arrived daily.

There was one group of seventy-five from Kansas City, Missouri; more than one hundred came from

Maine, intent upon founding a city of their own in the Hills. There was a large party from Connecticut; one from Ypsilanti, Michigan; and many others. From Shenandoah, Pennsylvania came seventy Cheyenne-to-Deadwood gold bugs, each armed with a Winchester, a hundred pounds of ammunition, hunting knives, and much camp equipment.

And in addition to the many prospectors and businessmen, a large number of "unmarried females" departed for the Hills. Many of them were in the employment of one Al Swearenger, dance hall operator.

On march 21, the Cheyenne and Black Hills Stage company sent 168 passengers to Deadwood. Six fine horses pranced in front of the Concord coaches, each loaded with eighteen passengers, plus about sixteen hundred pounds of baggage. Fifty pounds of luggage was allowed on each first class ticket. In addition to the coaches there were wagons carrying passengers and express, second and third class.

The company at this time stressed the fact that it had "fast horses, easy coaches, first class eating stations and division agents who take all pains to secure the comfort of passengers." It also said that the route was "well protected, having three military posts on the road, leaving only 45 miles between military camps, insuring safety over the entire route."

One day in march, Voorhees found it necessary to insert a notice in the local newspapers in order to stop a rumor that had spread to the effect that the stage company had passengers booked to fill all coaches for two weeks. The stage superintendent assured the public that the company was fully prepared to "carry all who wish to go to the Hills at once."

On the morning of march 26, 1877, the stage superintendent received the following telegram in Cheyenne from his Deadwood agent, Isaac H. Gray:

Deadwood, march 25   Road agents attempted to rob the coach about 2½ miles from here tonight. They killed Johnny Slaughter and wounded Mr. Iler.[46] We start after body now   Notify Johnny's father.   Gray

A second dispatch read:

Deadwood, march 26   Coach got in at 12   J. Slaughter was shot through the heart with fourteen buckshot, about 2½ miles from here We have been out and brought him in We found him lying in the road He looked as if he never knew what hurt him. The team ran about one-half mile and stopped Iler was shot in the arm, a flesh wound Smith was shot through the coat on shoulder but not hurt There were five masked men who did the deed They were seen by two men who say they went up over the hill near the timber Johnny dropped twenty feet I have him in the hotel and the sheriff offers $500 reward for the murderers.   Gray

Immediately upon receipt of the first telegram, Luke Voorhees notified City Marshal J. N. Slaughter of Cheyenne, father of the murdered driver. Slaughter left on the first stage for Deadwood.

Johnny Slaughter, who had lived in Cheyenne some seven or eight years was "highly esteemed" and he had gained a large number of friends in the Dead-wood area during the short time in which he had been driving. Voorhees had assigned Johnny to the danger-ous, mountain division because he considered him his most outstanding six-horse driver, fearless and depend-able.

Funeral services were held at the Grand Central

[46] Walter Iler was a representative of the Iler Distilling Co., of Omaha, Neb.

hotel in Deadwood on the evening of march 27, with Rev. Mr. Norcross officiating. A large number of women attended the services, in addition to the men. A second funeral was held in Cheyenne, april 4.

The hearse, drawn by six white stage horses, provided by Luke Voorhees, was followed by more than forty carriages. This was said to have been the longest procession ever seen in Cheyenne up to that time.

Records of the Lakeview cemetery, Cheyenne, show: "Johnnie Slaughter Age 26 yrs. Killed by road agents Buried 4/4/77"

A plain stone marking his grave bears this inscription:

> John H   son of   J. N. & E. Slaughter
> Died March 25, 1877   Aged 27 years

The shock of the death of her son evidently hastened the demise of Mrs. Slaughter, who passed away at the age of 54 years, on april 29, 1877. She was laid to rest beside Johnny.

In fact and fiction the name of Johnny Slaughter has become synonymous with the Deadwood stagecoach.

Many thought that the holdup of the stage was the work of Persimmon Bill[47] and his gang, but others were willing to bet large amounts that Bill was not even in the Hills at the time.

Later evidence pointed to the Joel Collins-Sam Bass

[47] On october 18, 1876, Persimmon Bill gave two half-starved miners $20 each and a horse at Alkali springs. That was the last news item found concerning him. No mention of him was found in the Cheyenne papers relative to stage holdups after the intimation that he was implicated in march 1877. Special Agent Furay, however, listed him among those suspected of robbing coaches in 1878. According to Malcolm Campbell, Persimmon Bill Chambers returned to his old home in Tennessee and was hanged for an old murder of which he was accused.

gang as the perpetrators of the holdup. Those mentioned as having taken part in the attempted robbery were: Joel Collins, Sam Bass, Frank Towle, "Reddy" McKemma (McKemna, McKemmie), Heffridge, and possibly Jim Berry. It is certain that some of these men did take part in this and other similar holdups along the line.

Although "Reddy" McKemma said several years later that Joel Collins fired the fatal shot that killed Johnny Slaughter, G. E. Lemmon, a Dakota pioneer, insisted that Joel Collins "came near killing Heffridge for his inhuman and unnecessary act of shooting Johnny Slaughter, since that caused the gang to lose the loot."

On the up stage following the one driven by Johnny Slaughter, was a demure little, dark-eyed woman, a direct descendant of John and Priscilla Alden. Her name was Hattie Durbin. She was on her way to join her husband, Thomas F. Durbin, who was prospecting in Deadwood gulch. In a bag with her baby's bottles, Mrs. Durbin carried another bag that contained ten thousand dollars, said to have been the "loot" which the robbers had hoped to take from Slaughter's coach. With this ten thousand dollars W. R. Stebbins opened his new Deadwood bank, which was honored by a grand ball at Grand Central hotel, april 6, 1877.

In relating her story of being a "bank messenger," Mrs. Durbin said:[48]

In 1876 my husband and his cousin Baily, went to the Dakota gold

[48] Related personally by Mrs. Thomas F. Durbin of Cheyenne, Wyo., to the author in 1936.

rush with a wagon train. They bought the mine that afterwards was the Golden Terry, later Golden Terra, a companion to the Homestake.

I decided I would go where my husband was, so in the spring of 1877, I left Cheyenne in a stagecoach, headed for Dakota. There were three women in the back part of the coach, three men in the middle seat. We had to sit dovetail to keep knees from knocking. One of the men was Bolthoff of the Bolthoff and Hendrie firm of Denver, who was furnishing iron and machinery for the mines. Brother John Durbin would not let me go alone. He was in the middle seat. There was a woman who looked elderly to me then because I was so young. One woman had a baby and I had my baby.

Stebbins and Post intended to open a bank at Deadwood, and had given out word that there would be plenty of currency in a few days.

We started in march. There were six cayuse ponies dragging the stage. Just before we left, Post in a casual way, handed a package to John and asked him to hand it to Stebbins. John buttoned it in his overcoat. When the first change of horses came and the folks got out to stretch, John said: "This is some money. Put it in your handbag with the baby's bottles. No one will suspect you of having it."

I didn't know how much there was but I knew enough to keep my mouth shut. I carried that with me six days and nights, but did not dream there was $10,000 in it!

The night before we got to Fort Laramie, the "elderly" woman was sick at her stomach and let fly out the coach door. Later she felt better and asked, "How many of you gentlemen have been in Deadwood before? What are the chances for a woman to get married there?"

That gave the men license to play horse with her for six days. Whenever they came to a stage station they'd take the old girl in and say: "Anybody here wanting to get married?" Then they'd all laugh.

When we got to Hat creek, Tom Smith's folks had the stage station or road house. Usually a man and his wife kept the road houses. The "old girl" got into the road house ahead of me and got the only bed. The woman at the station had a colored mammy and she said she'd take the mammy in with her and that the "old girl" and I could have the mammy's bed. I wouldn't sleep with the "old girl" so I sat up all night with my little bag of money behind me. There was a coverlet on the floor for the baby. At night they always made a corral of wagons to keep the horses in. They did the same with the freight wagons, too. We went through Red canyon where the Metz family had been killed. They said Indians had killed them, but I'm sure that it was the road agents disguised as Indians.

When we got to Red canyon station, John took the baby and I hurried ahead and got the bed. I never saw the "old girl" all night. Next morning she was there for breakfast. She may have spent the night in a freight wagon for all I know. Red canyon was like a cake cut in two and the pieces shoved back a little. You couldn't see the sky unless you put your head out of the coach. Pleasant Valley station was up out of Red canyon.

Our next stop was Custer City. Nothing there but slats and battens. Here was a two-story building. I slept upstairs but could hear glasses clinking at the bar all night. I was scared they would shoot up through the ceiling. I took the bag of money to bed with me.

It was a day's ride to Deadwood. Word came that the "stage was attacked last night by road agents. They shot Johnny Slaughter through the heart. . . The horses ran away." Johnny's father was marshal here in Cheyenne at the time. There were buckshot holes in the stage when it came into our station. We transferred into it though and sat there trembling as we looked at the bullet holes. During the early afternoon we went through the mountains. The road, called the dugway, was cut into the side of a hill, just wide enough for the stage. There was a terrible torrent of rushing water below. I was certainly nervous. I was so young and did not know much about the world, but I was determined to live with my husband wherever he was.

As we came around a curve, someone said: "Look up there." We could see a man off his horse in a long ulster, behind a cluster of trees. There was a log across the road. With the help of some of the passengers, the driver rolled it off like lightning and drove on.

About two miles from Deadwood the frost was out of the ground and the stage bogged down and stalled. The horses couldn't move it.

"Whip the horses," one man commanded, but the driver wouldn't do it. We all got out and the men helped to unload the stage. The "old lady" sat on a log beside me and we watched the men unload. My baby took the croupe there but nothing more serious developed. I had a big Saratoga trunk and saw them unload it. We should have gotten into Deadwood at eight o'clock, but we got in at 2 A.M.

I had telegraphed that I was coming. Tom was in the cabin on Whitewood creek cooking supper, that is, he was keeping the food warm for me, and he was almost frantic with worry over our delay. The stage came by the cabin and when he saw it he hurried into Deadwood. When he saw the money bag with the $10,000, he said: "O, my God, Hattie! It is because of the money in this bag that Johnny Slaughter's body is waiting to be taken to Cheyenne."

Before the body of Johnny Slaughter had reached Cheyenne for burial, robbers were again at work in the Hills. On march 30, two armed men stopped Edward Moran, of Cheyenne, on the stage road about five miles from Deadwood, tied him to a tree and took from him two hundred and sixty dollars in dust, some currency, and a watch.

For some time the Cheyenne and Black Hills Stage and Express owners had been endeavoring to purchase the Western Stage line, said to be a "sickly outfit" operating between Sidney, Nebraska and Rapid City, Dakota territory.

Colonel M. T. Patrick succeeded in getting a contract from the Post Office department for seventeen thousand dollars for temporary mail service, six times a week, over this route, from april 20 to september 20, 1877. The distance to be covered was 270 miles one way.

In march, Gilmer and Salisbury bought the interest of one of the partners in the Western Stage line, Jim (Modoc Jim) Stephenson, and soon afterwards transferred some of their equipment from Montana and Utah and established daily passenger service on the Sidney route to the Hills. This new line was put into operation during the latter part of april and relieved the Cheyenne route of some congestion.

On april 10, 1877, the Cheyenne and Black Hills Stage line put on the first night runs over the Cheyenne to Deadwood route.

In the latter part of the month, George P. Wallihan, city editor of the Cheyenne *Leader,* who wrote under the pen name of "Rapherty," went north on a coach in which the passenger list included General Dan Casement, noted railway builder; J. M. Studebaker of Studebaker Brothers (wagon makers); secretary of Wyoming territory, G. W. French, Judge Whitehead, G. M. Brown, and others. Wallihan reporting from Hat Creek station said that all of them had camped out before and all were "enjoying themselves splendidly." He said they had tried to do justice to the excellent meals furnished at the stations. In a lighter vein he reported that:

Judge McLaughlin is developing an alarming appetite for pie; Dan Casement flirts with all the pretty girls he sees along the road; Studebaker and Judge Whitehead devote their entire attention to caring for our female freight; Brown has taken charge of a 50-pound sack of ginger-snaps which were dropped by some careless pilgrim; while John Featherstun, division superintendent, who joined us at (Fort) Laramie, and your correspondent, both armed to the teeth ride "ontop" and keep vigilant watch over the outfit.

For months the roads between Custer and Deadwood had been in a condition reported to be "better calculated for rafting than staging." It was a daily occurrence for passengers over that part of the trail to dismount and choose footing on the hillside, while the stage driver and his horses plodded through deep mud, which in some places seemed to be bottomless. When a nineteen-inch snowfall came about the middle of april and melted quickly, the northern roads were turned into "one long slough."

In assuming the temporary mail contract, the stage company adopted a new schedule out of Cheyenne. Mails for Custer, Deadwood and way stations were closed at 6:45 A.M. and the stage pulled out of the "Magic City" promptly at 7 o'clock each morning. Letters weighing half an ounce or less, directed to Custer or Deadwood, now required a three cent stamp. The first official documents from the Post Office department to the new post office at Deadwood, bore the following address: "Deadwood, Crook county, Wyoming territory." The boundary line had not yet been officially surveyed and checked. In fact, the survey, in charge of R. J. Reeves, did not go into the field until the latter part of may 1877.

Under the government contract[49] the mail had to be delivered safely on a certain time schedule. Beginning may 1, 1877, the stage was limited to three days for mail to Deadwood with a day and night travel required. Failure to get the mail through on time resulted in monetary penalty to the company.

---

[49] Contract for Route no. 37116, which later was awarded to the stage company, covered the period from october 1, 1877 to june 30, 1878 and provided for service seven times a week, leaving Hat creek daily at 8 A.M., arriving at Deadwood the next day by 7 P.M. The return trip was scheduled to leave Deadwood daily at 8 A.M. and to arrive at Hat creek the next day by 7 P.M., "or in close connection with Route no. 37109, Cheyenne to Hat creek." The contract provided for a remuneration of $34,293 per annum and required a bond of $30,000. A rate of 3.4 miles per hour was called for in summer and 2.6 miles per hour in winter.

During the first three weeks of carrying the through mails to Deadwood, the Cheyenne and Black Hills Stage company made a remarkable record. Despite the terrible condition of part of the route, the mail was delayed only once, and then only for a few hours.

Knights of the Road

Parts of Wyoming territory, in the middle and late 'seventies, offered a perfect background for the operations of road agents, horse thieves, and desperadoes. The so-called Indian country, just being opened legally to the white men was a vast, uninhabited area made up of thousands of square miles of gulches, breaks, canyons, valleys, and rolling hills which provided innumerable getaways and hideouts.

There was practically no law enforcement in northeastern Wyoming above the Platte river at that time, as the county seat, Cheyenne, lay ninety some miles south of the river and from two hundred to three hundred miles from various parts of the area. There were few trails and fewer roads.

By the time a crime was reported to the law in Cheyenne, and a posse could be organized, the perpetrators of the outrage would be hundreds of miles out of reach.

Even before the gold rush began to the Black Hills, a well-organized band of horse thieves was at work running stolen horses from Idaho to Dakota and Minnesota, from Montana to the Dakotas, from Wyoming to Colorado and New Mexico, and from Wyoming to Idaho and Utah through Jackson Hole. They were said to be operating "all over the scenery."

The Hole-in-the-wall in north-central Wyoming (*see plate* 13), which later became notorious as head-quarters for railway robbers, cattle and horse thieves, and other renegades, had not yet come into prominence. There were so many other hideouts such as Robbers' Roost along the Cheyenne river, Pumpkin buttes near Powder river, and similar places close to the Black Hills routes, that the Hole-in-the-wall was not needed in those earlier days, except as a place through which to travel.

A favorite haunt for some of the worst early criminals Wyoming ever knew was up near the foot of the Big Horns. When O. P. Hanna, the first settler near Sheridan, Wyoming reached that country in 1878, he found that Frank and Jesse James and some of the "boys," already had a hideout cabin and stables in secluded Little Goose valley, which gave them ready access to Montana northward, and was on a straight line with the Union Pacific railroad far to the south, as well as being within easy riding distance of the Black Hills.

Not only did the Big and Little Goose creeks, Rock creek, Prairie Dog creek, Shell creek (over the Big Horns), Soldiers creek, and Wolf and Tongue river valleys offer protection from the eyes of the law, plus plenty of good brush, timber, and forage for horses, but the Powder river breaks also offered plenty of protection. The "Big Nose George" Parrot gang was known to have had a hideout near a spring under the rim of North Pumpkin butte not far from the Powder river country.

There were yet buffalo and plenty of wild game in the area. Many of the outlaws, in the guise of buffalo hunters, moved their camps around the country and plundered or murdered at will.

There was not just one band of road agents that operated along the Black Hills stage routes, but many. As soon as one bandit leader was killed, captured, or chased out of the country, another one mushroomed into his place to carry on the lawlessness. That Frank James was with some of the agents when the Cheyenne and Black Hills coaches were "stopped" is probably true. Heffridge, a spotter for the James boys, no doubt, was present. No positive proof, however, is at hand to show that Jesse James helped rob these coaches though he was known to have been working with some of the same men who were caught in connection with stage robberies. Jesse was arrested and put in jail on one occasion by N. K. Boswell of Laramie City, but was released because of lack of evidence. At the time, Boswell did not know the outlaw's identity.

The men, who for the most part harassed the Black Hills stagecoaches, were hardened criminals. Some were escaped convicts, others had come up the cattle trails from Texas, some came down from the mining camps of Montana. A few were adventurers who had gone broke in gambling in the Hills, or had failed to make a stake and had turned to outlawry.

Soon after the wheels of the daily stages started to roll smoothly and regularly between Cheyenne and Deadwood, road agents came on the scene.

One pilgrim, William Price of Somerville, New

Jersey, who walked to the Hills in the spring of that year, recorded in his diary:

TUESDAY, may 1, 1877. On the Road Among horse thieves, Gamblers & a few honest men the further I go the more I am impressed I will never live to see my familey in this world again

WEDNESDAY, may 2. On the Road feet and legs swollen badley Snow again tonight Hear bad news from Deadwood Men starveing and all returning that can

SUNDAY, may 6. Still on no day is given to the Lord in this country of horse thieves and gamblers and greedy gold seekers God bless my wife and little ones

Some of the Hillers en route to Custer in may, were robbed of their stock while camped in the vicinity of the McGinnis ranch, north of Fort Laramie. When they trailed their horses and were about to recover them, a party of outlaws stopped them, took the horses that they were riding, relieved them of their guns and money and told them to get out of sight within twenty minutes.

The Hillers went to Fort Laramie, as fast as they could, to report the affair. Lieutenant Thompson, with a detail from Company D, Third Cavalry, accompanied by two civilians, Hauphoff and Breckenridge, started in pursuit of the thieves. They succeeded in catching five men, who had in their possession some stock stolen from Hauphoff's stable that adjoined his saloon at Fort Laramie. The thieves were turned over to the civil authorities.

One of the thieves had a copy of a so-called "constitution" belonging to the outlaw band, in which each man was registered by number. The numbers ranged from one to ten. But the captured men refused to give details of their organization.

During the spring of 1877 there was a great shortage of supplies in the Hills for several weeks because of the bad weather and almost impassable roads for hauling. Food prices for a time went "sky high." A Deadwood physician reported a number of men sick in their cabins from exposure and destitution. Some of these desperate unfortunates were lured into highway robbery, no doubt, by the newspaper stories of gold discoveries and shipments. For the most part though, the road agents were not "driven" into their work. They chose it.

In june 1877, a cut-off from Hat Creek station, via Old Woman's fork and Jenney Stockade was finished by W. M. Ward and thirty-two workmen, which shortened the route more than sixty miles. Stage stations were transferred as soon as possible.

Although many persons had earlier left Custer City to go to the northern mining camps, the little town on French creek began a steady growth in the spring of 1877. By may it was prospering and supplying mining districts along Castle, French, Spring, Battle, Little and Big Rapid creeks.

The establishment of the new stage route via Jenney Stockade, some thirty-five miles west of Custer, was a severe blow to the citizens of the "discovery" town. They felt that Custer was entitled to regular, direct stage line connections with the outside world. To meet their demands, the Cheyenne and Black Hills Stage company improved a short-cut from the main line that branched at Cold Spring ranch to connect with Custer, thirty-six miles away.

The new main route north from Fort Laramie branched from the old one at Government Farm, ran west of Raw Hide Buttes, thence down Sage creek to Little Beaver, up Beaver some thirty miles and then over a good level country, striking Whitewood creek about fifteen miles from Deadwood. The route then paralleled the creek down to the little mining center, entered what was known as South Deadwood, followed Sherman street, crossed the stream over the Lee street bridge and brought up on Main street, at the stage office next door to The Place saloon.

While the transfer of equipment was being made to new stations, the company suffered a distinct loss on may 20, in the death of John Featherstun, the superintendent of the northern division. Featherstun's neck was broken when he was thrown from a stage wagon during a runaway near Mountain City.

Featherstun, who had served as deputy U.S. marshal in Dakota territory, under George M. Pinney, had a reputation for fearlessness. Too, as a leader of the Montana Vigilantes, he had helped rid that territory of a band of vicious outlaws. It was rumored that road agents in the Black Hills had been giving Featherstun "a wide berth."

Thomas Mitchell, veteran stage man, took Featherstun's place from june 3 until june 23, when he was succeeded by Ed Patrick, of Omaha.

There were always unforeseen things to be met and overcome by those running the stage line. On june 18, a terrific deluge of rain, carrying much hail with it, struck the Chugwater valley, near Hunton's ranch at Bordeaux. A strip of country for a half mile in width was a sheet of rushing waters, while creek beds that had been dry for six years, suddenly became seething rivers fifteen feet deep in places. Both bridges across the Chugwater were swept away, and the banks were plowed with deep gullies at numerous places.

After much difficulty in fording heretofore dry gulches, the up stage reached the Chugwater stage station about half-past one in the morning. It was forced to remain there thirteen hours until the water subsided. The coach from Deadwood, in crossing the upper ford of the Chugwater at eleven o'clock the morning of june 19, with five passengers aboard, "floated like a raft, while the horses were obliged to swim . . . passengers and baggage were thoroughly soaked."

From may 20 until june 15, the daily coach left Cheyenne at 2 A.M. and reached Deadwood in sixty hours of travel. The fare was thirty dollars. Beginning june 15, stages left Cheyenne upon the arrival of the Union Pacific express from the east and the down stages reached Cheyenne before the departure of the east bound express, thus enabling passengers to make connections without a lay-over in Cheyenne.

Changes in personnel of the stage company were made in june, when Isaac H. Gray, who had been Deadwood agent since october 1876, resigned to go into mining. Gray was succeeded by W. F. Bartlett, who had served for several months as agent in Cheyenne. H. A. Iddings took Bartlett's place on june 19.

The last of june, the stage company advertised for hay contracts for all stations between Cheyenne and

Deadwood. The various contracts called for not less than twenty-five tons each, "free from weeds, brush and old grass, to be put in good and well built stacks at each station, not less than 17 ft. high, not less than 20 ft. wide at bottom of stack." The hay was to be measured by the company's agent after thirty days from time the entire amount had been delivered. Checking up on this hay was no small job in itself.

From january 1 through june 30, 1877, Gilmer, Salisbury and Patrick carried 3,128 first and second class passengers with fares amounting to $48,766.22. In the same period the company also hauled 5,680 express packages for $19,471.44.

An inventory of the company's property at that time showed about two hundred thousand dollars invested in Concord coaches, six hundred sturdy horses, and other equipment. The seven thousand dollar monthly payroll carried eighty men.

Soon after the new cut-off was put into use, Jack Gilmer made a careful inspection of the entire line and recommended that the road be shortened from ten to twenty miles, by using a natural draw north of Fort Laramie, and going in almost a bee line to Hat Creek station. The new section of the road was built in july. The stage company established two new stations, one at Raw Hide Buttes and the other at Running Water, but was delayed in transferring stock to this second cut-off because of unexpectedly heavy work involved in digging wells at the new stations. The actual removal of stock to the new stations was not completed until the middle of august.

The official survey of the new route from Cheyenne to Deadwood, made by Captain W. A. Stanton, chief engineer of the department of the Platte, and his

assistants, which was finished on august 25, 1877, was
as follows:

From Cheyenne to	Miles
Horse Creek	25.66
Phillips's Chug	47.86
Owen's Chug Spring	66.13
Fort Laramie	88.28
Government Farm	103.22
Raw Hide Butte	116.50
Niobrara River	133.07
Hat Creek	147.80
Lance Creek	176.54
Cheyenne River	196.62
Beaver Creek	220.86
Cold Spring	242.61
Whitewood	263.79
Deadwood Post Office	266.19

The highest altitude recorded on the route was 6,509
feet, the observation being taken from the extreme summit of a hill a short distance from Spring canyon, about
230 miles from Cheyenne.

With the various improvements in the roads, the
stage line operators focused attention upon cutting
down the traveling time and much publicity was given
to the various runs. It was not uncommon for the six
horses drawing a heavy stage to average six to eight
miles an hour. During the summer, Voorhees succeeded in reducing the actual traveling time between
Cheyenne and Deadwood to forty-eight hours. Several
times only forty-seven hours were required. The average usually was from fifty to fifty-two hours.

Early in july, the distance from Cold Spring ranch
to Deadwood was cut considerably when a new cut-off
was built from the spring across a prairie for nine
miles to a crossing of the Spearfish river, then to White-

tail, Poorman's gulch, through Central City, Gayville, and down into Deadwood.

Within ten days after the death of division Agent Featherstun, there began a series of holdups along the division north of Fort Laramie, that kept the owners and employees of the stage company constantly harassed.

On the night of june 1, the down stage with Driver George Drake, was stopped about eight and one-half miles north of the Hat Creek station by a horseman who rode into the middle of the road, ordered a halt, and fired a pistol. Two more road agents came from some bushes just as the passengers, heavily armed, jumped from the coach. The three outlaws fled.

Superintendent Voorhees immediately telegraphed his agent at Deadwood, to send two armed guards – "shotgun messengers" – out on every coach that carried treasure, with orders to shoot the first armed man who approached a coach, either by day or night. As quickly as possible, the company installed heavy iron "treasure boxes" under the seats of the Concord coaches, to carry the gold dust and other valuables.

A layover of twelve hours at the Hat Creek station each night, was ordered until the drivers could become acquainted with the new road north from Sage creek.

Soon after this, the body of W. McLachlan, who had disappeared some time before, while hauling supplies for the Black Hills Stage line, was found near Pole creek by J. W. Bush, a ranch hand. Evidence showed that McLachlan had been shot down in cold blood, evidently by thieves making off with his horses.

About half-past eight on the morning of june 14, two road agents with blackened faces, sprang into the road ahead of the stage horses in a narrow ravine about twenty-five miles north of Hat Creek station. While one robber covered the driver with his rifle, another one ordered the shotgun messenger, Skinner, to throw out the treasure box.

One report said that Skinner threw out an empty box; another, that the robbers obtained $3,050.

A week after this robbery, Luke Voorhees received a telegram from Agent Gray which read:

Deadwood, D.T., june 21 Last tuesday three horse thieves Louis Curry James Hall and A. J. Allen were captured near this place and horses stolen from the stage company were taken from them the thieves were lodged in the jail at Rapid City on wednesday night the jail was broken open and the thieves taken out and hanged by unknown parties

Several days after the hanging, the bodies were buried and a pine board was erected over the triple grave which read:

A. J. Allen	Louis Curry	Jas. Hall [50]
Age 35 years	Age 29 years	Age 19 years

HORSE THIEVES BEWARE

Here lies the body of Allen, Curry and Hall.
Like other thieves they had their rise, decline and fall;
On yon pine tree they hung till dead,
And here they found a lonely bed.
Then be a little cautious how you gobble horses up,
For every horse you pick up here, adds sorrow to your cup;
We're bound to stop this business, or hang you to a man,
For we've hemp and hands enough in town
    to swing the whole damn clan.

[50] J. S. McClintock in *Pioneer Days In The Black Hills* (Deadwood, 1939) p. 176, states that the boy was innocent. He had been trudging along a road and had been offered a ride by Allen and Curry. According to pioneer Richard B. Hughes: "the evidence as to the guilt of the three was unmistakable."

There was a brief lull and then on june 25, 26, and 27, the road agents struck three times in rapid succession, netting about $3,400 in cash from the passengers, [51] blowing up one treasure box which contained between ten and twelve thousand dollars in gold, and making way with two more boxes, the contents of which were not made public.

F. B. Reed of Denver, a passenger in the june 25th holdup who "gave" the boys one hundred and twenty dollars in cash and a gold ring valued at four hundred dollars, reported that all of the passengers were asleep and the curtains of the coach were tightly buttoned when the command came to halt. The horses, in pulling up out of a gully, had slackened speed. Garret Crystal, a freighter riding the coach, was "fleeced to the tune of" seven hundred dollars in currency and a gold watch; Alex. Francais, formerly of Denver, was relieved of three hundred dollars; and Irwin, a miner from Potato gulch, contributed $198 in currency.

In the holdup on the 26th, five masked men stopped the down coach about ten miles from the Cheyenne river and "went through" the passengers' pockets and belts where they obtained three gold watches valued at $1,025 and about four hundred dollars in cash. Several shots were exchanged, one of which struck the driver, Hawley,[52] in the side, but the wound was not serious.

After blowing the lock off the treasure box and removing the contents, the robbers returned the guns taken from the messengers and one or two pistols taken

---

[51] Passengers were: J. M. Mattison of Ophir, Utah; J. H. Holliday of St. Louis, and a man named Pierce.

[52] Some months later, "Reddy" McKemma, after his arrest in Ohio, confessed to having shot Hawley.

from passengers. They swore about the wooden treasure box from Custer, which had been found empty the day before, and said they would go over and burn Custer City if treasure wasn't sent out from there soon.

Again the next day, june 27, the stage was stopped near Cheyenne river and both treasure boxes were taken, but were said to contain no treasure. The passengers [53] were not molested.

After requesting that the treasure boxes be carried loose in the coach hereafter, in order to save time and trouble, the road agents sent word by the driver to Voorhees to send them a pair of gold scales. They said that "dividing dust with a spoon is not always satisfactory."

Later, when Voorhees received a mysterious note extending thanks for the gold scales, he was puzzled. But not for long. Shortly he received notice from Agent Bartlett at Deadwood that he had just reimbursed a man for a pair of gold scales that had been stolen from the northbound coach!

According to "Reddy" McKemma, these three consecutive june robberies were the work of a gang comprising: Bill Bevans (Blivins), Clark Pelton alias Billy Webster, Dunc Blackburn, James Wall, and himself.

"Reddy" said that the gang, after the holdups, struck out for the Sweetwater country. While McKemma and Webster went into South Pass to buy supplies, a "disreputable woman" who had accompanied the road agents from the Hills, remained in camp and heard Bevans and the others planning to kill "Reddy" and

[53] Passengers: Mrs. M. G. Tonn, Miss M. M. Bogy, J. W. Miner, Dr. J. L. Edwards, W. L. G. Soule, Charles Wilson and Pat Keeley.

Webster. When "Reddy" returned, the woman told him of the plot.

"Reddy," with her help, got the others drunk, took eight thousand dollars in gold, nearly all of the greenbacks, and the best arms and fled. He and the woman struck the Union Pacific at Point of Rocks station and went from there to St. Louis, where he gave her one thousand dollars and left her. Thence he went to Texas and later back to his old home in Hillsboro, Ohio.

Dovetailing into this story by "Reddy," is the fact that Bill Bevans was arrested near Lander shortly after the robberies on the Black Hills trail. On Bevans at the time of his capture was the fine gold watch, which had been taken from J. H. Holliday, on june 26. Bevans was turned over by Sheriff J. W. Dykins of Green River City, to Sheriff T. Jeff Carr of Cheyenne.[54]

Who was the woman that fled from the Robbers' Roost country to the Sweetwater with Bevans, "Reddy" and the gang, after the stagecoach robberies?

In an interview some years later, Calamity Jane insisted that *she* was the woman. Realizing Calamity's love of a sensation, it is conceivable that she might have been the "woman road agent." But it is more likely that she gave rein to her imagination while recalling the past.

[54] Only five years previous, Bill Bevans was a well-to-do and respected citizen of Montana. Through gambling he lost everything he had. His first arrest was in october 1876, when he was charged with stealing some horses from Robert Foote of Elk Mountain, Wyoming. He was tried, convicted and sentenced to serve ten years in the penitentiary. While his case was being appealed, Bevans with several others, escaped from jail in Laramie City. Two of the escapees, Clark Pelton alias Webster, and Dunc Blackburn, became partners in crime with Bevans along the Black Hills trail. Bevans attempted an unsuccessful jail break in Cheyenne, july 28, 1877. He was released from prison in 1886 and died soon afterwards.

About two weeks after the 1877 holdups, the following item appeared in the *Rocky Mountain News* of Denver:

The Nebraska Press tells of a Black Hills character known as "Calamity Jane" who is strangely like one of Bret Harte's heroines. As she sits astride her horse there is nothing in her attire to distinguish her sex save her small, neat-fitting gaiters and sweeping raven locks. She wears buckskin clothes, gaily beaded and fringed and a broad-brimmed Spanish hat. She comes from Virginia City, Nevada of a family of respectability and intelligence. Donning male attire in the mining regions, where no restraints were imposed for such "freaks," she "took the road," and has ever since been nomadic in her habits – now one of a hunting party, then in a mining stampede, again moving with a freight train; and it is said she has rendered service as a scout. She has had experiences as a stage driver, and can draw the reins over six horses, and handles the revolver with dexterity, fires it accurately as a ranger. She is still in early womanhood, and her rough and dissipated career has not altogether "swept away the lines where beauty lingers." [55]

On july 6, about nine days after the stages were "stopped" by highwaymen, Calamity Jane called at Terry and Hunter's livery barn in Cheyenne and wanted to rent a rig. Frank Hunter refused to let her have it, as he recalled that on another occasion she had taken a horse and buggy from Abney's stable, ostensibly to ride to Fort Russell, but had not stopped until she reached Fort Laramie.

[55] There was a second "Calamity Jane," who died in Denver in august 1878, from injuries received in a runaway accident, during a "spree." She was a great favorite of the underworld in Denver and Central City, Colo. At the time of her death there was some confusion in the press as it was not well-known that there were two women by that name. Said the Cheyenne *Leader* of september 11, 1878: "The *Deadwood Times* says that the Calamity Jane recently killed in Denver was *not* the Calamity Jane so extensively known in the Hills."

The next day, the editor of the *Leader* described a visit of Calamity Jane to his office. He said that she entered his sanctum, cracked her whip at a big fly on the ceiling, hitting it on the left ear and knocking it "out of time." Whereupon the editor climbed upon a convenient desk, sprang through the skylight, and hid in a friend's office. He reported that:

Half an hour later he returned to the sanctum, which was in complete confusion. Tables, chairs, desks, and books were piled up in every outlandish shape conceivable. A note was tacked to the door, which had been written by the devil who dropped in for copy, and who was pressed into service by Calamity Jane to write it. It said:

"Print in the *Leader* that Calamity Jane, the child of the regiment and a pioneer white woman of the Black Hills is in Cheyenne, or I'll scalp you, skin you alive and hang you to a telegraph pole. You hear me, and don't you forget it.

                                    Calamity Jane."

There is a vacant chair in our sanctum. The city editor has gone to Borneo.

What inspired the editor to write in such vein is unexplained. Although he had mentioned that Calamity Jane was just "in from the Black Hills," had she, instead, just arrived via railway from St. Louis or Point of Rocks?

Some eight years later, in 1885, a special correspondent wrote from Lander, Wyoming to the *Democratic Leader* in Cheyenne, saying that Calamity Jane had decided to settle in the Lander valley. In relating various items pertaining to her career, the reporter said:

. . . Suddenly her trooper life failed to interest her, and deserting, she joined one of the most desperate gangs of road agents in the hills.

Here she was in her element. Retaining the manly costume, she rode with the band on all their raids, and soon wielded no small authority. In the summer of 1877 she laid the plan and personally superintended the execution of a most daring and successful stage robbery. The booty secured was large and the gang sharply hunted. They scattered for safety and Calamity accompanied by her then lover, Bill Blivens (Bevans), and a man known as "Red," made for Miner's Delight . . . there was a split in the robber camp and Calamity had long been growing tired of Blivens and she now told him that if he did not leave her and "Red," she would kill him. Blivens left and rode to Lander, while Calamity and her new lover started for the railroad. . .

The account from Lander was expanded with details of a fight with the miners from whom the outlaws stole some fine horses, and other ramifications which savored of the blood-red columns of Beadle or Munro.

In an interview on june 21, 1887, Calamity Jane, then Mrs. Steers, said that after having made at least ten trips skinning mules between Deadwood and Cheyenne, she had gotten tired of that life and had "embarked in a business that you nor no one else will ever learn anything about from me; but I will say that I became well acquainted with every road agent who helped to hold up a Black Hills coach."

Was Calamity capitalizing on the confession made by "Reddy" back in Ohio and upon the Lander correspondent's story? Historians now following the crisscross trails of Calamity Jane, may someday unravel the threads of the many tales that have been woven about this enigmatic character of early western days. Many of the tales were spun by Calamity Jane herself out of whole cloth, no doubt, just for the fun of it.

Research has not thus far proven conclusively that Calamity Jane ever drove stage for the Cheyenne and Black Hills Stage company over the Deadwood-Cheyenne route, though she did, no doubt, drive elsewhere. She certainly could handle the ribbons.

John Hunton, who ran the stage station at Bordeaux, and who lived in that vicinity from 1867 until the last wheel of the stages stopped rolling, said:

Jane often stopped at my place, especially during the years 1876-1878, while the Cheyenne and Black Hills stagecoaches were in full swing, but I seldom ever saw her. She went out with Dodge's expedition in 1875 [56] and remained with the expedition until the expedition train returned to Fort Laramie. The wagon master, old Jim Duncan, demurred at the order, but saw to it that she went back to Fort Laramie. She then resumed her old life at the Cuny and Ecoffey ranch and other places of similar character at Fort Laramie and Fort Fetterman, until the organization of Crook's army in may 1876, when she and three other women of the same character smuggled out with the command and remained until found out and ordered back.

Ernest A. Logan, one of Cheyenne's pioneers and an old-time stage driver, who had seen Calamity Jane many, many times remembered her dressed in men's clothing skinning six-mule teams. She was, he said, one of the few women who could "live off the country" with a gun, that is, she could kill game enough to keep herself alive. He often saw Calamity and her pals, Soldier Frank, Laramie Kate (by all odds the best looking one), and Frankie O'Dare or O'Day, loafing around Cheyenne or attending a variety show at McDaniels theatre [57] (see plate 14).

[56] A letter by Capt. Jack Crawford from Custer City, february 1876, published in the Cheyenne *Leader,* february 24, 1876 said: "Calamity Bar is a fine mining claim about three miles from Custer on this gulch. . . Calamity Bar derived its name from a woman who accompanied the soldiers last summer. They called her Calamity Jane."

[57] Information given by E. A. Logan to the author, 1936.

But to return to the summer of 1877. On august 7, a news item stated: "Calamity Jane is tripping the light fantastic toe in a Deadwood dance house."

And on september 20, 1877, the Deadwood *Times* said:

Among the passengers on the Cheyenne stage last evening was a young woman attired in men's apparel. She was from Hat creek, home of our Robin Hoods, and immediately on arriving here she struck for a bar. In the course of time she got drunk, drunker than a biled owl, and kicked up a considerable rumpus on the streets. The matter coming to the ears of Sheriff Bullock, he gobbled her and lodged her in jail. . .

Who was the woman from Hat creek? Had Calamity Jane dropped by there to visit with Dunc Blackburn and Webster?

Mrs. Boney Earnest, pioneer of Alcova, Wyoming, one of the passengers who was robbed on a coach in the summer of 1877, said she looked down the barrel of a shotgun held by a "woman agent."

"Dunc Blackburn was in charge of the gang and his wife was with him," said Mrs. Earnest. "They took two dollars which I had in my pocketbook. I had other money sewed in the hem of my ulster and jewelry sewed in the velvet of my hat. I called to the woman with the shotgun saying, 'Madam keep that away.' A man passenger on top of the coach called down. 'Never mind. I'll make it right with you – five dollars and six bottles of beer.' The robbers even searched my hair."

After the flight of "Reddy" and the woman, and the arrest of Bevans, Dunc Blackburn, Webster, and Wall returned to the Cheyenne river area.

By the middle of july 1877, the whole northern country was beset by road agents, who stopped coaches on the Fort Pierre, Sidney, and Cheyenne to Deadwood routes.

When the southbound coach on the Cheyenne trail was stopped on the night of july 17, near Cheyenne river, the passengers were compelled to give up money and valuables. The treasure box was found to be empty.

In almost the same location, the next night, five masked agents again stopped the coach. In addition to making the passengers get out of the coach and stand in line as was the usual custom, the robbers made their victims take off their boots, coats, and pants in order that a thorough search might be made for loot. T. A. Kent, banker and cattleman, and J. T. O'Connor of Cheyenne were among those robbed. One passenger stated that he had been searched three times.

After finishing with the passengers, the agents unloaded the coach and went through all of the baggage, selected what bedding and clothing they wanted, opened the treasure box, but found no gold. The entire plunder amounted to only about three hundred dollars.

After having been detained for about an hour, the coach reloaded and continued on its way. Twelve miles farther south it again was stopped by four robbers, who took part of the blankets and all available arms. Because the treasure box again was opened, it appeared that the second robbery was committed by a different crew from the first.

The northbound coach also was stopped that night near Robbers' Roost at the Cheyenne river. The "take" amounted to only about thirteen dollars.

For some time Jack Gilmer, the senior partner of

the stage company, had objected strenuously to carrying treasure on the coaches, but he had been overruled by the other members of the firm, who felt it could be done if more shotgun messengers were employed.

Salisbury, Gilmer, and Voorhees all headed for Deadwood at this time to size up the situation. Salisbury was reported to have made the trip through from Cheyenne to Deadwood in forty hours, a record run over the system.

When the next particularly large consignment of gold was ready to leave Deadwood via coach, Jack Gilmer armed himself with a double-barrel shotgun, strapped himself on the platform at the rear of the coach, called the "rear boot," placed driver Fred Hopkins and "Quick-Shot" Scott Davis on the front boot, and took the coach with its precious load through to Cheyenne, without molestation.

About four days after the triple-holdup of coaches had occurred, Deputy Sheriff Hays of Fort Laramie, received a tip that some road agents were at the Six Mile ranch. Hays left at once with an assistant and Adolph Cuny of the Three Mile ranch. They quickly found and arrested two men who gave their names as Duncan McDonald and Billy Webster. Later they were identified as none other than Dunc Blackburn and Clark Pelton alias Billy Webster alias The Kid.

While Hays and his assistant were searching for other members of the robber gang, one of the agents shot Cuny, who died instantly. The two desperadoes fled. They were seen three days later by Henry Chase, a ranchman living at Castle ranch about twenty-five miles north of Cheyenne. Chase immediately sent word by two of his men to Sheriff T. Jeff Carr.

Next it was reported that two horsemen had held up a watchman at one of the railway snowsheds near Sherman station and had robbed him of one hundred and fifty dollars. It was evident the pair of road agents was headed toward the Laramie plains.

Sheriff Carr at once dispatched Deputy Jim Talbot, with Sergeant Major Gome and a squad of four picked men from Fort D. A. Russell, in pursuit of the men. The two couriers from the Chase ranch accompanied them.

Talbot and his men crossed Cheyenne pass, stopped at Fort Sanders for fresh mounts, and pushed on to the North Park country. Then they came back down the Laramie river. At one time, when they were at Fort Sanders, they were within about two miles of their quarry as Blackburn went into Laramie City to buy supplies. When he read in the newspaper that the posse hunting him was in the vicinity, he burned up the road getting back to his camp on Rock creek, some forty miles north.

Blackburn and Webster hid out for a time, then the two struck out for Fort Pierre, where they separated. Pelton soon fell in with "Laughing Sam" and the two of them stole horses, stopped freight teams, and were the terror of ranchmen and stagecoach passengers.

Said the Cheyenne *Leader* after Pelton's arrest:

Having gathered some $4,000 or $5,000 by his bad practices, he and his chum, Laughing Sam, crossed the Missouri and engaged themselves to an honest Iowa farmer at $18 per month. Burying their booty on the farm they worked faithfully for some time, and were beginning to believe that they had been forgotten by the detectives. But Nemesis was on their path, and one fine day a neighbor of their employer, who had just returned from the Black Hills, rode along past the field in which they were working. He had met Laughing Sam on a moonlight night a few weeks before, and Sam had held a pistol at his head and forced him to give up his money and valuables. He stopped and talked until he knew he was talking to his despoiler, then rode away.

Setting an officer to watch Sam, the man went to Omaha to inform the United States authorities there of his discovery. The marshal at once arrested Sam, and as The Kid seemed a suspicious character, he, too, was placed in jail, and both being soon after fully identified, were taken to Rapid City for trial.

"Laughing Sam," whose name was Samuel S. Hartman, was tried in Rapid City, on the charge of highway robbery, and was sentenced to serve eight years in the penitentiary.

"The Kid," who plead guilty to grand larceny, was sent to the penitentiary in Minnesota for one year. Upon his release on may 21, 1879, Clark Pelton was immediately arrested and taken by Sheriff George Draper to Wyoming to be tried for the murder of Adolph Cuny.

He was defended by an able young lawyer named Charles N. Potter, who later became chief justice of the supreme court of Wyoming. Pelton's mother attended the trial. He was sentenced to from one to four years for manslaughter.

In the meantime, Jack Wall, who already was well-versed in stagecoach robbery technique, teamed up with Dunc Blackburn and was often confused in the press with Bill Webster, "The Kid."

The stage owners succeeded in having a troop of cavalry assigned for special patrol duty along the stage route in the neighborhood of Hat Creek station, in addition to having soldiers ride inside the coaches. But because of the vast, broken, and isolated country over which the knights of the road worked, it would have taken a whole brigade of soldiers even to have attempted to keep track of the outlaws.

During that summer of 1877, the same swaying Concords and stage wagons that took the gold southward, hauled large quantities of California fruit to Deadwood from Cheyenne. The fruit, however, went through unmolested and in excellent shape. Too, tons of vegetables went north the same season, on the company's wagons.

There was a slackening in the holdups for a time while the company held back gold shipments, pending the installation of the so-called "salamander," a specially designed, green, oblong, iron box or safe, 16 x 30 inches, lined with chilled steel. It was manufactured in Cincinnati, Ohio, for the stage company. The sides, end, top, and bottom of the box were three inches, with a space 10 x 24 inches for the storage of valuables. The manufacturers "warranted" that with the latest style Yale lock, the safe could not be opened inside of six days, by any means except a knowledge of the lock combination. Superintendent Voorhees and Scott Davis, then captain of the Guards, escorted the "salamander" on its first trip, on august 24.

Arrangements were made to have a cavalry escort ride beside the coach on the night run between Jenney Stockade and Hat creek. On its second trip, which was completed on august 31, a dozen or more sacks of gold and retorts valued at thirty thousand dollars went through to Cheyenne in safety. Davis and another "trusty messenger" were on the boot.

Late in august, a peculiar incident occurred in Deadwood, which resulted in the imprisonment of three suspicious characters. D. Boone May, a "shotgun messenger," who had been robbed of a valuable rifle in one of the july stage holdups, was walking along the main street with Ike Goldman, who strangely enough, had been a passenger on the coach that was robbed. May and Goldman at the same time, recognized Prescott Webb, who was standing on the street, as the man who had taken May's gun.

Goldman slapped Webb on the shoulder in greeting. Webb evidently thought May was after him and began shooting. He hit May in the arm. May returned the fire and a running fight ensued. Webb jumped on a horse that was tied to a rack in front of the post office. As he sprang into the saddle and was about to make his getaway, his horse was shot out from under him by Deputy Sheriff Cochrane. May wounded Webb under the shoulder blade, and he surrendered. While Doctor L. F. Babcock was dressing Webb's wound in jail, the latter warned the physician to handle him more carefully. "I come from a good family even if I do look rough," he said.

Later in the day, Sheriff Seth Bullock arrested Webb's two companions, C. P. Wisdom and G. W. Connor, at a corral where they had five horses, a mule, and their saddles. They attempted to resist but were overpowered.

All three men said they had come up the Texas trail with cattle. Webb and Connor had since then been whacking bulls for freighting outfits. That is, until they had gone to hunting wild game in the vicinity of Canyon Springs stage station. They had no permanent camp, they said, but carried a tent and followed the game. They claimed to have delivered several loads of elk and deer meat in Deadwood.

Later the stock tender at the Canyon Springs station

reported that he had been robbed of a hat and suit of clothes, which one of the arrested "hunters" had wanted to buy from him.

Wisdom insisted that they had just come to Deadwood to sell their stock and were planning to leave the Hills.

Deputy Sheriff J. W. Murray took the three men to Cheyenne on the stagecoach and delivered them to the authorities on september 1. From Jenney Stockade to Fort Laramie the coach had a cavalry escort. The men were given a preliminary hearing and were bound over to the district court in bonds of one thousand dollars each. In default of bail, they were committed to jail.

From the time of the killing of Johnny Slaughter in march, Luke Voorhees had followed every clue, employed detectives, purchased robber proof safes, and had expended money with a lavish hand, in order to catch the road agents and thus put a stop to the holdups. His detectives scoured the northland, visited ranches and hang-outs of the robbers and did not give up until they "got their man." Through his efforts the following appeared in the *Black Hills Times,* on september 1, 1877:

NOTICE

We offer two hundred dollars for the arrest and conviction, or dead body, if killed resisting arrest, of any of the men who were implicated in robbing the coach and the passengers on the Cheyenne and Black Hills Stage road within the last sixty days.   E. Nagle;   A. H. Swan, County Commissioners Laramie County, Wyoming

For several weeks after the installation of the new strong box, the coaches went up and down the line without being stopped. The little green "salamander" was referred to as the "road-agent-proof-safe."

In fact, early in september, the headlines about road agents and their pilferings, gave way to stories about Buffalo Bill locating a cattle "ranche" on the North Loup river, in partnership with Major North; the funeral of Brigham Young; and a visit paid to Deadwood by Madame Lake Hickok,[58] the widow of the late "Wild Bill," and one about the northern cattle round-up for the season of 1877. There also was a story of General Crook hurrying to the Spotted Tail agency, on an emergency call and being upset in a stagecoach; a story of two soiled doves in Deadwood having a fight to see which should retain the affections of a certain prominent business man; and a paragraph about a Chinese physician's office in Chinatown in Deadwood where a number of "our citizens, both male and female, besides the pigtailed gentry, assemble to indulge in the vicious and extremely perilous habit of smoking opium."

And the passengers on the Deadwood coach, instead of firing guns at road agents, were reported to have killed two deer on the Cheyenne road, as the southbound coach ran into quite a band of the animals.

On september 1, 1877, the Cheyenne and Black Hills Stage company advertised tickets to all parts of the east for sale at reduced rates.

During the month arrangements were completed to issue through tickets to St. Louis, at the same rate

[58] Early in september 1877, Madame Lake Hickok, accompanied by Charles Dalton (Buckskin Charley) and wife, and George Carson, arrived in Deadwood. The widow visited Wild Bill's grave and proposed that "as soon as it is definitely settled that the graveyard will not be disturbed, to erect a fenced monument to his memory, in which kind action Buffalo Bill, Texas Jack and Buckskin Charley will assist." On september 27, Mrs. Hickok married George Carson in Cheyenne. The groom was said to be a "frontiersman widely and favorably known."

as to Chicago. Through tickets from Deadwood to St. Paul and St. Louis were listed at $45 and $41.15, respectively.

With the miners cleaning up their summer's work and going out of the Hills for the winter, the stages were taxed to capacity every day.

On september 23, there arrived in Deadwood, a new division superintendent, Alex Benham, to replace Ed Patrick, who was being transferred to the Sidney line. Benham, who had worked for Ben Holladay and Wells, Fargo & Company, on the Overland Stage line, was known far and wide as one of the best and most experienced men in the entire western stage world.

While Benham was on his way to the Black Hills there occurred at Big Springs, Nebraska one of the most daring train robberies in the annals of the west. It was reported that the gang of masked outlaws obtained from sixty thousand to seventy-five thousand dollars in loot from the passengers and railway express.

Among the gang were Joel Collins, Sam Bass, Bill Heffridge, and Jim Berry who were credited with the holdup of the Black Hills stage on march 25 of the same year.

It was hoped by the stage company's officers that these outlaws had moved on to "bigger game" and that the stage line would have a breathing spell from robberies.

Such, however, was not the case. There still were plenty of bandits along the Black Hills trail. The coach which left Deadwood on the morning of september 26, had Scott Davis and John Denny as messengers on the rear boot, with Alex Benham, the division agent, the driver and a stock tender on the top. Soldiers were taken on at Jenney Stockade to ride inside.

When the horses, at a walk, entered a swale in the Cheyenne river bottoms, there was a sudden command to halt. According to Scott Davis, he and Denny jumped to the ground and cocked their guns. When the robbers ordered everybody to get down and to leave their arms on the coach, the soldiers and the stock tender fled. Benham and the driver took hold of the horses.

As soon as Davis located the robbers lying nearby he opened fire, and when at last his weapon failed and he attempted to get another gun, the robbers shot him in the right leg just below the hip. The bullet fell into his boot.

Davis claimed that the soldiers and stock tender came running back to the coach crying, "We give up, we give up." He said that the robbers, who wore heavy black masks, knew him and called him by name. They took the "bulldog" revolver which Benham was carrying in a side pocket, then gathered up all of the arms, and inquired if the safe was on the coach. They did not try to open it, but said they thought they were tackling a regular passenger coach and had expected to get a few hundred dollars.

Davis ridiculed them into giving back Denny's watch, which they had taken. He implied that Denny had made no resistance to the agents.

Later, Dunc Blackburn and Wall visited a hay camp in the vicinity and told of the holdup. They claimed that Denny fired the first shot and did not "show the white feather."

Immediately the Cheyenne and Black Hills Stage company offered a reward of one thousand dollars for the arrest and conviction of the men who had attacked the coach, or two hundred dollars each for their dead bodies.

While attention was being concentrated on the breaking up of the gangs of road agents operating north of the Hat Creek station, along Cheyenne river, the stage was stopped in a new locality. On october 3, two men held it up near Eagle's Nest, about twelve miles south of Fort Laramie. The passengers [59] who were asleep, roused and climbed out of the coach upon the command to stand in line, with their hands up. By the light of matches, one robber searched the passengers, while the other stood guard.

Mrs. King, who had hidden a roll of bills in her hair, was searched twice. The second time she was compelled to take her hair down and her money was discovered there. The sum of two hundred and forty dollars was taken from the men.

The wooden treasure box was broken open, but no treasure was found. The papers in the box were left undisturbed.

On the boot with the driver, O. R. Manchester, was an extra driver, H. E. Barnett, who later was driving the treasure coach in the Canyon springs holdup.

After this robbery almost within the shadow of Fort Laramie, the editor of the Cheyenne *Leader* asked, "Is there no God in Israel? Is there no law in Wyoming?" And he vigorously urged the use of "hemp," saying that "the people are paying for protection from lawlessness and are not being protected." He ap-

---

[59] Mrs. Ella King, A. C. Schryver, S. M. Wheaton, William Smith, W. J. Scott, and one unidentified man.

pealed to men in power to rid Wyoming of this "dark incubus."

About a week later, on october 9, both the north and south bound coaches were stopped by Dunc Blackburn and Jack Wall. The robbers took about one hundred and fifty dollars in cash, arms, and ammunition, jewelry, some blankets, and several articles of underclothing from the six passengers on the down coach, which they stopped near Cheyenne river. They informed the passengers that they were going "to take" the next treasure coach without fail.

Jack H. Bowman, proprietor of the stage station at Hat creek, who was a passenger on the up coach, reported when he reached Deadwood, that he had been on the boot with George Chapman, the driver, when the stage was stopped. Said Bowman:

We were booming along at a pretty good pace, when we heard the command to halt. The night was dark and we could see no one. George didn't pull up quick enough, and we heard the gun locks click. They hallooed to George to "make that man get down." I at once recognized the voice of Blackburn, as he used to work for me, so I replied, "O, no, you don't want me to get down." They came up to the coach, and inquired who in ——— I was, and ordered me to get down. I laughed at Dunc and he recognized me. They pulled off their masks, and passed up a flask of whisky, and then wanted to know if they had any money. I said "No," but told them I had some. They replied, "O, ———, we don't want your money." Dunc asked me what was being said in town about the frequent robberies, and who was getting the credit for it, and when I replied they were, Dunc said, "O, I suppose so." I told them that soldiers were on the road, which made both of them laugh and drew from Wall the remark, "I wish they would put a company of cavalry on our trail, we could make some money out of their horses." I asked Dunc if they were mixed up with the Homan robbery and he said, "No," although he knew he had the credit for it. Turning to the driver he said, "Well, George, I will never ask you to put the brakes again, we are going to quit the road; business is too ——— bad."

Evidently Blackburn spoke the truth, because that was the last time he was identified with a coach holdup. Soon afterward, Sheriff Bullock was tipped off that Blackburn and Wall were in the vicinity of Deadwood.

With three deputies, Bullock stationed himself on the stage road in the outskirts of Crook City to watch for the pair. About midnight, two men appeared from the brush. Just as Bullock ordered them to halt, one of his own men accidentally discharged a gun.

Shots were exchanged, but the outlaws regained the brush and escaped. The next day Blackburn appeared at a ranch nearby and sought assistance in the dressing of two wounds in his arm. He was bitter in his denunciation of Sheriff Bullock. He declared that he would kill him within twenty-four hours.

Wall had a brother named Jim, who ran a dance hall in Deadwood. The officers planned a trap there for Blackburn and Wall. But their blockade of the hall failed and the outlaws escaped. Jim Wall was arrested and put in jail on october 25, charged with aiding the escape of the pair.

On november 3, the Black Hills coach was stopped and robbed about three miles south of Fort Laramie. Although the robbers at first were suspected of being Blackburn and Wall, they proved to be two "amateurs," named Babcock and Rines (Ryan).

Among the passengers on this coach, which numbered seven, was U.S. Marshal Sweesy. Evidently recognizing him, the outlaws told him to step aside. Then they proceeded to relieve the others of everything of value including hats, coats, boots, money, jewelry, blankets, and overcoats.

Early the next morning the same pair robbed a freight outfit comprising four wagons. They took all the blankets except those belonging to a woman and two little children. They robbed a Chinaman in the outfit of everything he had and then thrashed him with a teamster's whip.

As if on a wild orgy, this pair of agents robbed six men during the day, as they went north along the Black Hills trail.

As soon as word reached Voorhees of the coach robbery, he telegraphed stage agent, John W. Ford, at Fort Laramie, to get in touch with Lieutenant George F. Chase and to follow the culprits until they were caught.

Chase, with a detachment of Third Cavalry, and accompanied by William A. Reid, an experienced man at trailing thieves, took the trail of the robbers. Agent Ford rode with the party until forced to quit because of a recent injury.

Late in the afternoon, after a whirlwind wind-up that lasted for about five miles, in which the robbers threw away a gun and various heavy articles, the soldiers captured the agents north of Government Farm, about twenty-six miles from Fort Laramie. Several shots were fired at them before they surrendered.

Two gray horses, which the outlaws were riding, were at once identified as stolen property of the Cheyenne and Black Hills Stage company. The men had with them a number of articles taken from the coach the night before. The thieves were kept in the guard house at Fort Laramie for several days and were then removed, under heavy military escort, to the jail in Cheyenne.

Lieutenant Chase later received from the Laramie

county commissioners a reward of four hundred dollars for the capture and arrest of these men, whose full names were given as John F. Babcock and Fonce Rines or Ryan.

In recognition of their capture, the Wyoming legislature passed the following resolution on november 10, 1877:

RESOLVED, By the Council and House of Representatives of the Territory of Wyoming, That the thanks of the Fifth Legislative Assembly be, and are hereby tendered to Lieut. George F. Chase, U.S.A., and the men under his command, for the gallant, prompt and efficient manner in which they have recently pursued, captured and delivered into the custody and charge of a civil officer of Laramie county, two of the notorious highwaymen who have for some time past been a scourge and annoyance to travelers within the boundaries of this Territory, and that in thus ridding the public of such outlaws, Lieut. Chase has endeared himself to all good citizens of this Territory.

John F. Babcock, a native of New York state, claimed to be 34 years old and unmarried. After serving in the Union Army for two years, he came west in 1865. He had worked part of the summer of 1877 for John Hunton at Bordeaux and had gone to Deadwood on august 26. He returned to the Hunton ranch for a short time but decided to go back to the Hills. He said he was trudging along between the Breckenridge and McGinnis ranches north of Fort Laramie when overtaken by Fonce Ryan, known as "The Kid." Ryan was riding one horse and leading another. After passing the time of day, Ryan suddenly covered him with his Colt's revolver, telling him to throw up his hands or he would shoot him. Babcock did as ordered. Ryan relieved him of his weapon and

$20.25 in cash. Then, after removing the cartridges from the gun, Ryan returned it saying, "You can't harm me now. I've use for you; we'll go and rob the stage coach."

Although both Babcock and Ryan declared that Ryan laid the plans and bossed the robbery of the coach, Babcock was found guilty and was sentenced to ten years in the penitentiary.

Fonce Ryan (Rines), alias "The Kid," alias George F. Duncan, who had a previous penitentiary record for grand larceny, confessed to having robbed Babcock and to having held up the stage. Although he insisted that he had come from Texas, Cheyenne residents were positive that he had grown up in their city and had started early on his crime career there. He was sentenced to an aggregate of twenty-three years and three months.

Early in october, four fine black horses, about the best on the entire stage system, which had been stolen from the company near Fort Laramie, were located at Fetterman and Fort McKinney. On the same day that the horses were returned to Fort Laramie, october 27, the two men who had stolen them, Lowe and Jones, ran amuck in a valley near Sidney, Nebraska, while attempting to run some more horses out of the country. In trying to escape arrest, Jones was killed. Lowe was caught and returned to Rawlins, Wyoming, where he was wanted on a previous horse stealing charge.

In addition to troubles from horse thieves and road agents, the stage company, in the fall of 1877, suffered the loss of considerable trestle work on its road south of Deadwood, when a fire in that area did much damage.

But despite the many handicaps, the company received much praise for the courtesy, care, and caution of its messengers; for the skill and promptness of drivers; for the strength and fleetness of its horses; and for the comfort and ease of its coaches. The eating houses all along the line were highly praised.

Charley Hedges, with a train of twenty-four wagons, transported 109,000 pounds of grain to Deadwood, at this time, for the feeding of stage stock. And the regular weekly treasure coach, with its "salamander" filled with dust and bullion, continued to reach Cheyenne on schedule. Although the agents had threatened to "get" Boone May, who was now riding as messenger instead of Scott Davis, the coach came through unmolested.

By late october, Davis had sufficiently recovered from the wound in his leg to be around with a cane. He was back on duty soon.

About november 1, Davis telegraphed Voorhees that Dunc Blackburn and Wall had stolen eight horses from the Lance Creek station. And, although a two-foot fall of new snow blanketed the entire Fort Laramie area, Davis asked authority to go after these thieves.

With a detail of four men and a non-commissioned officer from Fort Laramie, Davis started out. Acting on pure "hunch," he struck westward and soon picked up what he believed to be the right trail. Swiftly he led the escort of soldiers to Fort Fetterman, then to old Fort Caspar, past Independence Rock, Devil's Gate to Split Rock in the Sweetwater valley. In the meantime heavy snows had fallen and the soldiers refused to go on. They said that their horses were played out. They stopped and put up at a ranch.

Scott Davis, thoroughly disgusted with the men, pushed on alone and late that night when his horse gave out, stopped at a ranchman's barn where he found a horse tied in a stall. Without consulting the owner, Davis exchanged horses and pushed on. He knew that every minute counted in overtaking the thieves. On through South Pass he went, crossed the Continental divide and continued to South Pass City and Atlantic City.

By that time the trail was entirely obliterated by deep, new snow, so Davis left his horse, took his saddle and guns and boarded the southbound stage at South Pass for Green River. On the way down he again followed a hunch. Getting off at the Alkali stage station, he woke up Broncho Jim, the man in charge. When questioned if he had anyone staying at the ranch or if he had seen any strangers with horses, Broncho Jim at once answered, "No."

Just then a door inside of the house was pushed open and a woman thrust her head into the room at the entrance to which Davis was standing.

"You know very well," she said, "that those men are sleeping in the haystack."

The station keeper became excited and talked in a loud voice, evidently hoping to give the outlaws some warning. But Davis did not hesitate. He went at once to a haystack in a hay corral nearby. In the bright moonlight he could see two men asleep in a bedroll in the edge of the haystack.

"Throw up your hands," he commanded.

The pair came up out of bed and, according to Davis, "They came up shooting." Then they started to run. Davis fired and the men returned the fire. One man went down, wounded in both legs. The second man dodged around the corral and escaped into the night.

"You have put a pair of shackles on me that I can't get off," gasped the man on the ground, whom Davis recognized at once as James Wall. The man insisted that his name was Thomas Woodby.

Davis knew now that his three hundred and seventy-five mile ride across bleak, unmarked, snow-covered wastes had not been in vain. He did what he could to care for Wall's wounds and placed him in care of Charles Brown, a deputy from Green River, who took the outlaw down on the first stage. Before he left, Wall told Davis that his partner could not survive long in that extreme weather, as he had fled without his coat, shoes, or hat. In the haystack Davis found a pistol belonging to himself, which had been taken in a coach robbery. He soon recovered the eight stolen horses and followed the southbound stage.

Upon his arrival in Green River, Davis spread word around town that he was expecting the outlaw to head that way. About eight o'clock that night, a man minus coat and hat, and with his feet tied in a pair of under-drawers, entered Barrett's store. J. R. Morgan, a citizen, reported the incident at once to the police and Davis. They immediately began to "keep cases on the new arrival."

Within fifteen minutes after he had gone into the store, the man emerged wearing a new hat, overcoat and rubber shoes, and hurried into Pete Appel's restaurant. There, as soon as he had finished eating, he was arrested by Deputy "Pawnee Charlie" Gorsuch. The man readily admitted that he was Dunc Blackburn.

"I'd stand you off if I had my gun," he said as he surrendered. "But I hid it outside of town." Later he showed Davis and the deputies where the gun was hidden. He gave it to "Pawnee Charlie" as a gift.

Blackburn, when searched, was found to have three buckskin money sacks containing some old coins, a watch and about one hundred and fifty dollars in currency.

When the Overland Express of the Union Pacific thundered into the Cheyenne station the next day, november 23, it carried Scott Davis, the two road agents, plus an express car filled with the recovered stage horses.

A large crowd, including Sheriff T. Jeff Carr and his deputies, swarmed the platform as the engine wheels ground to a stop.

"Why the crowd?" Davis asked Voorhees with a puzzled expression, as he left the train.

"They came down to get a look at a man who had nerve enough to capture two road agents," Voorhees assured him.

In turn, Voorhees looked around and asked Davis where the soldiers were. The superintendent was dumbfounded when told by Davis that they had quit him over on the Sweetwater. The soldiers had not yet reported back to Fort Laramie. When they did come straggling in, they were courtmartialed for neglect of duty, and it is said they were sent to the federal penitentiary in Leavenworth, Kansas.[60]

---

[60] This account of the capture of Blackburn and Wall was told to Russell Thorp by Scott Davis. According to a Green River newspaper reporter, Scott Davis first came on down to Green River on the stage. Upon his arrival he received a telegram from Big Sandy station saying men with horses had passed there. Davis then took two deputies and went back up the line. Since Davis was a man of integrity, his story is accepted.

Both Blackburn and Wall, when arraigned in district court in Cheyenne, early in december, plead guilty to four separate indictments: for obstructing the United States mails, for highway robbery, for assault with intent to murder, and for grand larceny. Each was sentenced to the state penitentiary for eight years with a $99 fine.

George Draper, a member of the Wyoming legislature, which was then in session, introduced a resolution of thanks that was adopted by the lawmakers. It read:

RESOLVED by the Council, the House of Representatives concurring, that the indefatigable exertions and signal bravery displayed by Mr. Scott Davis in his recent capture of the notorious "road agents," Dunk Blackburn and Wall, deserves recognition by the fifth legislative assembly of Wyoming Territory, and that the thanks of the assembly are hereby tendered him for his services in bringing these marauders to justice.

Resolved, That the Hon. G. W. French, Secretary of the Territory of Wyoming be requested to furnish Mr. Scott Davis with a copy of this resolution.

Several claims for a reward were presented to the Laramie county commissioners, and after some delay, the commissioners on january 12, 1878 allowed the claim of Scott Davis "for the arrest and conviction of Blackburn and Wall, in the sum of four hundred dollars."

While awaiting removal to the state penitentiary, Blackburn and three other prisoners attacked Sheriff Carr and attempted a jail break. Perry, Wisdom, and Webb who were in the jail at the time, awaiting trial, did not take part in the attempted break.

On Christmas day 1877, Deputy Sheriff Martin took Blackburn and Wall, and three other prisoners to Laramie City in a caboose, attached to a guarded Union Pacific pay car. They were whisked from the Laramie railway station and taken "over the river" to the state penitentiary as quickly as possible. At last they were barred from future depredations along the Cheyenne and Black Hills trail. Later, they were transferred to the Nebraska State penitentiary as Wyoming "boarders."

Blackburn claimed to have come from respectable parents. He said he came west in 1870, worked as a teamster, then had taken hay and wood contracts until he began "trading horses." While in prison he learned the trade of a saddler.

The county commissioners of Lawrence county, Dakota territory, of which Deadwood was the county seat, had a standing offer of two hundred dollars reward for the capture or arrest of each robber or for the dead body of any robber killed while resisting arrest or capture on the stage and wagon routes. Sheriff Bullock and his deputies, including Captain A. M. Willard, an outstanding officer, waged continuous war on the outlaws.

As winter came on, it seemed as if the road agents who had not yet been caught, went into "hibernation."

By the last of november the snow was drifted so deeply in the gulches that it was necessary to put the stagecoaches on runners between Jenney Stockade and Deadwood. It was not uncommon for a driver to experience the "pleasure" of an upset or to have to hold the ribbons on days when the mercury registered far below zero.

The year 1877 came to a close with the whole north country buried in snow, and reports from Deadwood said, as the new year was ushered in, that it was "still snowing."

But the Cheyenne and Black Hills Stage company continued to go through, regardless of the weather and the many obstacles that beset the trail over which the wagons rumbled or the runners creaked.

The Reign of Terror

By the beginning of 1878, the mining business in the Black Hills had settled down to substantial proportions. In two years this country had changed from a trackless, unexplored region into one of the richest gold producing areas of the world. Already ten million dollars in gold had been added to the wealth of the United States from these timbered gulches.

In the vicinity of Deadwood big strikes had been made that now demanded development through the expenditure of large capital. Between six hundred and eight hundred stamp mills were at work with twice that number needed.

The hectic days of helter-skelter stampedes were over and the prospectors who still were looking for something better "just over the next hill," shouldered their picks and shovels and struck out for new "diggings." Reported discoveries beckoned them to Crazy Woman creek near the Big Horns, to Douglas creek in the far reaches of the Medicine Bow range, over to the Grand Encampment valley south of Rawlins, and to Dale creek near Cheyenne. New finds also were reported from the Sweetwater and South Pass areas and later in the year glowing stories came from Sitka, Alaska and from Leadville, Colorado.

Jack Gilmer and Monroe Salisbury were interested not only in transporting gold over their stage line, but also in mining it. They induced California and Nevada bonanza kings to inspect the Black Hills mines. In addition to their holdings near Deadwood, they invested heavily in various properties at Lead, including the Homestake, in which George Hearst and other Californians also were interested.

Gilmer pronounced the Black Hills to be the "best mining country in the world" and said he anticipated an influx of capital that would bring "a better class of travel," over the stage line. The day of the bonanza king, indeed, was at hand. Great strings of freighting outfits now labored northward, loaded with heavy mining machinery in addition to carrying supplies.

With clocklike regularity the wheels of the weekly treasure coach rolled into Cheyenne with Captain Walter Scott Davis and D. Boone May on the boot with the driver. And the "salamander" continued to disgorge its golden treasure, much of which was shipped to New York by the bankers, Stebbins and Post. The coach on january 18, 1878, brought a "button," valued at $7,400, for the Black Hills Gold Mining company, product of the last cleanup from Hidden Treasure Mine and mill of which Tim Dyer was president, and I. C. Whipple, treasurer.

At this time some of the miners left Deadwood to rush to the Jenney Stockade district where oil had been discovered bubbling from a spring. And within a short time the prairies west of the Stockade, which were traversed by the Cheyenne and Black Hills stage route, were dotted for miles with "claim cabins."

Lieutenant George F. Chase, who had made a reputation for catching road agents, and who now was in command of troops at Red Cloud agency, organized a stock company for the purpose of sinking a test well near the new petroleum springs.

A new branch mail route was inaugurated, around the western base of the Black Hills, from Jenney Stockade to Sand creek in northeastern Wyoming, where a number of miners were busy panning for gold. There was considerable talk of organizing "Lincoln territory" from the parts of Wyoming, Montana, and Dakota[61] where the recent gold had been discovered, but the measure proposing it did not pass congress.

There had been a respite from holdups by road agents during the winter, but the stage company officials and local authorities had kept up the pursuit of the outlaws who already had perpetrated crimes against the stages.

Thomas Flood, suspected of being one of the gang who shot Johnny Slaughter, was arrested in january 1878, by U.S. Deputy Marshal M. F. Leach, at Sidney, Nebraska. George Healy, also said to be a road agent, was arrested in Deadwood. And during the month, ex-sheriff Seth Bullock received a tip that "Reddy" McKemma (Robert McKimmie), was in Hillsboro, Ohio. He went east at once to investigate. McKemma had bought a fine farm, then traded it for a store and had settled down in Ohio as a merchant. Bullock at once recognized McKemma as a road agent, who had worked in the Black Hills. He arrested him. Complications immediately developed, as "Reddy" had money enough to employ good lawyers, who fought extradition. Bullock telegraphed to Luke Voorhees to come on to help out with the case and the Black Hills stage superintendent left immediately for Hillsboro.

[61] 45th Cong., 2 sess., Senate report no. 110 (Washington, 1877).

Realizing that there would be considerable delay before the prisoner could be brought west for trial, Voorhees returned to Wyoming. Bullock went to Michigan on other business, but warned the sheriff at Hillsboro to use the utmost precaution in handling "Reddy," as he was a desperate character.

The local authorities, later dubbed by the Cheyenne press as "The Buckeye boobies," evidently regarded "Reddy" only as a "home town boy." They permitted "Reddy's" wife and friends to visit him in his cell, without being searched.

On february 11, "Little Reddy" escaped from jail, but evidently did not return to his old haunts in the Hills. He was caught a year later, after being involved in robberies in Kentucky and Ohio, and was returned to Hillsboro for trial. Wyoming saw no more of "the scourge of the road."

Although a considerable trade was maintained between Custer and Cheyenne after the main route of the stage line was changed and the cut-off was constructed from Cold Spring ranch to Custer, a shorter, better road was badly needed by the freighters. Largely through subscriptions of Rapid City business men, a new "cut-off" from the Hat Creek station to Horse Head, a connection with the Sidney route, was built and used during the spring of 1878. This greatly increased activity around the Hat Creek station.

As the longer, warmer days of early february melted the snow in the gulches, the stage company took its sleighs off of the run between Jenney Stockade and Deadwood and the yellow spokes of the Concords again chugged through the water-filled ruts.

But it was not long until "runners" again were in

vogue, for on march 7, a blizzard began which raged
for five days, said to be one of the biggest and worst
storms ever experienced in the western country.

Pioneers of Cheyenne often told how guests at the
Inter-Ocean hotel walked out of second story windows
on top of the drifts. There was a drift about five miles
south of Cheyenne, said to be "a mile wide and eighteen
feet deep." Store roofs caved in and families were
marooned in their houses without food until they could
be "dug out" by the "relief committee," headed by
Marshal Slaughter. The roof of a mule shed owned by
Benjamin Smalley, a freighter, caved in and five of his
valuable mules were suffocated. Smalley moved his
kitchen furniture into his living room and housed ten
of his mules in his long, lean-to kitchen until the storm
abated. Snow was fifteen inches on the level along the
Black Hills trail between Cheyenne and Chugwater.
Many sheep and cattle perished.

A number of herders and freighters, caught out
without shelter lost their lives or were badly frozen.
Innumerable horses, mules, and oxen with freighting
outfits on the road between Cheyenne and Deadwood
died from exposure or starvation.[62] Telegraph lines
were down and mail and passenger services were temporarily suspended.

Some items describing the storm said:

The City Hall is full of snow . . . one hundred men with five
engines and snow plows (u.p.) didn't get more than five miles from
town during the day. . . The Denver Pacific is in the vicinity of
Summit and is expected to arrive in Cheyenne this afternoon. . .

[62] A. J. Parshall of Cheyenne, lost all except nine head, of the 100 head of
oxen in the freight teams, with which he was hauling machinery for the
Homestake.

The Colorado Central is at Taylor's and the prospect for its arrival here today is exceedingly slim. . . The eastern bound Union Pacific train is yet at Laramie. . . Snow drifted two feet deep upon the floors of the officers' quarters at Fort Russell. . . The snow in Deadwood is over five feet deep on the level. . .

On the third day of the storm, Luke Voorhees sent the mail north to Deadwood from Cheyenne, by "pony express." Mail from the southbound coach, which had reached Chugwater, was transported southward also via horseback. The next day, Voorhees, on horseback, escorted a Concord coach load of passengers north from the "Magic City," for five miles, to make sure the stage had a good safe start.

Freighters who reached Cheyenne some two days later reported that they had seen this northbound coach near Nine Mile ranch "winding its way off the road among the snowdrifts." But it went through to its destination "right side up." At this time the winter schedule for mail called for delivery from Cheyenne to Deadwood within 107 hours, without penalty; the summer schedule required delivery in 83 hours.

The Omaha *Bee* at this time paid the following tribute to the superintendent of the Cheyenne and Black Hills stage line:

Mr. Voorhees is one of the best stage superintendents in the western country, possessing pluck and energy, which qualities are essential to success in his line of business. Under his administration fifteen of the principal road agents who operated on the Black Hills road last summer were captured, and only one — Reddy McKemma — managed to escape through the carelessness of a sheriff in Ohio, where he was traced and arrested.

Among the Cheyenneites detained in Deadwood by the big snow blockade in the spring of 1878 was

Francis E. Warren, later governor and United States senator of Wyoming. Warren often related how he made his way out of the Hills on the first stage that left Deadwood. He and the driver started in a sled but had to abandon it in the deep drifts. They then tried to go on horseback and had to give up that mode of travel. They made it at last to Jenney Stockade on foot. Warren came on to Cheyenne on the first southbound coach that came through.

The spring schedule for the Cheyenne and Black Hills Stage company as advertised in may 1878, in the Deadwood *Times,* by the Union Pacific railroad was as follows:

CHEYENNE AND BLACK HILLS STAGE COMPANY
Sidney coach leaves daily at 5:30 A.M.
Cheyenne coach leaves daily 5 A.M.
Express packages and mail matter must be in the office by 9 P.M.
previous to day of departure.
Tickets all parts of the East for sale at reduced rates
Express Envelopes for Sale
This Company will take every pains to make passengers comfortable.

———

THE UNION PACIFIC R.R. AND ITS CONNECTIONS
Including first-class Stage Lines via
Cheyenne and Sidney and the Colorado Central R.R.
recently completed to Cheyenne,
offers unrivaled advantages to Denver City,
all points in Colorado and New Mexico
and to the
East, West, North, and South

———

By it you avoid the snow of the far North and Bad Lands of Eastern and Northern Dakota; the dangerous hunting grounds of the Sioux Indians and the delays and dangers of Missouri River navigation.

These are the only lines open the whole year round and by which nine-tenths of the people in the Hills have come here. The only lines on which the Military Posts and Telegraph Lines are established; the only lines that bring the mails in four days from Chicago, and run daily the whole year. By it you secure all rail transportation from Cheyenne and Sidney and the finest road-bed and equipments in the world —

Steel Rails, Miller Platforms and Air Brakes. The finest Pullman Sleepers attached to all Passenger trains. Rates always as low as by any other line. Full information and a new map of the United States, showing the great Overland Route, its connections, etc., with view of scenery, will be cheerfully furnished on application to

THOMAS L. KIMBALL, Gen. Pass. and Ticket Agt., Omaha, Neb.

or T. A. RUSSELL, Traveling Agent, Deadwood, D.T.

THE TREASURE COACH IS BUILT

Up to this time the so-called "treasure coaches" were just the regular Concord coaches which carried either wooden or iron treasure "boxes." Now, however, Gilmer, Salisbury and Patrick knew that with the large new developments in the Black Hills and the resultant shipments of gold, the road agents would swarm along the stage route as the summer came on.

They therefore employed A. D. Butler of Cheyenne, to build a coach designed purely for the carrying of valuable express. Butler lined the interior of a coach with steel plates five-sixteenths of an inch in thickness, capable of withstanding any rifle bullet. A test showed that the contents of the heaviest charged rifles fired at the plate at a distance of only fifty feet had no effect. There were two port holes in the doors to permit the messengers within the coach to get the so-called "dead wood" on any and all road agents. Because of the weight involved, the roof of the coach was not lined with metal.

The specially built chilled steel safe, "the salamander," that had carried so much treasure out of the Hills during 1877, was put into the new coach and fastened to the floor with heavy bolts. This new coach, which was ready for use the latter part of may 1878, was called "The Iron Clad," also, "The Monitor."

This was the only real treasure coach used on the stage line until a second one was completed in september, which was dubbed, "The Johnny Slaughter." Superintendent Voorhees ordered that no passengers should be permitted to ride on these special treasure coaches because of the danger from attacks by road agents.

William M. Ward, who was one of the first Cheyenne businessmen to promote a stage line to the Black Hills and who had worked closely with George Homan, jr., of Omaha, on the proposed establishment of a stage line in 1875, was now the superintendent of the northern division of the Cheyenne to Deadwood stage. With Jim May he had recently built the short-cut road from Hat Creek station to Jenney Stockade, so was entirely familiar with the country and knew its dangers.

Ward's first real troubles began when on july 2, road agents stopped the stage at Whoop Up canyon, about sixty-five miles south of Deadwood. In the coach, driven by John Flaherty, were E. S. Smith and J. S. Smith of New York; A. Liberman and H. Liberman of Chicago, Mrs. M. V. Boughton of Cheyenne, and

Daniel Finn, a former freight conductor on the Union Pacific railroad.

Only two agents came into view and after placing the passengers in line and robbing four of them of various amounts of money and two gold watches, they advanced to Finn, who drew his revolver and shot one of the robbers. The robber, later identified as John H. Brown, fell on his knees, then rallied. As Finn was about to shoot again, an accomplice of the robber, Charley Ross alias James Patrick, who was lying in ambush, shot Finn through the nose and mouth, inflicting a painful but not serious wound. The robbers then retreated, firing several shots, wounding E. E. Smith in the leg below the knee and A. Liberman in the thigh. Both were flesh wounds and although painful, were not dangerous. Mrs. Boughton was not molested.

The coach proceeded to Hat creek where the wounded were made comfortable and then proceeded to Cheyenne. Ward, with Boone May and Billy Sample, attempted to trail the robbers, but was unsuccessful. Brown and Ross, later however, were brought to justice.

Heavy spring rains in 1878 carried off several bridges along the Cheyenne to Deadwood road, including those across the Cheyenne river, Lance creek, and Old Woman's fork and, hence, when the streambeds were filled with water the stages were delayed. The coach that left Deadwood for Cheyenne on july 23, was detained at Jenney Stockade because of high water ahead and when it proceeded, was stopped about two o'clock in the morning near Lance creek, about twenty-eight miles from Hat creek. The six masked men who ordered the coach to halt found only one passenger on board, the Rev. J. W. Picket who was sitting beside the driver. The agents did not molest him, but turned their attention to the mail sacks and robbed them of registered letters and other valuable matter. They also broke open the treasure boxes but found them empty. After half an hour the robbers ordered the driver to go on. This robbery was an important milestone along the trail of crime and banditry in the Black Hills, as it was the *first time* on the *through*-Cheyenne-to-Deadwood route, that the *United States mails were robbed*.

Up to this time the road agents operating between Fort Laramie and Deadwood, had confined their depredations to robbing passengers and plundering the treasure boxes. But now with the treasure heavily guarded and being transported in the steel-lined "Monitor" coach, they cast their eyes on something easier,—the registered mail, which went over the road every day.

The next day after the mails had been robbed, six road agents again stopped a coach near Lightning creek. They were taken quite by surprise by E. S. Smith, a shotgun messenger, who was escorting this coach on horseback, instead of riding the boot. Smith opened fire on the robbers at once. His horse was killed almost instantly by the robbers, but Smith kept firing until he had discharged about twenty shots to the agents' fifty shots. The outlaws left without molesting the coach. Smith was highly praised by the passengers for his coolness and bravery.

With the robbing of the mails, the United States government at once took a hand, in the person of special Agent John B. Furay, of the Post Office department. Furay was a seasoned frontiersman, who had soldiered with the 11th Ohio Volunteer Cavalry along the Oregon trail, under Colonel William O. Collins in the 'sixties. He had now just completed forty thousand miles of travel in the west in less than a year, inspecting the official bonds of all postmasters in Nebraska, Wyoming, Dakota, Utah, Idaho, and Montana.

Upon his arrival in Deadwood, Furay began his investigations and soon opened up "an avenue" through which he had access to valuable information regarding the outlaws. This "avenue" was E. E. Cunningham, who owned a quartz mill at Central City, and who was on friendly terms with a young desperado, also named Cunningham. Through the latter he was able to pick up much information.

Inspector Furay reported that: "The fact that Jackson Bishop, the Colorado murderer and outlaw, Frank Towle, Jack Campbell, Tom Reed, and a deserter from the Third Cavalry, with Persimmon Bill were the six men who stopped the stage on july 25, is well known to me still there is not a particle of legal proof of the fact as they were closely masked, and the passengers and driver could not, as they say, possibly identify them." Later, Furay added that possibly Jack Watkins also was with the gang. Some thought that "Big Nose George" Parrot also was among them.

Furay informed D. B. Parker, chief special agent of the Post Office department in Washington, D.C., that there were several gangs of road agents at work along the Cheyenne and Black Hills trail.

"Indeed," he said, "the whole country in the vicinity of old Fort Reno, now Fort McKinney,[63] and east of

---

[63] Fort Reno was on Powder river. In october 1878 Fort McKinney was established on Clear creek fork of Powder river near the present site of Buffalo, Wyoming, and old Fort Reno was moved fifty miles north to this new location.

there for 150 miles is infested with various gangs of the
most desperate outlaws[64] to be found anywhere perhaps on this continent. They have various places where
they receive food and information, which places are
well known, but the buffalo are in the country in which
they are staying and they profess to be 'hunters' and
when they rob the stages and mails, they know that
they can not be identified sufficiently to make a conviction. The few settlers there are honest, will give no
information, knowing full well that their lives will
pay the forfeit if it becomes known. The only way to
get evidence is to buy up certain members of the 'confidence gang' at Custer, Lead City, Central, and Deadwood, have them go out and join outlaws, be captured
with them and then turn state's evidence."

Furay estimated that it would cost from three thousand to seven thousand dollars to carry out such a
plan and said *money* was needed, not *promises*. He
reiterated the fact that Fort McKinney was the "hard-
est spot" in the United States and called attention to
recent congressional legislation prohibiting the use of
the U.S. Army as a *posse comitatus*. The clause of the
army bill referred to, had been designed to give im-
munity to violators of revenue laws in southern states,
but it immediately worked hardship on the people of
the west as the troops could now not be called upon to
guard the mails.

Furay further stated that in the country infested by
the robbers there was no civil authority whatever and

---

[64] Jesse James and his gang had a hideout in the Little Goose valley not
far from new Fort McKinney, about forty miles north. The cabin and stables
were there in 1878 when O. P. Hanna went into the valley to settle. George
Beck and T. J. Foster, as well as Frank Gruard all stated the James Boys
were there.

said that now the highwaymen knew there was nothing to fear from the army forces. One band of renegades even dismounted and disarmed a cavalry escort of a mail coach between Fort McKinney and Fort Fetterman!

On the Cheyenne and Black Hills route another coach was stopped about the first of august, four miles from Jenney Stockade, but the road agents merely asked the driver concerning the movements of the treasure coach and went on their way.

About this time an attempt was made to derail the westbound Union Pacific pay car east of Carbon, a small coal town near Medicine Bow. The plan was foiled by a section worker who discovered the loosened rail and stopped the oncoming train. In trying to track down the outlaws who had made the plans for the train wreck, two men, Tip Vincent and Robert Widdowfield of Carbon county, Wyoming, were killed near Elk mountain. This tragedy incensed the entire state. Part of the gang who made the attempt were afterward identified as working along the Black Hills stage line. Among them were: "Big Nose George" Parrot, "Dutch Charley," Joe Manuse, Frank James, John Irwin, and Frank Towle.

In the latter part of august, another coach was waylaid. This was a northbound stage, which was stopped between Cheyenne river and Lance creek. Only three agents were in evidence and were said to have been: "Texas Charley," [65] "Sitting Bull," and Joseph Boyd alias Charley Osborn, known also as "The Kid."

[65] On august 8, the father of "Texas Charley" visited the Hills looking for his son. The father was described as being a quiet, inoffensive, old gentleman. "Texas Charley" was supposed to have helped in the train robbery at Percy, Wyo., in may 1878.

After compelling the passengers to throw up their hands the robbers went through their pockets, took two watches, and a small amount of money and then cut open all of the mail sacks and took the registered letters. They left the balance of the mail strewn over the ground.

Shortly after this, Postmaster General Key and his official party visited Wyoming, on their way to the Pacific coast. Inspector Furay and Colonel M. T. Patrick were among those who spent some time with the party in Cheyenne. The officials of the stage asked that they be allowed to carry registered mail from Deadwood on all coaches as usual, as they felt if the mail were allowed to accumulate for the treasure coach, the Dakota patrons would soon use the mails, instead of the more expensive express, and that would mean a considerable financial loss to the stage company.

General Key granted the request, with one proviso, that registered mail matter going up to Deadwood should be carried only on the treasure coach.

Business in Cheyenne during the summer of 1878 was dull as compared with that of the previous year. Aside from the excitement of the arrival of coaches that had been robbed, there was little out of the ordinary except some trouble now and then in the western section of the "Magic City," known as "Chicago," where the colored troops from Fort D. A. Russell "hung out."

The daily routine of the little city on the plains was varied by such incidents as an inebriated cowboy dashing down Sixteenth street on horseback and running over "the little boy of Mrs. O'Donald" and breaking his arm. Upon realizing what he had done, the cowboy gave Mrs. O'Donald a bill of sale for his horse, bridle, and saddle.

One afternoon Mrs. Elizabeth Herndon struck Mrs. Callahan with a parasol, demanded a jury trial, and was fined ten dollars and costs, which amounted to $51.30.

There were running and trotting races quite often at Sloan's lake between Conley's Sorrel, Emery's Badger Boy, and O'Brien's Chalk Line.

Then there was an evening upon which all the Cheyenne hotel proprietors vied to have as guest one R. L. Potter, the man with a wheelbarrow, who had walked 2,687 miles in 92 days, on his way from Albany, New York to San Francisco. And speaking of wheelbarrows – Officer James A. Bean one evening found a drunk in an alley and wheeled him in a wheelbarrow to the city hall during a terrific storm. The inebriated man thought the storm was for his benefit and tried to make a speech from the barrow.

Much conversation went the rounds this season concerning a bill before the U.S. Senate providing for the incorporation of the National Pacific Railroad and Telegraph company, the object of which was to construct and operate a railway and telegraph line from Cheyenne to Deadwood and from Fort Laramie to Fort Fetterman, thence toward the Yellowstone river, near the mouth of the Big Horn river, thence to Helena, Montana, and on to the Pacific ocean.

Early in 1878, the board of directors of the Union Pacific railroad voted to construct, during the summer, one hundred miles of railway from the main line of the Union Pacific in the direction of the Black Hills, but construction was delayed.

A standing committee [66] of Cheyenne men had been appointed a year before relative to the Colorado Central, and Cheyenne, Black Hills, and Montana railroads. Late in january 1878, the voters of Laramie county approved the issuance of one hundred and fifty thousand dollars in bonds to the Colorado Central railroad in an effort to make certain that Cheyenne would be the starting point for the Hills railway, instead of Sidney.

In april, Captain E. L. Berthoud, chief engineer of the Colorado Central, arrived in Cheyenne with a surveying party to ferret out, if possible, a more direct route to the Hills than previously outlined.

In the meantime, no rails were being laid, and the Cheyenne and Black Hills Stage company kept its wheels rolling.

In that summer of 1878 there was much interest in Wyoming in the total eclipse of the sun, which occurred on july 29, but little publicity was given to the "tall, slim looking fellow, with thin face and restless eyes, very nervous who talked fast and put on but little style, wearing a huge mustache," named Thomas A. Edison, who went through Cheyenne on his way to Rawlins as a member of the Henry Draper Astronomical expedition. The party made scientific observations of the eclipse from Creston, on the Continental divide. "Most people," said the *Leader,* "would take Edison for a second lieutenant in the regular service."

It was claimed that on this trip, Edison, while sitting on the shore of Battle lake, (near what is now Encampment, Wyoming), stripping strands of bamboo from a

[66] Committee comprised: F. E. Warren, E. Nagle, J. H. Nichols, I. C. Whipple, A. R. Converse, A. H. Swan, H. Glafcke, J. Joslin, W. R. Steele, and L. Murrin.

fishing rod, conceived the idea of a nonconducting filament that made possible the incandescent electric lamp.

There really was much more of a ripple of excitement over news from the Swan ranch near Chugwater, about the killing of a buffalo, than there was over Edison's visit. Two days after the scientist was in Cheyenne, a ranchman reported that "A monster buffalo bull was killed two miles north of William Swan's ranch, about sixty-five miles from Cheyenne." It was said that the animal weighed nearly seventeen hundred pounds and was killed with revolvers!

In addition to Edison, other Cheyenne visitors of note that summer were: Daniel Frohman, who came as advance agent for the Georgia Minstrels; Henry Ward Beecher, who was on a lecture tour; and Mrs. Maude Collins, widow of the late Joel Collins, reputed leader of the Big springs train robbers.

That, too, was the summer that Buffalo Bill, in a glass ball shooting match, broke 23 out of 25 balls thrown into the air. He used a rifle *without* sights.

Probably the most excitement of the season occurred the day a severe hailstorm struck Cheyenne and six teams were seen on Seventeenth street running away at the same time. This same storm, on august 10, struck the Black Hills stage near Government Farm. The driver vowed that stones fell there that were as large as hen's eggs. It was with the greatest difficulty that he kept the horses attached to the coach, as they ran at great speed.

When miners, with their summer earnings, began to come down from the Hills, and heavy shipments of dust and bullion from fall clean-ups of the many mines were taxing the treasure coach to the limit, Voorhees assigned six "shotgun messengers" to regular duty.

On the night of september 10, three armed men stopped the down coach between Lance creek and the Cheyenne river. The brigands robbed the four passengers and plundered the mail. Just then the northbound coach arrived. They stopped it, robbed the passengers and cut open the mail sacks. They also broke open the treasure boxes and took their contents.

Messenger Smith, who had remained in the coach, intending to stand off the robbers, was compelled to come out by an agent who placed a passenger in front of him as a shield.

During this robbery the arms of the passengers were tied behind their backs. One of the thieves, who wore no mask, was thought to be "Lengthy" Johnson, a notorious horse thief. Shortly afterward, Deputy Marshal Horn arrived in Cheyenne with a man, in custody, named William Wallace (Lengthy) Johnson, who owned a ranch near Red Cloud agency. He later was released because of lack of evidence.

In quick succession, beginning about the middle of september, outlaws struck in all directions in eastern Wyoming. They robbed the mail near Dutch Charley's place at Trabing, where the Fort Fetterman stage road crossed Powder river; they took supplies, watches, and firearms from men repairing the Cheyenne and Black Hills Telegraph line; and they robbed S. M. Booth, a Custer merchant of twelve hundred dollars and a fine team of horses, while he was on the Cheyenne river road.

Shortly afterward, packers reported finding a camp of outlaws, in a dell completely hemmed in by rugged and steep hills in the vicinity of Harney's peak. They claimed there were fourteen men and two women in the hideout.

At this time, Superintendent Voorhees went north to make preparations for some important changes in the stage route. Because of the difficulty experienced during the summer as the result of the unusual rains in the Hills, plus the constant holdups by road agents, he proposed to change the route almost entirely. He outlined a route that would leave the old road at or near Raw Hide Buttes station, veer in a northeasterly direction leaving Custer City to the left, thence proceed to Deadwood by the way of Crook City.

Voorhees ordered new stations built and proposed to have everything in readiness to make the switch in routes, without loss of time, and with no inconvenience to passengers. Thirty head of new horses were shipped in from the east, and additional stage equipment was acquired.

Wyoming had had a change of governors earlier in the year, when Governor John W. Hoyt had been appointed to succeed John Thayer as the chief executive of the territory. Governor Hoyt immediately became active in trying to obtain protection for the railway and stage lines against the inroads of robbers. He appealed to the War department saying that "Threatened depredations are imminent, points of attack uncertain. The laws of Wyoming do not fully meet the exigency, and the end to be gained is clearly and properly within the duties and powers of the federal government. . ."

Although it was kept a secret from the public, the Post Office department appropriated two thousand dollars to be used in detective work in the Black Hills. Special Agent Charles Adams at Deadwood, working under Inspector Furay's direction, was placed in charge of the work and was sworn in as deputy U.S. marshal. He selected and deputized Scott Davis, D. Boone May, and eight others, and equipped them with good horses and ammunition. These men were to be paid five dollars a day and two hundred dollars from the United States government and two hundred dollars from the Laramie county commissioners for every road agent they captured, dead or alive.

The Laramie county commissioners also employed five men, under the leadership of Ed Ordway, at one hundred dollars per month each, to aid in "the good work."

Six men robbed the mail on the northbound coach about 11 o'clock the night of september 13, at Old Woman's fork. After taking ten dollars from a passenger named Goldworthy, they returned it because he said he was a laboring man. They did not molest the other passenger, a woman.

This coach soon met the southbound coach and warned its driver that robbers were in the vicinity of Old Woman's fork. Boone May and John Zimmerman, who were riding about two hundred yards in the rear of the down coach, dropped back farther and kept out of sight. When the coach reached the general vicinity of the recent robbery, it was stopped by a command from the outlaws.

As soon as the robbers had "gone through" the passengers, they put the mail sacks on the ground. Suddenly they realized that the shotgun messengers were closing in on them. The outlaws opened fire. May and Zimmerman returned the fire instantly. A robber, afterwards identified as Frank Towle (or Toll) fell, fatally wounded.

According to Boone May, he recognized one of the robbers as Frank James alias Tom Reed.

"Get into the coach and drive on," the robbers shouted to the passengers as they began to retreat. They kept up a steady fire, in the direction of the messengers.

May and Zimmerman soon realized that they could not dislodge the outlaws, so mounted their horses and joined the coach. The mail was left in the road near the body of the fallen robber. The next morning when the mail was retrieved, there was a pool of blood in the road beside the rifled sacks. What had happened to Towle's body was learned by the law some three months later.

C. H. Brown, of Denver, a coach passenger, who was robbed of ten dollars and a satchel, praised the messengers very highly for the way they conducted themselves during the attack.

For weeks the western press had been crying for a "war of extermination" against the road agents, but at the same time it continued to exercise its right of the "free press" to publish all news concerning the movement of gold. For instance, on september 18, 1878 there appeared the following in the Cheyenne *Leader:*

Special telegram to the *Leader*   Deadwood, Dak.
THE TREASURE COACH LEAVING TOMORROW TAKES $250,000 BUL-
LION FROM THE HILLS

Such items perked up the "road agents" considerably, but they irked the "special agents" no end.

Of course, it must be admitted that the *Leader* tried to print all of the news. On the same day that it headlined the shipment of gold bullion it published a report that the dead bodies of two men named O. B. Davis and George W. Keating, well known horse and cattle thieves, were found hanging to a tree, five miles north of Spearfish, and said it was thought to be the work of the Vigilantes, "as tracks of a dozen men were found to and from the spot."

The Wheels of "The Monitor"
Are Stopped

TREASURE COACH ROBBERY – CANYON SPRINGS

After the stagecoach holdup, in which Frank Towle was killed, there was a lull like that which precedes a cyclone. No trouble from highwaymen along the Black Hills trail was reported for almost two weeks and then came the most daring, bloody, biggest, and last holdup on the Cheyenne to Deadwood route. This was the Canyon Springs robbery.

Canyon Springs station, in a lonely, rough, and heavily timbered country along Beaver creek was about thirty-seven miles south of Deadwood and nineteen or twenty miles north of Jenney Stockade. Since it was maintained only as a relay station for coach horses, it comprised a combination stable and living quarters, in which there was a room for the stock tender.

It was not nearly so well known as Cold Spring Ranch station, two or more miles up the canyon to the north, where a short-cut from Custer City joined the main Cheyenne-Deadwood road. Hence, the big hold-up of the treasure coach is often referred to as the "Cold Springs robbery." Within a month after the affair, the stage was routed over an entirely new road and Canyon Springs station, later known as the C. V.

Smith ranch, became only a dim memory as a part of the Cheyenne and Black Hills stage system.

According to Luke Voorhees, there were in the fall of 1878 the following regular "shotgun messenger" guards employed by him: Scott Davis, captain, Jesse Brown, Gale Hill, Boone May, Billy Sample, Eugene Smith, and Johnny Zimmerman. Others were employed as "specials" as needed.

Voorhees instructed division Superintendent Ward to accompany the treasure coach from Deadwood to Hat creek on this particular trip. Ward, however, disobeyed orders and only remained with the coach to the Pleasant Valley dinner station, where he turned back to Deadwood. The cause of this disobedience is not of record.

On the up trip with the "Monitor," Jesse Brown, Boone May, and Billy Sample remained at Beaver station, about ten miles south of Canyon springs, to be in readiness to pick up the loaded coach on its down journey and to accompany it on horseback from Beaver to Hat creek, via Jenney Stockade.

According to John McClintock of Deadwood, one agent, called "Red Cloud" because he had come from the agency, loitered around Deadwood and when the "Monitor" was ready to start southward, stole the fine pacing horse owned by Blanch White, a woman of the town, and dashed ahead to notify the robber gang then hiding out near Canyon springs.

As the coach approached Canyon springs about three o'clock on the afternoon of september 26, Gene Barnett was driving the six horses, with Gale Hill on the boot beside him. Scott Davis and Eugene Smith were inside as guards, with Hugh O. Campbell, an employe of the

Black Hills Telegraph company, who had been permitted to ride from Deadwood to Jenney Stockade, where he was to take a new assignment.

Gene pulled the team to a stop on the slope about ten feet from the front of the log barn at Canyon springs, where William Miner, a stock tender, usually stood ready to assist in the seven-minute change of horses. No one was in sight. Gale Hill called to the stock tender, but receiving no answer, jumped down from the coach and picked up the chock block to block the back wheels of the coach. As he raised up from placing the block and started around the rear of the coach to go into the barn, he was met by a volley of gunfire from the stable. Hill was wounded in the left arm, but managed to use his gun with one hand and wounded one of the robbers. Then a shot from a large bore rifle struck him in the breast, passing through his body and knocking him down. With blood pouring from his mouth, he grasped his gun and wounded another robber, who it was thought died the next day. Hill managed to crawl to the rear of the stable out of the line of fire.

A shot fired through the top of the coach grazed Messenger Smith's head and he slumped down stunned. Scott Davis thought at first that Smith was killed. Davis said:

I fired a good many shots from the coach into the barn door and the port holes from which the robbers were firing, but from my position in the coach was unsuccessful in hitting the attacking foe. I told Campbell that I was going to get out of the coach and go across the road to where there was a large pine tree from which I could get better aim. . . Campbell said he was going to the tree with me. We both climbed from the coach but Campbell had no gun with him to defend himself. I turned and backed my way across the road, shooting at anything and everything that looked like a robber. When we were about half way across the road, Campbell swerved to the left while I kept shooting at the port holes, hoping I might hit a hidden robber. Suddenly Mr. Campbell went down on his knees in the middle of the road. The holdup men then fired another volley, killing him instantly.

Before I reached the tree, one of the robbers appeared at the head of the horses. I had been urging the stage driver to make a run for it and leave the coach. The instant I saw the robber at the horse's head, I turned quickly and fired. The shot wounded him badly. He threw up his hands, fell over backwards, crawled around behind the horses and made his getaway to the back of the barn.

As soon as Davis gained the protection of the large tree and began firing toward the stable again, a robber appeared from behind the coach and ordered Barnett to get down from the boot. Then he pushed him toward the tree where Davis was stationed.

"Surrender!" the agent yelled at Davis.

"If you come an inch farther I'll kill you," Davis shouted.

Barnett, who was being used as a shield for the robber, cried out: "For God's sake, Scott, don't shoot."

When Scott Davis saw that he could not hit the robber, without killing Barnett, he suddenly recalled that Voorhees had said that any time the treasure coach was held up, he could rely upon the guaranteed safe to hold the money for twenty-four hours. He then backed away through some brush and pine trees, and made his escape.

He went on foot about seven miles to the Ben Eager ranch, where he obtained a saddle horse and struck out as fast as possible for Beaver station. Soon he met Jesse Brown, Billy Sample, and Boone May, messengers, who had started up the road to look for the coach when it failed to appear on scheduled time. Davis told what had happened. All headed at once for Canyon Springs station and reached there just after the robbers had left.

Just exactly what happened during the plundering of the coach is not clear from the records, as so many conflicting stories were told during the excitement and were amplified in being repeated. Some were changed entirely down through the years.

William Miner, the stock tender, in a statement made to Voorhees, soon after the robbery said,

Shortly before time for the stage to arrive from Deadwood, a man on horseback rode up and asked for a drink of water. Upon dismounting, he ordered me to throw up my hands, which I did. He then pushed me in the grain room of the stable. By this time the band of five (I thought there were six of them) all got in the stable and proceeded to make arrangements for the capture of the coach.

They removed the mud or chinking from between the logs near the door of the stable, where the stage always stops, and on its arrival they opened fire from their position on the inside. After the killing of Campbell and wounding of Gale Hill, Scott Davis got away from the coach and, taking a position behind a tree opened fire on the robbers. Soon after this the band rounded up all of the men about the place and tied them to trees, saying that at 10 o'clock a man would be along to release them. Immediately upon securing their victims they removed the safe from the coach and opened it. . . This required several hours of work.

Eugene Smith said later that the robbers made him come out of the coach and give up his guns, then they ordered him back in and drove out with Barnett to the timber out of sight of the road. They tied Smith and Barnett to the coach wheels and with a sledge hammer and cold chisel broke open the safe in about two hours.

They took the money, bullion, and jewelry valued at about twenty-seven thousand dollars, packed them on horses and fled. Most of the plunder was in gold dust and bullion, there being only about thirty-five hundred dollars in currency, about five hundred in diamonds, and a few hundred dollars worth of jewelry.

In the meantime, as soon as he could release himself, Miner, the stock tender, struck out on foot through the timber for the Cold Spring ranch. There he obtained a saddle horse and went on to Deadwood to report the robbery and to obtain medical aid for Gale Hill. Doctor F. L. Babcock went south at once and gave Hill attention at the Cold Spring ranch to which he had been taken. While there he was in the care of Mrs. Frazier and Mr. Snow, the ranch owner. Later he was removed to the hospital in Deadwood. Two years after the holdup, a ragged piece of bullet worked its way out of Hill's arm.

The body of Hugh O. Campbell was taken to Deadwood where his funeral was conducted by the Masonic lodge. He was buried in Mt. Moriah cemetery, in which rested the remains of "Wild Bill" Hickok and "Preacher" Smith.

Upon being apprised of the robbery, the stage company officials posted the following notice:

$2,500 REWARD

Will be paid for the return of the money and valuables and the capture (upon conviction), of the five men who robbed our coach on the 26th day of september 1878, at Canyon Springs (Whisky Gap), Wyo. Ter., of twenty-seven thousand dollars, consisting mostly of gold bullion. Pro rate of the above will be paid for the capture of either of the robbers and proportionate part of the property.

LUKE VOORHEES, Supt. Cheyenne and Black Hills Stage Co.
Cheyenne, Wyo., sept. 28, 1878

News of the holdup of the treasure coach and the killing of Hugh O. Campbell struck Wyoming and Dakota like a bombshell. So many minor holdups had occurred that the public had been accepting them as a matter of course. Now, however, with the murder of an innocent man involved, the law abiding citizens had "blood in their eye." The size of the rewards offered for the capture of the culprits, too, may have had something to do with the way men roused to action.

It was as if a whole fourth of july celebration had been set off at once. Innumerable posses were organized and struck out in various directions on the man hunt. For a week or so there was a man with a gun behind every bush and tree along the trails and highways to stop all passersby, either to ask for news or to demand explanations of travelers as to why they were there. Rumors flew thick and fast. Facts were distorted. Lurid stories were fabricated from flimsy whisperings. The citizens of Cheyenne flocked down to the stage office each night for news and swarmed around "The Monitor" when it completed its first trip down, after being stopped at Canyon springs.

Scott Davis led a party of robber-hunters into the Inyan Kara country, but soon decided he was "off the scent" and veered southwest toward Raw Hide Buttes. Sheriff Manning of Deadwood and his men headed toward Fort McKinney and the Powder river area. A party under Seth Bullock, including Captain W. M. Ward, division agent, J. H. Burns, June Dix, and three others went south toward Robbers' Roost and Harney's peak. D. Boone May, Bill May, detective Noah Siever and their companions hit the trail toward Pactola on Rapid creek and soon learned that the outlaws had bought a dead-axle wagon and two ponies at Slate creek for which they had paid two hundred and fifty dollars in cash. One of the outlaws had been so badly wounded, it had been necessary to transport him. It was believed that the outlaws had made a wide circle around Rapid City and had gone over the Divide to Boxelder creek to the Pierre trail.

May's party was joined by a posse from Rapid City, in which were: Sheriff Frank Moulton, Doctor Flick, Ed Cook, and others. Now hot on the trail of the "dead-axle wagon," they met freighters coming westward who gave them news of the fleeing highwaymen.

The pursuers hastened on to Wasta Spring Road house, eighteen miles east of Rapid City, where they stopped to rest their horses and to eat supper. There Bullock and his party, who had also gotten on the trail, joined them.

Although for a time the trail of the outlaws was dim, the posse decided that the thieves probably had made camp near Pino springs, off the main road. Bullock and Moulton wanted to attack at once when they felt they had located the men. Cook, however, insisted on waiting until morning.

By daylight, the "birds had flown." They had abandoned the wagon and it was supposed that the wounded bandit, probably Frank McBride, described as a small man about twenty-four, had died en route and been buried. The posse pushed on.

Dr. Whitfield of Rapid City, who was riding a Mexican pony, could not keep up with the others, so turned back for home. When he reached the place where the bandits were supposed to have camped, he stopped to investigate. He kicked the ashes of the campfire and suddenly saw a pair of old overalls a short distance away. He took a kick at the garment and found that it contained a gold brick valued at thirty-two hundred dollars! The doctor later received eleven hundred dollars, upon the return of the brick to the stage company.[67]

A man named Gouch, who was said to have been an advance guard for the robbers in the wagon, was later arrested at Fort Thompson and taken to Rapid City. He was instrumental in locating some retort valued at about eleven thousand dollars that had been buried near Pino springs.

W. M. Ward and his party hurried on to the Missouri river. There some of the men turned south. Ward went on to Pierre, where he learned that a man, answering the description of one of the road agents had crossed. Ward followed his trail to Atlantic, Iowa, where he captured and arrested Thomas Jefferson Goodale. From infancy the young man had been known as "Duck" Goodale. His relatives were among the best and most respected citizens of the town and his arrest caused little less than a furore. It was said that young Goodale had left Atlantic the previous may, and had sent back favorable reports of what he was doing in the west.

Upon his recent arrival in Atlantic, he had given to his father, Almond Goodale, a banker, a gold brick weighing twenty pounds. He asked that it be put in the bank vault for safekeeping. It was marked "no. 12" and was valued at forty-three hundred dollars. Young Goodale, it was reported, had told his father that he had sold his interest in a very valuable mine and had gotten the brick in payment.

Goodale was found to have in his possession, in addi-

[67] Information obtained from scrapbook of C. I. Leedy, Rapid City, S.D.

tion to the brick which weighed 248.87 ounces, one ladies' gold watch and chain, two silver watches, a seven set diamond ring, two plain gold rings, one shot gun, and two revolvers.

As soon as Governor Gear of Iowa, granted a requisition, Ward started back to Wyoming with the prisoner and the prisoner's lawyer. Shackles were riveted on Goodale's leg by a railway blacksmith at the depot in Council Bluffs, Iowa.

Upon reaching Lone Tree, Nebraska, Goodale, with permission of Ward, went to the wash room, in the rear of the railway car. That was the last seen or heard of him by the public. When Goodale's escape was discovered, the train was stopped and backed about a half mile to the place where it was thought he had jumped off. Later the shackles were found in the toilet room. One theory was advanced that he must have climbed to the top of the train and ridden into Ogallala or some other station, instead of having jumped off. How he got out of the shackles was never explained.

Ward returned to Cheyenne empty handed and "under a cloud," as it was rumored that he had received three thousand dollars for the "escape." Superintendent Voorhees went at once to Atlantic, Iowa and arranged for the recovery of the stolen property, which had been turned over to the county authorities by Goodale's father. The Cheyenne and Black Hills Stage company offered seven hundred dollars reward for the recapture of Goodale, and Laramie county added two hundred dollars more to the offer. The rewards were never claimed.

A week after Ward's return to Wyoming, Voorhees stated that W. H. Ward no longer was in the employ of the stage company.

In the great round-up of road agents during those last days of september 1878 and early october, arrests were made of many suspects and almost to a man, the villains were brought to justice for one crime or another.

A day after the robbery, John H. Brown was arrested at Canyon springs. Brown, who had been under suspicion, had been employed by the stage company "for a purpose." Although it was at first reported that he had confessed to being implicated in the Canyon springs robbery, he later swore that he was involved only in the one at Whoop Up canyon on july 2, when passenger Finn had been shot. Brown was "escorted" to Cheyenne by J. L. Jelm and placed into custody just four days after the attack at Canyon springs.

Arrested with Brown, was Charles Henry Borris, who it was said, was forced to confess that he had taken part in the big holdup. He readily acknowledged that he had assisted in two other stage robberies, including the one at Whoop Up, and said he was with the party that had stolen the horses and property at Noble's camp earlier in september.[68]

Borris had been sent to the Wyoming state penitentiary three years previous to this time, on a charge of stealing government stock. He was then known as Charles Henry. Subsequently he had escaped from

[68] About september 8, 1878, five men robbed the camp of W. H. Noble, on Lander creek, near Atlantic City. The robbers took 14 horses, all of the provisions in camp, guns, ammunition, three new saddles, blankets, spurs, and the like. They tied up the herders and spent the day at the camp. They talked freely about ranchmen along the Sweetwater and Green river and seemed to be well posted in matters concerning Wyoming, Utah, Idaho, Nevada, Oregon and Washington, as well as Colorado, New Mexico, and Texas. Worden Noble, a New Yorker, had come to Wyoming in 1866 as a bookkeeper. In the spring of 1868 he opened a store at South Pass City and was a contractor for Camp Stambaugh. Later he went into stockraising.

the prison. When arraigned before U.S. Commissioner Fisher, Borris was held in five thousand dollars bail for appearance at the next term of district court. He was taken at once to Laramie City for safekeeping.

Later he denied that he had been at Canyon springs and said that he had gone to Deadwood to sell some dust and some of the horses stolen from the Noble camp. While there he was drugged and failed to get over his spree in time to join his comrades at Canyon springs. Meeting the robbers after the robbery, he said he "came near being killed by them on suspicion that I had been 'blowing on' them." Borris was convicted on november 27, of obstructing the mails. He was sentenced to pay a fine of one hundred dollars, pay costs of prosecution and to stand committed until paid.

Other early arrests were those of Lew Hagers, keeper of a ranch at the crossing of the Cheyenne river on the old Custer trail, and George Howard alias Tony Pastor, a notorious horse thief, who was taken into custody when he arrived at Hagers's ranch. Hagers, who was arrested by detective Noah Siever on the strength of a letter found under the treasure coach which had been written to him by a notorious woman in Lead, was later released. Pastor admitted that he had been on a horse thieving expedition, but denied any connection with the stage holdup.

Men arriving in Cheyenne on october 10, stated that they had found two bodies hanging to a tree seven miles from Jenney Stockade about four miles east of the Custer road. They said from the appearance of the corpses that the men must have been dead about a week. The victims, said to have had light hair and moustaches, were wearing California riveted brown clothing. It was rumored that Scott Davis's party did the "good work."

On october 18, the southbound coach rolled out of Deadwood with Jesse Brown and Jim May in charge of two road agents, William Mansfield and Archie McLaughlin, who were said to have admitted implication in the Canyon springs robbery, and also to have taken part in the affair at Whoop Up canyon.

These men had made overtures to Deadwood citizens relative to the disposal of considerable bullion. Acting under the direction of special Agent Adams, the citizens had endeavored to negotiate with Mansfield and McLaughlin but were unsuccessful.

Later the pair was arrested and escorted to a secluded spot. Both men were "drawn up a tree" until they confessed to having participated in recent robberies, including one in the Cariboo country, and the one at Canyon springs.

Mansfield and McLaughlin were kept in jail in Cheyenne until november 3, and when it was then learned that the next term of court would not be held for several months, the authorities decided to return the pair of "black legs" to Deadwood, where they could be tried immediately for grand larceny. Accordingly they were placed on a northbound coach, again under guard of Jim May and Jesse Brown.

When the coach reached a place on Little Cottonwood, about a mile north of Fort Laramie, five masked men suddenly appeared, but they were not after gold.

The stage messengers were relieved of their arms and were set afoot for the time being. The Vigilantes then tied the outlaws' hands, placed ropes around their necks, and put them on top of the coach. Quickly the coach was driven to a large cottonwood tree near the river bank, not far from Watson's saloon. The ropes were tied to a tree limb. The coach drove off and the men were left dangling.

It was said that young Billy Mansfield, a carpenter by trade, shed tears and begged for mercy and asked to write to his mother, but the avengers of the law were not moved by his pleas. Archie McLaughlin, also known as Cummins, was made of harder stuff. He defied his captors and refused the opportunity to confess the whereabouts of the hidden spoils of the recent stage robberies. He said he had eight thousand dollars cached away where it could be reached by friends, but declined to answer all questions put to him. He died cursing his lynchers.

At daylight on november 4, F. L. Greene, deputy coroner at Fort Laramie, was notified and rode to the scene where he found the bodies and gave the agents decent burial. No coroner's jury was held, nor were the names of the five masked men ever made public. The general sentiment at the time seemed to be that a necessary job had been done in ridding the country of two dangerous outlaws, who if given a wee chance, might escape and again ride a trail of murder and banditry. One editor declared that the region now could "enjoy a lasting peace."

The alleged head of the gang to which Mansfield and McLaughlin had belonged was Tom Price, an acknowledged desperado. Price was captured in a camp about ten miles southwest of Lead City by a party including Jesse Brown, Boone and Jim May, and Wes Travis. He was wounded before being captured and lay in a hospital in Deadwood for several weeks.

By february 1879, he was able to travel and was escorted to Cheyenne by D. Boone May. Between the stage office in Cheyenne and the court house, May and his prisoner were followed by a large and curious crowd. Price was sentenced in may 1879, to five years in the penitentiary and was committed to prison in Lincoln, Nebraska. Price confessed to having been in the Cariboo robbery, but denied he was with the Canyon springs gang.

During the whirlwind round-up of road agents, an excellent piece of detective work was performed by Deputy U.S. Marshal M. F. Leach, a merchant of Ogallala, Nebraska. Leach earlier had helped catch the Big springs robbers and had given Bullock a tip that had resulted in the arrest of "Reddy" McKemma in Ohio.

Voorhees was tipped off that Al Spears, a questionable character, had written to Cheyenne about a trunk. Almost at the same time, Leach contacted Voorhees and said that he suspected Spears of being one of the Canyon springs robbers as he had just disposed of about five hundred dollars worth of jewelry at Ogallala and eight hundred dollars in gold dust. Voorhees instructed Leach to arrest Spears, if possible.

It was not long until Leach surprised Spears in the act of disposing of some of the stolen goods at Grand Island, Nebraska. Spears reached for his gun, but Leach was quicker on the draw. When arrested, Spears had on his person a quantity of the jewelry stolen from the Black Hills treasure coach, also a gun which had been taken from Gale Hill, after he was wounded.

On the way to Cheyenne, Spears told Leach that the Canyon springs robbery was his first and last venture of that kind and said that he had been coaxed into it by others, as he had been hard up all summer. He insisted that there were only four others in addition to himself, and said that he had failed to get his just share, as the loot was divided in his absence. His confederates told him they "didn't make much of a haul."

Spears told several stories about where the stolen gold was buried, but upon threats from Voorhees of hanging, he finally said it was on Wood river.

Despite his protestations as to his innocence of past crimes, the Cheyenne officers declared that Spears was a well known cattle thief and a "hard customer." He plead guilty to murder in the second degree in the killing of Hugh Campbell and received a life sentence on november 27, 1878. He served in the penitentiary at Lincoln, Nebraska as "Alber Spurs."

In less than six weeks from the time of the Canyon springs robbery, three-fifths of the stolen property had been recovered by the Cheyenne and Black Hills Stage company,—a real accomplishment, in view of the vast expanse of country which had been covered in corralling the outlaws.

Charles Carey, said to have been the leader of the gang, and described as 27 years old, with light brown hair and about six feet tall, was not apprehended.

Could he have been one of the pair found hanging to a tree near Jenney Stockade? He was said to have been a former scout with General Custer. Carey first came to Deadwood in 1876 and worked as a taxidermist. According to John McClintock, who lived just across the street from Carey's cabin, his gang at first was "all as good boys as you'd find." McClintock claimed that later Carey stole his shotgun and began a life of banditry.

In response to an appeal from Governor Hoyt, special Agent Furay, and officials of the stage company, also Congressman Corlett, the war department ordered troops to protect the Cheyenne and Black Hills mail route. Company F of the Fifth Cavalry, in command of Captain Payne, established headquarters at the old Hat creek barracks, which had been evacuated the previous march.

Monroe Salisbury went to Cincinnati to make arrangements for the construction of a burglar-proof safe to be used in the treasure coach. The safe, designed to weigh one ton, was guaranteed by the manufacturers to withstand the operations of stage robbers for 56 hours of uninterrupted work. It was to be delivered in two weeks. Records are not available as to its performance, but a similar safe which was delivered from Cincinnati to the stage company some five months later, was opened single-handed by Superintendent Voorhees in one and one-half hours!

The owners of the stage line gave patrons every assurance that they intended to continue to carry valuable express and registered mail over the Cheyenne and Deadwood route.

Early in december, a letter came to Cheyenne requesting a copy of the *Leader*. Through that letter, one of the road agents, Charley Ross alias James Patrick and by some thought to have been "Jack Campbell," was traced to Eureka, Nevada and apprehended. He was brought back to Wyoming by Sheriff T. Jeff Carr, was tried and sentenced to twelve years in the penitentiary. He committed suicide while in prison at Lincoln, Nebraska on february 16, 1885, because of suffering from tuberculosis.

Soon after Ross was brought to Cheyenne from

Nevada, a woman named Lurline Monte Verdi, who was lying ill in the "Magic City," sent for a *Sun* reporter and said she had a story that she wished to tell.

The reporter accompanied Dr. J. J. Crook, a physician, to her sickbed and wrote the following for his newspaper, as the woman told it to him:

I have sent for you for the purpose of telling what I know about Charlie Ross, who has just been arrested and is now in jail here. I had not intended to say anything about it, or to mix myself up in it, but as one of these robbers engaged in that Finn shooting affair [69] is dead and one has confessed, I don't think my oath binds me to silence. I am familiar with nearly all the members of the gang recently engaged in stage robbery. I was not in any way connected with their business; but my restaurant in Deadwood was a place of resort for some of the members of the gang, and there I learned much concerning their actions. But I paid little or no attention to them or their conversation. It was about the middle of last july that I became, reluctantly, connected with the gang. It happened this way.

One night a particular friend of mine, a young carpenter named Billy Mansfield, poor boy, he has been innocently hung since then, came to my restaurant and told me he must see me at a certain opium-smoking house that night, as a friend of his was sick. I had been in the habit of spending pleasant hours in that opium house with parties of friends, and thought nothing of the appointment. I told my husband where I was going and why, and, at the time appointed, I was there. Billy Mansfield then informed me that his friend was very sick and that I must go and see him. After some argument on my part, I accompanied him down the main street of Deadwood to a small house near the bridge, where I met McLaughlin and another member of the gang, and in the presence of these men I was made to take a solemn oath of secrecy. I was afraid to refuse, for a person's life was not worth much in that region.

I was conducted from the deserted shanty near the bridge to another

---

[69] The stage holdup at Whoop Up canyon, july 2, 1878. The man referred to as dead was presumably Archie McLaughlin. The one who confessed is John H. Brown.

not far distant, where the pretended sick man lay. There, in a dark corner, upon a pallet or bunk made of pine poles, lay a man whom I at once recognized as Johnny H. Brown, who is now lying in jail here in Cheyenne. The men told me he was not wounded, just sick, but I declined to believe it and insisted upon knowing the truth before I would prescribe. Brown was in a high fever and delirious. Blood and pus were thrown from his mouth during each convulsion. He was raving and would not permit anyone to approach him, saying that the gang wished to poison him or kill him to prevent him "giving them away." Finding that "taffy" and nonsense would not do, the men told me the truth – that Johnny Brown had been engaged in the robbery of the coach on the 3rd (2nd) of July, and had got shot. He had laid there ten days without medical attention, fearing that a regular physician would expose the gang if he were introduced.

I obtained control over the suspicious sufferer by means of chloroform, which I administered from the wounded man's head, while I held his pulse in my right hand. When I knew that the excitement was reduced sufficiently, I told him what I wanted to do was to save his life. He had a bullet in his side which I wanted to cut out. I asked him if he could stand the pain, or whether I should give him chloroform. He said, "No. I can trust you, as you are not interested in my death." I turned him over and found where the bullet had lodged between two of his ribs after passing through his side and liver. I cut out the bullet and inserted a wire loop I had prepared, and in less time than it has taken to tell you, I flipped the bullet out. Johnny, the brave boy, made but one groan during the entire operation. I was then permitted to go home, with the promise to return the following night.

Monte Verdi then told of how she went to see Brown every night until he was out of danger. During her visits she met many of the gang. On the second night she was startled by the discovery that two men were concealed beneath the wounded man's bed. She kept her presence of mind and pretended not to have seen them. It seemed that Charlie Ross and Burris (Borris), members of the gang, were suspicious of the woman and were listening to her conversation with Brown. On the first indication of treachery they intended to kill her. They were in the habit of spending the days in the woods and the nights in the shanty in Deadwood.

During her conversation with the reporter and Doctor Crook, Monte Verdi gave information to the effect that she had been married to a surgeon in the army, with whom she had studied surgery and medicine, and had practiced anatomical studies at the dissecting table. After her husband died, she became a tutor among the Sioux at the Red Cloud agency, then sat behind a table dealing "Twenty-one" in a fashionable gambling palace in a frontier town. Later she was the proprietor of a restaurant in Deadwood. One record shows that she was billed at the Bella Union theatre in Cheyenne in january, 1876 as a serio-comic singer, "The favorite of the public."

The New York *Tribune,* january 3, 1878 said: ". . . Then there is Monte Verde, with her dark eyes and tresses, who on her arrival in Deadwood stood upon a board and was borne through the town on the shoulders of four strapping miners and who now deals '21' and dances a jig with a far-off look in her left eye."

The Deadwood *Resident Directory,* 1878-9, lists "Lurline Monte Verdi" as living at Main near Wall. This probably was the location of her restaurant.

Other names assigned to the "woman physician of the road agents" have been: Mme. Vestal[70] (Belle

---

[70] William B. Thom writing for the Leadville (Colorado) *Herald-Democrat,* august 19, 1937 said in part: "When the Deadwood and other Black Hills gold diggings were creating excitement in 1876, Mme. Vestal (Belle Siddons) chartered a four-horse omnibus in Denver, had it modeled into a beautiful boudoir and bedroom, and attended by several of her attendant sporting men, with wagons loaded with tents and gambling furniture, started for the Black Hills. On her arrival there she opened her gambling palace under

Siddons), and Mrs. Hallet. According to some she was a daughter of a wealthy Missouri family and a one-time belle in the society of the state capital, Jefferson City. Some said she was a spy during the Civil War and served a prison sentence.

It was said that D. Boone May, one of the "shotgun messengers," won his way into Monte Verdi's favor and through information obtained from her was able to bring several of the Black Hills road agents to justice.

There are various intriguing stories about this "woman physician," who made headlines in the *Police Gazette*. That she did exist is evident, but which stories one should believe—that is a matter difficult to settle.

In this same month of december 1878, another person allied with outlaws was moved to "confession." Frank Howard, one of the gang[71] that planned to wreck the Union Pacific train near Medicine Bow in august, told ex-Governor Thayer, who owned a ranch and a hotel at Rock creek, that a gang was hiding out in the neighborhood getting ready to rob his hotel and to stop a train.

Thayer immediately sent word to Laramie City, but the sheriff of Albany county hesitated to act, because he said he could not get men to go with him to tackle the outlaws. Nathaniel K. Boswell known as the "Fearless man of the plains," acting as a representative of the Rocky Mountain Detective association, took thir-

canvas. There it was she became acquainted with Archie Cummings, who was a former guerilla on the Kansas border, and with whom this strange woman fell in love."

[71] Dr. John Osborne of Rawlins, Wyo., said that members of this gang were: "Dutch Charley," "Big Nose George" Parrot, Tom Reed (supposed to be one of the Younger boys), Sim Wan (thought to be Frank James) and Frank Towle.

teen men and went to Rock creek on a special train. Although the weather was about thirty degrees below zero, and the time was after midnight when the men reached Rock creek, Boswell hastily gathered horses and riding equipment and led his men across a network of ravines and gullies in search of the robbers' camp.

The daring detective captured the following men: Joe Manuse, "Dutch Charley," Frank Ruby, A. C. Douglas, Hank Harrington, and Charles Condon.

Joe Manuse had in his possession an overcoat which had been worn by Boone May on the night of september 13, when the Black Hills stagecoach had been held up.

Shortly after these men were placed in jail in Laramie City, another member of the gang, John Irwin, who had been sent to Cheyenne for provisions, was arrested and detained on a charge of firing his revolver while in McDaniels theatre. Boswell at once took him to Laramie City, also, as a suspect in the murder of Widdowfield and Tip Vincent, the previous august.

Under stress, Joe Manuse told the officers that "Dutch Charley" had told him that he had shot either Vincent or Widdowfield and that a dozen bullets from the other men's guns had brought down the other man when he tried to escape. This sealed "Dutch Charley's" fate. It was decided to transfer him from Laramie City to Rawlins for trial, since the murder of which he was accused, had occurred in Carbon county. En route, "Dutch Charley" was taken from the Union Pacific at Carbon, near Elk mountain, and was hanged by a mob to a telegraph pole.

A similar fate befell his confederate, "Big Nose

George" two years later at Rawlins, Wyoming. Having been arrested in Miles City, Montana in the summer of 1880, "Big Nose George" was brought to Rawlins, tried and sentenced to be hanged on april 2, 1881. The prisoner made an attack on Sheriff Rankin, in attempting to escape from jail. Vigilantes took him from prison and hanged him from a telephone pole. Dr. John E. Osborne, later governor of Wyoming, who was a young physician just newly arrived in Rawlins, was called to pronounce the outlaw dead. Dr. Osborne and a woman physician used the outlaw's corpse for a study in dissection and the former had a pair of shoes made of skin cut from the chest.

In the summer of 1881, the governor of Wyoming territory received a request to send a transcript or certificate of death to A. Lefaiore, consul general of France, relating to the "late George Parrot, alias *Au-Groz-Nez,* who was lynched in the beginning of last march at Rawlins. . . The aforesaid certificate of death is required by the widow of the victim."

Harrington, who was in the round-up staged by N. K. Boswell at Rock creek, turned state's evidence but was soon afterward shot by a man named Smith when he was on his way to Fort McKinney to identify supposed stage robbers. Smith claimed that Harrington had killed his brother.

A. C. Douglas, who had been employed by the Rock creek stage line, had not taken part in any robberies but was accused of assisting the stage robbers by notifying them when there was treasure on the coach. He was sentenced to a year in the penitentiary.

Joe Manuse and Ruby each received four years in prison.

Frank Howard was made a detective on the Union Pacific and gave valuable service to the company.

Irwin, the captain, and Condon, "The Kid," were sentenced for life.[72]

While in jail in Laramie, Irwin confessed to Boswell that he had taken part in the Black Hills stagecoach robbery in september when one of his pals, Frank Towle, had been killed. He described where he and another confederate had buried Towle. Boswell relayed the story to D. Boone May, who located the body.

Believing that he was the one who had killed Towle, May hoped to collect the reward money. He amputated the robber's head, put it in a gunnysack, tied it behind his saddle and rode 178 miles to Cheyenne. There he offered his gruesome "evidence" to the county commissioners.

His claim was delayed for some time and then was refused because of the lack of proof that he, May, was the one who fired the shot that killed Towle. May also filed a claim with the county commissioners of Carbon county, as it was in that county that Widdowfield and Vincent had been killed, presumably by Towle and his gang. The sworn affidavit filed in the court house at Rawlins read:

                              Territory of Wyoming
Carbon County, Wyo. T.   To Boon May, Dr.
For reward of Frank Toll one of the Murders of Widdowfield and
    Vincent
Territory of Wyoming, County of Albany
    Boon May being first duly sworn on oath says: That on the night
of 13th of september A.D. 1878 he shot and killed Frank Toll one

---

[72] Cook, John W. *Hands Up,—Reminiscences by Gen. D. J. Cook* (Denver, 1897).

of the murders of Widdowfield and Vincent on the Old Womans fork on the Black Hills Stage road running from Cheyenne to Deadwood that affiant has the head of the said Frank Toll in his possession sufficient to identify him and that affiant is prepared to prove that the man killed by him as above stated is the identical Frank Toll and the murderer of Widdowfield at Elk mountain in said Carbon county.   Boone May

Subscribed and sworn to before me this 29th day of january A.D. 1879
(Seal)   John D. Brockway, Notary Public

The records of the Carbon county commissioners do not show that the reward was ever paid.

There is an oft repeated tale in Cheyenne to the effect that some youngsters in later years who were drowning out prairie dogs or gophers north of town, discovered the bandit's head which had been buried there.

That these road agents were not the gallant Robin Hoods so often portrayed in western fiction, is shown in the following incident. It seems that John R. Smith, a ranchman on Powder river, who sold beef to Fort McKinney, was reputed to have considerable money at his place. When Frank Towle came to the ranch once and attempted to rob him, Smith shot him. Fearing it would "go hard" with her husband if the robber should die, Mrs. Smith nursed the wounded man back to health. Smith was tried in Cheyenne for the shooting and was exonerated. Later Towle stole Smith's horses, some of which were recovered in the Black Hills.

Despite the swift justice meted out to the road agents who were identified with holdups along the Cheyenne to Deadwood trail, in that intensive campaign against outlawry in the late autumn of 1878, the robbing of mails continued on the Fort McKinney route and along the Sidney and Ft. Pierre routes. Road houses were robbed in the Fort Fetterman area and there were holdups in the Green river country.

Horse thieving increased and cattle rustling began in earnest in Wyoming. A large gang of renegades lurked near the mouth of Lightning creek and along Old Woman's fork in 1879 and gradually the center of activity for the outlaws shifted away from Robbers' Roost and the breaks of the Cheyenne river, toward the Powder river country near Fort McKinney, then to the Hole-in-the-wall, and even on over into Jackson Hole.

After the big robbery at Canyon springs, the Black Hills coaches rocked along over the trail unmolested. The stage company continued to transport the bullion from the Homestake and other mining companies until 1881, when the railway from the east was completed into the Hills.

The Wheels of the Mills Grind on

The mail route from Cheyenne to Deadwood had
been run under a special contract from the Post Office
department from march 1877, to october 1, 1878, at
which time new bids were called for and the contract
was awarded to John E. Kemp at sixteen thousand dollars per annum. Kemp, finding that he could not afford
to carry the mail at the contract price, made statements
to the Post Office department to the effect that the government could save money and Deadwood and Cheyenne would be served just as well, by having the route
changed from Cheyenne to Horse Head, where it
would connect with the Sidney to Deadwood stage line.
Kemp claimed that by such an arrangement the price
could be curtailed to fourteen thousand dollars per
annum and he said the same time could be made as was
now being made by the way of Jenney Stockade.

Evidently upon his representation, the department
curtailed the route. And since the contract was not a
paying one, Kemp sublet it to M. T. Patrick, M. Salisbury, J. T. Gilmer and Luke Voorhees who were now
organized under the name of Salisbury and Company.

Early in the spring of 1878, Al S. Patrick, a brother
of Colonel Matt, had bid on carrying the mail to
Deadwood, but had not been successful. On october 1,
Colonel Patrick withdrew from the Cheyenne and
Black Hills Stage company and later became associated

with his brother Al, in a line from Rock Creek, Wyoming to Echeta, Montana, said to be the longest stage line in the region. On this new line, which traversed the Powder river area, the Patrick Brothers had to contend with road agents at every turn of the road.

Luke Voorhees, who already had been planning a change in routes to avoid the hilly, muddy country via Jenney Stockade, now arranged to have the mail carried over the newly designated mail route, by the way of Horse Head, south of Buffalo gap.

A new road and stations were completed with all possible speed, even though the change was made during the intensive round-up of Canyon springs robbers.

On the morning of october 10, 1878, the first mail went over the new route. It left the old line at Raw Hide Buttes and headed eastward fifty-five miles to Horse Head station, where a confluence was made with the Sidney line. North from there a six-horse coach made the run to Deadwood.

This new route almost entirely avoided the Hills. The road passed over a fairly level country now. Many passengers were pleased with the change as they felt they would escape being "all shook up," as they had been in the past, when negotiating the road through the hills, especially that part north of Jenney Stockade.

The settlers around Hat Creek station and north to the edge of the Hills, however, were much perturbed when the new route disrupted their direct mail service. After the post office at Hat creek was closed, they sent petitions to Governor Hoyt and to Delegate Corlett, urging that mail service be reestablished in that area, which was becoming a thriving cattle ranching country.

Residents of Custer City and adjacent camps strove

to have the Cheyenne coach enter the Hills by the way of Red canyon, as in earlier times, but the year 1878 closed with the stages rolling along by the way of Horse Head junction.

Three railways now brought gold seekers and others into Cheyenne, and all through the autumn many women and children arrived in the "Magic City of the Plains," and took the stages north to the Black Hills to join their husbands and fathers. Civilization definitely was on the march and yet, the Cheyenne and Black Hills stage line still spanned vast areas where life was lived on a widely varying scale.

While socialites in Cheyenne wore the stylish new "switches" and "lunatic curls," topped by ostrich feather evening hats, and served on their tables fresh grapes from California, oranges and bananas from the south, fresh codfish from Massachusetts and fresh salmon from the Columbia river, only a comparatively short distance to the north stray bands of Indians were constantly slipping away from their agencies to stampede cattle herds near Pumpkin buttes and Hat Creek station; "Dutch George" Werre, a professional hunter, was mauled and killed by a grizzly bear; English tourists were on buffalo hunting expeditions; and "sow belly" and sourdough biscuits still comprised the main diet in many a lonely shack, dug-out, or cabin.

In Cheyenne itself during 1878 much substantial building was accomplished, including the new McDaniels theatre block, a new Masonic temple, and the "fine brick mansion on Eighteenth street built by Miss Ida Hamilton," said to have cost fourteen thousand dollars, including a Springfield gas machine for lighting and a Salamander furnace!

And although much gold from the Black Hills

pouied into "Miss" Hamilton's palace of iniquity that autumn and winter, some of it also went into the coffers of the substantial churches which were within a stone's throw of Miss Hamilton's "place" on "The Row."

While raucous voices mingled with the tunes that were banged out by mechanical pianos in Cheyenne's numerous saloons and places of "entertainment," groups of God-fearing citizens met in the various churches for Bible readings, the singing of hymns, and the giving of classical recitations.

The Catholics held fairs and festivals to raise money for church work; the Ladies Sewing society of the Congregational church sewed for the needy and helped to raise money for the "yellow fever" sufferers of the south. Jewish residents celebrated Yom Kippur with much ceremony. Colored voters organized a political club and nominated one of their members, W. J. Hardin, a popular barber, to the territorial legislature. Hardin was elected and served with credit. Cattlemen continued to bring big herds to the plains surrounding Cheyenne and many of them erected homes of "elegance."

The "Magic City of the Plains" now had its roots down deep and had established itself as one of the most substantial young cities of the entire west, an acknowledged popular starting place for the world-famous Black Hills gold country, which could be safely reached by the already nationally known Cheyenne and Black Hills stage. The reign of terror of the road agents had come to an end.

A review of the general situation in the Black Hills at the beginning of 1879, showed that the gold produced during the preceding season just closed, had reached nearly three million dollars; the population of the Hills had reached approximately fifteen thousand; one hundred and fifty thousand cattle were grazing in the valleys; and thirty-eight quartz mills and eight hundred stamps were in operation. Deadwood, with a population of five thousand, was conceded to be the commercial center, with Lead and Central City, the ore crushing centers.

Where three years before there was practically untouched wilderness, there now were two telegraph lines, four stage companies, and seven newspapers in operation. It was reported that the California capitalists had paid four hundred thousand dollars for the Father De Smet mine. The Golden Terra had sold for eighty thousand dollars; the Homestake no. 1, for seventy thousand; Homestake no. 2, for fifty thousand; and the old Abe for two hundred and fifty thousand dollars. Attention was called to the fact that in Deadwood nails were worth ten dollars a keg; beer, three dollars a keg.

Down in the "Magic City" on new year's day, 1879, a Concord coach, belonging to the Cheyenne and Black Hills Stage company, rollicked on its thoroughbraces through the streets, behind the heels of eight mules. At intervals it drew up in front of first one and then another of the residences of the city's most substantial citizens. With as much dash as the driver of the mules could command, the wheels were cramped to permit the exit from the coach of four young gentlemen who were wearing top hats and their "sunday best." From house to house they went paying their respects to the various hostesses of the city, who were holding their annual "at home."

But that gay beginning of the month of january was no criterion of the days to follow, for soon Indians went on a rampage and endeavored to run off horses belonging to the stage company at its new Bluff station, about thirty miles northwest of Red Cloud agency; and before the month came to a close, one of the company's messengers, William Rafferty, was killed accidentally.

In telling of the Indian fight, which took place on january 9, near Bluff station, William Scanlon, Company C, Third Cavalry, said:

Some Sioux who had been captured and put in the guard house at Fort Robinson, killed their guards and escaped. It was a bitterly cold day. We found afterward that the squaws had smuggled guns in their clothing when we put them in jail. We went to the hills after the fugitives and found them ready for us, hidden from view, in a buffalo wallow from which they opened fire. They refused to surrender and every last one of them, including the squaws was killed. We lost several soldiers and many others were wounded.

For a week a number of Indians loitered in the vicinity of Bluff station, but did not attempt a raid as troops were camped close by.

It was at the end of his run into Deadwood, on january 22, that William Rafferty, messenger who had replaced the wounded Gale Hill, jumped from the boot and began to remove blankets from the coach. His pistol fell and the hammer struck the brake, sending a bullet into his body, killing him instantly.

During the spring, "Lame Johnny" Bradley, said to have participated in some of the stage holdups on the Black Hills trail, was taken care of by Vigilantes near Buffalo gap, while being taken to Rapid City, in the custody of "Whispering" Smith. A creek in the vicinity now bears the name of "Lame Johnny." His partner, Black Hank, was arrested the following november, accused of being a road agent, a murderer, and a member of "Doc" Middleton's gang of horse thieves.

Among the various hang-outs of the outlaws along the Cheyenne and Black Hills trail, was the dug-out home of "Old Mother Feather Legs" on Demmon hill between Raw Hide buttes and Running Water. "Old Mother Feather Legs" was so-called by the cowboys because the long red pantalettes that she wore tied about her ankles, fluttered briskly in the breeze when she dashed on horseback across the flats. According to one of her visitors: "Them drawers looked exactly like a feather-legged chicken in a high wind."

The woman was a go-between for road agents and other desperadoes and it was claimed she kept much stolen jewelry and money around her place. She had come to the Raw Hide country in 1876 and had opened a place of "entertainment" for travelers in the dug-out. A couple of tin horn gamblers and "rot gut" whisky were part of her equipment. No one at the time knew who she was or where she came from.

About a year after "Mother Feather Legs" opened up her establishment on Demmon hill, a man named Dick Davis, called "Dangerous Dick" because of a certain hang dog and evil look on his countenance, came to live at the place. Ostensibly he followed hunting and trapping for a living, but most of his time was spent loafing in the woman's shack. The two seemed well acquainted and to have known each other in the past.

One day in 1879, Mrs. O. J. Demmon, wife of a ranchman who lived at Silver springs on the stage road, decided to visit the "Old Woman," since she was the only woman living in the neighborhood.

Upon her arrival at the dug-out, Mrs. Demmon was horrified to find that the "Old Woman" had been murdered. She evidently had been shot while filling a bucket of water at the spring. In the soft soil about the spring were many tracks,—many were those made by moccasins, the kind of footgear always worn by "Dangerous Dick." The murderer had fled, taking with him the twelve or fifteen hundred dollars that the "Old Woman" was known to have had.

The body of "Mother Feather Legs" was buried in a grave near the dug-out.

It was later learned that "Old Mother Feather Legs" was "Mam," the mother of Tom and Bill Shephard, members of a gang of outlaws and cutthroats who lurked in the slimy fastnesses of the Tensas swamps in northern Louisiana, after the close of the Civil war.

With the return of the paroled Confederate soldiers, the doom of the band was sealed and its members were hunted like the wild beasts they were. Both the Shephard boys died by the swift judgment of the lynching rope. The gang was wiped out with the exception of "Mam" and a fellow named "The Terrapin." These two succeeded in making their escape, to appear years afterward on the Raw Hide.

After murdering "Mother Feather Legs," Davis, "The Terrapin," went back with the plunder, to his old haunts in the swamps. But there, after engaging in his old practices of murder and robbery, he was lynched within sight of where the Shephard boys had met their fate. Before he died, "Dangerous Dick" made a full confession and thus cleared the identity of the "Old Woman of the Raw Hide, Mother Feather Legs."

After the mail route between Cheyenne and Deadwood was curtailed and shunted eastward from Raw Hide Buttes to the junction with the Sidney route at

Horse Head station, considerable trade was lost to Cheyenne. Such trade now went over the Sidney and Pierre routes. But despite the change, some three million pounds of boilers and machinery awaited delivery from Cheyenne to the Black Hills on february 1, 1879.

Passenger traffic over the Cheyenne route continued heavy, stimulated to some extent by the development of the extensive ranching and other interests north of the Platte river. Cattlemen during the past three years had gradually pushed to the Raw Hide and Running Water, then on beyond the Cheyenne river toward the Belle Fourche. Fort Laramie, too, provided many passengers for the stage line.

For a few months the leaving time from Cheyenne was changed to two o'clock in the afternoon, but was changed back to the old 5 A.M.

Salisbury and Company continued to expand their interests and were constantly alert to new opportunities in the stage business. There was considerable talk in early 1879 of transferring some of the horses and equipment to better paying routes in Colorado and Wyoming.

H. A. Iddings, who had been agent for the company in Cheyenne for a year and a half, resigned that position to go to Helena, Montana to take over large interests for Salisbury and Company. He was succeeded by W. S. Tobey.

Soon after Tobey took charge of the Cheyenne office, he held a sale of unclaimed baggage and express then in possession of the company, and closed up the express office which the company had maintained in the Union Pacific depot. Future business of that nature was conducted in the one "uptown" office.

Business over the Cheyenne route received a decided

impetus in october, following the disastrous fire which on september 25, wiped out the business area of Dead-wood. Scarcely had the embers cooled, than the Dakota business men began raking them away and rebuilding substantial new store buildings and business houses. Immediately they ordered by telegram, new stocks of goods and supplies to be forwarded from Cheyenne by express. Salisbury and Company delivered the express with remarkable efficiency.

The "Monitor," or "Old Ironsides," the treasure coach, was now being sent over the Sidney line and on some runs carried as much as three hundred and fifty thousand dollars in gold. The road agents moved to that area. Their former haunts along Old Woman's fork and Lightning creek now became headquarters for horse and cattle thieves, who were operating on the vast ranges of the big stockmen.

Late in 1879, D. Boone May, assisted by W. H. Llewellyn, of the department of justice, succeeded in decoying an outlaw called "Curly," whose name was Lee Grimes. Curly was said to be an extraordinary gunman,[73] who had perfected a system of "rolling" the hammers of his guns with both hands and firing with tremendous rapidity and accuracy. He was a "dead" shot and evidently had invented a system of his own which would shoot his guns more rapidly than a trigger would operate them. Grimes was known to have driven eighteen head of horses from the Raw Hide Buttes area to the Hills.

May arrested Curly about fifty miles from Dead-wood, and in company with Llewellyn started to take the prisoner to Fort Meade near Sturgis. The ther-

[73] Information about Curly's gun ability obtained by author from James H. Furay, son of Postal Inspector Furay.

mometer was below zero, with a bad blizzard on. Some time after dark, Curly asked if the handcuffs could be taken off so that his hands would not freeze. He promised not to attempt to escape. May complied with his request.

It was not long until Curly made a dash for freedom. His horse, however, floundered in the two feet of snow off the trail and Curly was not able to make good his escape. Although ordered to halt, the fugitive urged his horse on. Both officers fired. Grimes was killed.

In the ensuing months there was considerable ugly criticism against May and Llewellyn for the killing, hence they demanded a trial in order to clear themselves. The trial was held and the jury rendered a verdict of "not guilty" without leaving the jury box in the court room.

A report of the Cheyenne and Black Hills Telegraph line, which connected with the Western Union at Fort Laramie, showed at the end of 1879, that 17,500 paid messages, in addition to nine hundred thousand words of press dispatches had gone over the wires from Deadwood during the year.

Within the year, O. J. Salisbury, who with Gilmer had invested heavily in the mines of the Black Hills, was elected president of the First National bank at Deadwood, and continued in that position until the bank consolidated with the American National bank of Deadwood some time later. He also became a substantial stockholder in the First National bank of Lead. The records show that Salisbury was an excellent director, the type that "directs" with firm decisions and close scrutiny of affairs at hand.

Less than a dozen years from the time that Monroe Salisbury and Jack Gilmer started as partners in the stage business in Utah, they were acknowledged to be "one of the most powerful corporations in the West." By 1880 they had more than five thousand miles of daily stage lines in operation and were using between six thousand and seven thousand horses. Their monthly payroll at that time was said to have been large enough to "come pretty near running the United States government under the John Adams' administration."

Shortly before Christmas, the Deadwood coach experienced a queer phenomenon, – a Chinook, while in the vicinity of Lead City. The snow and ice, which at five degrees below zero crunched beneath the Concord tires, turned to splashing slush, as the mercury skyrocketed to forty-two degrees above zero in just one hundred and twenty minutes.

Some three weeks later the driver of the southbound coach faced one of the worst winds on record, in the Cheyenne area. The air was filled with dust and small pebbles by a sixty-two miles an hour "breeze" that blew down chimneys in Cheyenne, tore away wooden awnings, felled fences, and sent large dry goods boxes scurrying along the streets as if they were band boxes.

In Cheyenne, the old year was ushered out and the new year welcomed with "a little random shooting on the streets and some more not so random." But it was reported that no particular harm was done.

Governor and Mrs. Hoyt, as well as "Mrs. General Merritt at Fort Russell" were "at home" on new year's day, 1880, but the day was reported not to have been nearly so festive as its predecessor in 1879, had been.

A New Eldorado Calls

In january 1880, the mail contract between Cheyenne and Deadwood was curtailed, the daily service going only as far as Raw Hide Buttes. A semi-weekly extension service reaching fifty-nine miles northeastward to Buckhorn post office and intervening places along the western edge of the Black Hills, was handled from Raw Hide by a buckboard driver.

The passenger service from Cheyenne to Deadwood via Horse Head junction continued as usual in the Concord coaches.

Luke Voorhees was a familiar figure those days as he went up and down the line in a two horse buggy, inspecting stations, horses, and equipment, and keeping things moving along smoothly.

A study of his notebooks shows that in addition to his regular stage work, he attended to innumerable errands for those along the route, not necessarily just the employees of the stage company.

For instance, among the items jotted down are:

For Lowrey: 5 gallon molasses, 1 wash stand, 1 cheap bedstead, wash bowl and pitcher, hat 7 1/8, dairy salt, stove flange, jars for butter, lamp chimney, dripping pan, door knob, camp kettle, 2 doz. large size milk pans, 2 four tine forks.

Send a man up to work for Patrick; quit claim deed for Patrick.

45 Needle to J. M. Jester, army cartridges, trunk lock, crash towel-

ing, wooden bowl, 10 ft. oil cloth for table, see about door, box of envelopes, looking glass, 3 sauce dishes, scouring brick, dried peaches, lard pail.

For Lathrop: canvas coat, buffalo coat, empty barrel.

For driver: Box 44 Cal 73 Model Centre fire, 38 Co revolver, 1 E violin string, beeswax, whip, caddie of Climax tobacco, pocket knife, tarpaulin.

Voorhees at this time was busy not only on the Wyoming stage line, but also on the Sidney line, and on a line from Fargo, North Dakota, to Pembina, Manitoba. He also established a "short line" from Fort Collins, Colorado to Mason City and had other Colorado mail contracts.

The records of 1880 have little to say about road agents or their confederates along the Cheyenne-Deadwood route, except to detail now and then the capture of some of the long-hunted desperadoes wanted for their past "work" along the line.

Johnson and Nolan were caught and convicted during the year through the efforts of Special Agent John B. Furay of the Post Office department.

Early in april, Sheriff N. K. Boswell of Laramie City, went to Yankton, Dakota to bring back "Cully" Maxwell, who had been indicted by the grand jury of Albany county on four counts. Maxwell, said to have been a prominent member of the Black Hills road agents' gang, had committed a number of thefts along the Cheyenne route. A reward of twenty-two hundred dollars had been offered for his capture: one thousand dollars by the Union Pacific railroad, one thousand dollars by the Cheyenne and Black Hills Stage company, and two hundred dollars by the Post Office department. Maxwell had eluded capture in Wyoming and had shifted his operations over into Dakota territory, when at last caught.

While Boswell was enroute after his man, Maxwell escaped from the Yankton jail. He was later captured at Cedar Rapids, Iowa, returned to Yankton, and chained to the floor of the jail, until he was delivered into the hands of the Wyoming authorities.

At this time, Corey Boyd, arrested for stealing horses, was identified by a ranchman as one of the agents who had taken part in the Canyon springs robbery. He was lodged in jail in Cheyenne and was reported to be a "very bad pill."

In the spring of 1880, a new Eldorado was discovered, much to the delight of Cheyenne business men and the owners of the Cheyenne and Black Hills Stage line.

The country from the Platte river near Fort Laramie, north to the Running Water began to swarm with prospectors, who claimed to have discovered gold bearing rock in the hills six miles northwest of Fort Laramie; a fine gold-bearing ledge six miles farther north; a lode of silver-bearing quartz three miles west of Muskrat canyon; fine showings of silver and gold-bearing ledges in the Raw Hide Buttes vicinity and outcroppings of similar nature all the way from that district to Running Water. Four miles west of Demmon's ranch at Silver springs, an immense ledge of silver-bearing rock was reported to have been located.

Over night, town sites [74] were laid out and mill sites were filed on. Lumber was in great demand. And

---

[74] In Raw Hide canyon was a townsite called Brackett City, in honor of General Brackett, one of the locators of the mines. Three miles above the stage station at Raw Hide Buttes was Maysville, so-called because of its proximity to the blacksmith shop run by Ed Mays. This adjoined the Victorine lode.

miners began to come southwestward from the Black Hills, as well as north from Cheyenne and Fort Laramie.

Wagon wheels rumbled toward this new Golconda from every direction. The Cheyenne Carriage works, with its ten first-class mechanics, was kept busy turning out equipment for prospecting parties.

And while the wagon spokes rattled, surveyors with transit and level were busy locating a short route for a railway between Cheyenne and Chugwater.

By the middle of march, fifteen lodes, covering 22,500 feet and extending four miles along Running Water, had been staked out.

Fred Schwartze, the well known stage station owner and rancher on Pole creek, was one of the most enthusiastic promoters of this Running Water area, where he staked out silver mining claims, and put a force of men to work.

The chief topic of discussion over the bars, in hotel lobbies, and at various other places where men congregated in Cheyenne that summer of 1880, was the new mines in eastern Wyoming. Considerable interest also was evinced in the horse races that season in the "Magic City," to which the Cheyenne and Black Hills stage company transported passengers at half-rate fare.

It was in this summer that a group of wealthy young cattlemen organized the "Cactus club," which became the nucleus of the famous old Cheyenne club, later known from ocean to ocean. Within its walls were served everything from pickled eels and Champagne Pierrier Brut to Hereford steaks and antelope roasts. And up to its doorsteps, innumerable times, during the boom days of the 'eighties, rolled the wheels of Harry Oelrichs's "drag," a vehicle imported from England, at a cost of more than four thousand dollars.

The cattle business, too, had penetrated the Hills. Said the *Carbon County Journal:*

One of the Deadwood girls is having a dress made and embroidered with the cattle brands of the various cattle men whom she counts among her admirers. It is evident that she is in cahoots with the coroner and surgeons and is taking this way to promote domestic encounters. *The Black Hills Pioneer* says the above is correct, and adds: "The dress referred to is not only receiving the brands of many of our thoughtless young stockmen but the initials of their names as well. An artistic seamstress in Fountain City is doing the embroidery, under a contract of $200. Some of the investors in the dress will no doubt be heartily ashamed of their foolish investment before they die, if not sooner. The brands and initials of her particular favorites cover the side of her neck and bosom, and the brands, etc., of those occupying but an indifferent corner in her affections are attached to the bottom of the skirt, and some are located so as to be frequently sat down upon. After reading the explanation her admirers will be enabled to discover at a glance their standing in the girl's sinful love, whenever she appears in her novel frock."

Civilization was certainly on the march along the old Cheyenne and Black Hills trail in more ways than one. A passenger on the Cheyenne coach into Deadwood in september wrote that as he sat by the side of "Little Billy," who was bringing his six horses up the street at a smart trot,

I was sort of dazed at the civilized appearance of the town. White shirts and collars, and brilliant neckties and blackened boots and broadcloth coats, and striped trousers, and charmingly dressed females, and pet dogs, and dirty pigs, and beer bottles, and other evidences of civilization abounded on every hand, and filled my heart with dismay as I pondered on my limited and primitive wardrobe. When I was shown my room in the Merchants' hotel, I sat down and debated long and anxiously as to whether I should go into the dining room or not. Finally I referred it to the landlord and he eased my mind by saying: "Of course, go in, but keep your coat on." [75]

And yet, the gentlemen who strolled the streets of Deadwood, dressed in their blackened boots and broadcloths, passed markets in which hung antelope saddles, mountain sheep quarters, bear meat, and innumerable buffalo hams offered for sale at two and a half cents per pound. There still was a herd of some ten thousand buffaloes skirting the fringe of civilization along the northern edge of the Black Hills.

Deadwood, stretching some eight miles up and down the gulch, with a population sometimes aggregating fifteen thousand comprised men and women who lived in cabins, houses, dug-outs, and shacks that clung precariously to the mountainsides. The shouts and cries of peanut roasters and flower vendors mingled with the shrill bark of dogs fighting on Main street. Fist fights, knock downs, shootings, and stabbings added to the continual turmoil of that one main artery of Deadwood's lifeblood.

In the early 'eighties the Gem theatre, run by Al Swearengen, and Patsy Carr's Green Front drew the biggest crowds of entertainment seekers. Mike Russell, a friend of Buffalo Bill, ran a saloon that was well-equipped with faro layouts and roulette wheels, and was said to be "on the square." Mike treated all alike, drunk or sober.

And while the milling crowds pushed in and out of

[75] The Cheyenne *Sun*, september 16, 1880.

the batwing doors along the plank sidewalk, smaller groups tripped the "light fantastic toe" in the parlors of the I.X.L. or the Grand hotels.

But the whole camp turned out when the click of the Concord wheels in the sandboxes could be heard and the six horses trotted down Main street with the swaying stagecoach crowding their heels.

The railway later brought to Deadwood a more settled life and a more even tempo, but the days of romance, excitement, and pioneering were the stagecoach days.

With the coming of 1881, more mines were discovered along the stage route, or close by. Among the richest ones were the copper strikes in the Hartville Uplift northwest of Fort Laramie. The original claim, staked by a ranchman named Miller, was called the "Green Mountain Boy," and produced approximately a million dollars in copper ore within five years. Another big producer was "The Sunrise," now owned by the Colorado Fuel and Iron company.

A smelter was built at a place called Fairbanks, on the Platte river. The copper boom brought considerable business to the Black Hills Stage line, especially to the lower division. In addition to the passengers transported by the coaches, various individuals patronized private hack lines that were established between Fort Laramie and the mines. A new Concord was added to the Black Hills Stage company's equipment and was said to be "resplendent with its Mexican canary wheels."

Dark shadows began to cloud the horizon of the two stagemen, Gilmer and Salisbury, during 1881, in the form of government investigation of star route contracts,[76] followed by suits filed by the government against many mail contractors in the West.

The Cheyenne to Deadwood route was not involved. The Fargo, North Dakota, to Pembina route, which had been let to Voorhees, came through with "no indictment." And incidentally, about nine years later, Voorhees won a suit against the government and was awarded fourteen thousand dollars as the balance due on a star route mail contract, which he had held in 1878.

Special Inspector John B. Furay and his assistants, who had been so popular with the public, in running down "road agents" now were ridiculed and blocked at every turn as they attempted to assemble evidence pertaining to misuses in the star route systems. They, however, did their work courageously.

It was claimed by the investigators that over-payments on fraudulent service had been made on forty routes, approximating $2,172,132.87 and that not only contractors, but persons in high official positions had participated in the frauds.

The method of obtaining the money illegally was to present affidavits for increased service, including

[76] The designation of "star route" was given by the Post Office department to all mail service that was not performed by railway or steamboat companies. Attention to frauds in star route contracts was first called to public attention through the increased expenditures under the administration of Thomas J. Brady, second assistant postmaster general, under President Rutherford B. Hayes. When a subcommittee of the committee on appropriations made an adverse report concerning the granting of increased appropriations for covering a large deficit in the Post Office department, the searchlight of public opinion was turned on the so-called "Star Route Ring." Upon receiving various information concerning the star route contracts, in the spring of 1881, President Garfield directed officials to proceed at once with criminal prosecutions, without regard to who might be injured.

increase of men and horses on various routes, without having such service.

Although the Star route cases were said to have been "undoubted and enormous," the prosecution was not successful, due, it was claimed, to the magnitude of interests involved and to deficiencies in the criminal statutes of the United States.

In 1881, the postmaster general in Washington, D.C., ordered the mail service between Cheyenne and Raw Hide Buttes cut to three times a week, instead of seven times. Through the efforts of Wyoming officials, however, the daily mail was retained with a weekly "swing run" to Buckhorn. Luke Voorhees held these mail contracts.

In a notebook bearing the date november 1881, Voorhees recorded the following:

Route	Miles
Cheyenne to Horse Creek	28
Horse Creek to Little Bear	3½
Chugwater	22
Bordeaux	14
Ft. Laramie	31
Raw Hide Buttes	30
Buckhorn	59

The following april (1882), a new contract was in operation from Hat Creek, Wyoming to Spearfish City, Dakota, a distance of one hundred and fifty miles and back, once a week. The mail under this contract was carried over a new Black Hills route, which skirted the western side of the Hills and reached Spearfish by the way of Sundance mountain in Crook county, Wyoming.

Ernest A. Logan, early Wyoming pioneer, carried

the mail at this time from Raw Hide Buttes to Hat creek on horseback, and also in a buckboard. Later he drove the route from Raw Hide to Fort Laramie.

Luke Voorhees tried to induce Logan to take over the mail contract north from Raw Hide Buttes, but Logan could not see his way clear to do so. He knew though, that O. J. Demmon, who owned the Silver Springs ranch, was "hoss poor" and that he had a corral full of unbroken horses that were eating up feed and bringing in nothing. Logan talked Demmon into taking the mail contract off of Voorhees's hands.

With the help of two of his older boys, Demmon broke the horses while carrying the mail and then sold the animals to prospectors who were beginning to come in with the mining rush to Muskrat canyon. Demmon paid all of his running expenses with the passenger and express money, had the mail contract money clear, and the money for the sale of his horses was surplus cash.

While Superintendent Voorhees was busy with the Cheyenne and Black Hills route, Gilmer and Salisbury established a four-horse Concord stage line to run between the terminal station of the Northern Pacific railroad and Helena, Montana via Bozeman, thus enabling the railway to form a through connection from St. Paul and Minneapolis to Helena, where connections were made with stage lines for Fort Benton, Butte, Deer Lodge, and Virginia City.

As soon as the new arrangements in Montana were completed, the company took off the stage line from Sidney to the Black Hills and Cheyenne became the chief southern entrance to the Hills, as in the earliest days.

About a year later, the Cheyenne *Leader* ran the following announcement:

NOTICE

Gilmer, Salisbury & Co., having this day sold the Cheyenne and Black Hills stage line to Russell Thorp, request that any person owing them will call at their office in Cheyenne, and settle, at once. All accounts against the late firm will be settled at once on presentation to Luke Voorhees.

May 15, 1883   Gilmer, Salisbury & Co.

Gilmer and Salisbury now devoted their attention to their extensive Montana and Idaho interests.

Luke Voorhees, who had purchased a herd of thirteen hundred head of cattle from George Hill and Company on Raw Hide creek under the brands, 918, 96, and NP, in the fall of 1881, now quit the Black Hills stage business and organized the Luke Voorhees Cattle company with a capitalization of five hundred thousand dollars. The brand of the new company was LZ.

Vigorous, fearless, and aggressive, Luke Voorhees kept the wheels of the pioneer Cheyenne and Black Hills Stage line rolling for more than seven years. When he turned the reins over to Russell Thorp, sr., he gave them into the keeping of a most worthy successor, a man already widely experienced in stage line management and thoroughly schooled in the ways of the west.

Raw Hide Buttes Becomes the "Home Station"

Russell Thorp, sr., who purchased the Cheyenne and Black Hills Stage line from Salisbury and Company in may 1883, brought to the business fifteen years of experience accumulated in pioneer Wyoming territory (*see plate 3*).

Thorp had been buying, selling, and handling livestock including particularly fine horses, since 1868. Upon moving to Cheyenne in 1875, he purchased the T. A. Kent Livery stable on Sixteenth street, "second door from the corner of Ferguson."

He was reputed to have the "faculty of harboring the best horse flesh in this country" and to keep the best "turnouts" in Cheyenne. When he added a modern hearse to his livery equipment, he was appointed city sexton.

In 1877 he launched a street hack and a bus between the Union Pacific depot and the Inter-Ocean hotel. Early in 1878 he established and managed the stockyards of the Union Pacific railroad at Cheyenne, at which all stock in transit over the railway was fed.

Russell Thorp's livestock sales business became extensive and he sold many horses and mules in the vicinity of Leadville, Colorado, as well as personally trailing herds of fine horses to Deadwood, Dakota territory. Despite the fact that "Doc" Middleton and his band of horse thieves were then operating in the Black Hills, and hostile Indians were on the warpath, the young Cheyenne liveryman delivered his stock in safety to the Deadwood purchasers. He often was entrusted with the care of extremely valuable shipments of horses and pure bred bulls that came into Cheyenne.

In 1880, Thorp became superintendent of a stage line for Patrick Brothers between Tie Siding, Wyoming and a new mining district in North Park, Colorado. At this time he also entered into a copartnership to carry on the business of a livery firm and sale stable[77] with William Wightman. The new firm leased Terry's IXL barn in Cheyenne.

Early in 1882, Wightman bought Thorp's interest in the barn and it was rumored that Mr. Thorp would "shortly open a sale and exchange room for carriages and similar equipment." He, however, had his eyes on farther horizons. After accompanying his family east on a trip, he returned with a "stylish team of black flyers," and at once headed north toward the new mining district near Raw Hide Buttes, along the Cheyenne and Black Hills stage route.

His first investment in the area was in the Deadwood mine on the north side of Raw Hide creek, in close proximity to the Wolverine mine. By september his team of "black flyers" unloaded several hundred pounds of rock from his holdings, in boxes in front of Masi's book store in Cheyenne. The ore, copper bearing, promised to net one hundred dollars per ton in Chicago. Soon Masi and Thorp purchased the Wolverine and began its development.

Later, Russell Thorp became owner of the Old George lode and pushed work on it as fast as possible.

---

[77] The Idleman block later was built on this site for forty thousand dollars.

By the autumn of 1882, the mines at Muskrat canyon and Raw Hide Buttes were reported to be in full operation, with new claims being located every day.

In november, Thorp purchased the Raw Hide Buttes ranch from Charlotte H. Atkins for thirty-five hundred dollars, and began extensive improvements. The ranch, then a stop on the Cheyenne and Black Hills stage line had a fine blacksmith shop where horses were shod at two dollars each; a well stocked grocery and dry goods store; stage station, telegraph office, post office, and road ranch accommodations.

Although heavy snows blanketed the north country the following february, the new owner of the Raw Hide ranch transported a force of carpenters to his holdings and made extensive changes in the store and residence. As quickly as possible, he moved his wife and five-year-old son, Russell, jr., to their new home.

Mrs. Thorp, being born of pioneer stock, readily adjusted herself to this frontier surrounding, and it is of record that: "Anyone who ever stayed over night or for a meal at the Thorp's home station will bear out the assertion that the welcome and entertainment there were of the best western character, and the meals, prepared by a Chinese cook (Friday), something to be long remembered."

On may 15, 1883, Russell Thorp purchased the Cheyenne and Black Hills stage line and at once made Raw Hide Buttes the Home station (*see plate* 15). With his headquarters here, the new proprietor was at the center of activity and was able to keep in touch with every phase of the line's business. From that time on his name and "Raw Hide Buttes" were synonymous. He was notary public, postmaster, justice of the peace, stage line owner, and leading livestock man.

One guest at the ranch said: "Raw Hide station was truly an oasis in the desert of sand, cactus, and loneliness surrounding it. Mrs. Thorp's charming personality, her kind neighborliness, the comfortable air of hominess so rare at that time on the Wyoming plains, as much as the busy life around the station, drew to these fine people the warm regard of all those who made up the fast-growing community. Mr. Thorp was one of the salt of the earth."

Soon after the change in ownership of the Black Hills stage line, the country over which the stage route ran between Cheyenne and Fort Laramie, experienced the worst high water in ten years, which damaged the approaches on both sides of the bridge at Pole creek; washed away the bridge at Horse creek; took out the upper bridge at Kelly's ranch; and spread the Chugwater out to a width of one hundred yards at Hunton's ranch, where it washed away the approach to the bridge on the south side.

A passenger who made a trip over the line within a few days after Mr. Thorp had purchased it, wrote the following account,[78] which illustrates some of the problems that faced the new owner:

The first eighteen miles of my journey in the stage were made under circumstances which prevent me from saying anything about the features of the country. At 4 o'clock on saturday morning, the hour when the stage started, it was raining, the streets (in Cheyenne) were a mass of liquid mud, and the air was chilly. When the stage called for me, I found that the two back seats were occupied by two passengers, and the two front seats were piled roof high with express packages, and valises. Room was made for me by the driver removing some goods to the top of the coach and placing the valises on the passengers' knees. Once inside, the curtains were pinned down, and

78 Cheyenne, *Daily Leader,* may 23, 1883.

we passengers not being able to see out, glared in the dim light at each other. The two men opposite me I found to be Texas cowboys, on their way to a northern ranch. They proved to be pleasant fellow travelers. At the stable, Mr. Russell Thorp, the owner of the stage line, became a box passenger.

The stretch to Schwartze's ranch, eighteen miles, was a dreary ride. It rained steadily, the wind blew a gale, and it was, so one of the boys said, as "cold as the devil." Beside me was piled on the seat, a sack of flour and several boxes, the topmost being a twelve by sixteen wooden packing case, that appeared to be almost empty from the ease with which it tumbled on my head at every second jolt of the stage. A score of times I was tempted to hurl it out in the mud, but the thought of the possible value restrained me. I saw that box opened here at the Chug. It contained nothing more than a lamp shade packed in hay.

After some hours of sparring with this box, trying to thaw out the frozen cowboys, and listening to the wheel spokes pelting the puddles, a voice outside called out, "Have you boys got your lives insured?"

We tore open the curtains and looked out. We were at the edge of a line of hills, and the road ran steeply down to a swollen stream, in a deep valley, studded with numerous lakes that stretched along in the meadows. We emerged from the stage and took to the mud. Several men and a team were at work about the approaches to a bridge over the torrent, dumping sand in great holes that had been washed out. The bridge was standing askew, and it looked as if it were about to be washed away. In front of the stage a figure ran about, gesticulating and directing the driver to the safe part of the road. This figure was that of our friend, Fred Schwartze, and he succeeded in piloting the stage to a point near the bridge and the party to the barroom. We spent about four hours at Fred's, and an excellent meal was served there. One of the Texans said, "There ain't no chuck nowhere to beat that."

When the bridge approaches were repaired sufficiently for temporary use, the stage was carefully taken over, and our journey resumed. I took the seat beside Driver Brown, and facing the wind and rain, now somewhat diminished in violence, proceeded in the interest of my inquisitive tenderfoot friend in Cheyenne, to "interview" him for all he knew about the country. But I found him fully occupied in the task of driving with a short whip a pair of fast walking wheel horses hitched behind a pair of slow walking leaders. It takes talent to do it, but Brown succeeded, by ignoring my questions, in making all four horses pull alike.

My friend, the "topography" of the plains between Fred Schwartze's and Goodwin's ranch is the topography of a row of pillows laid side by side. It is as rolling as the waves of the Atlantic. The picture, repeated the entire distance mentioned, is a big hill in front of you, then a valley, then a hill. All the hills are today a fresh green. Nothing was seen to the right or left but other hills, except far to the west the white frame to the picture formed by the snowy range.

At the end of a ten mile drive we arrived at Goodwin's. Horse creek was quite as high as Pole creek had been. Schwartze had said that Pole creek was higher than it had been in fourteen years. Goodwin was at hand when we drove to the stage barn to report that Horse creek was higher than it had been for ten years. The rivalry between Goodwin and Schwartze is well known, and Fred will be glad to know that, while he kept his bridge in place on its fourteen-year flood, Goodwin let his bridge float away on a little ten-year flood.

Goodwin had a budget of news about swollen streams and accompanying mishaps. He wanted us to believe that many of the wagons we saw in camp about his place had left Cheyenne about the first of april. Turpin's train was stuck near Nine Mile ranch, and the Wyoming Copper company's train was axle-deep in the water close to his ranch. He had heard about the loss of two teams "up north," Lem Smith's and Snyder's, both having their horses drowned in crossing swollen streams. We have since had reason to believe that he was not joking about this, as the report is confirmed. Goodwin was also working up sums in addition to see how much the county commissioners would have to pay for new bridges. He gave me this schedule as his bid for the jobs:

> Pole creek, repairing............................$ 300.00
> Horse creek, building a new one................ 500.00
> Chugwater, two bridges......................... 1000.00
> Bordeaux, new bridge........................... 500.00
> Platte river, repairing approaches............. 5000.00

. . . After a good night's rest in a good bed at Goodwin's, I made the trip today to Kelly's, twenty-two miles. The "topography" was carefully watched by one of the cowboys while the rest of us lay sea sick from the jolting of the coach over the ruts. The face of the land as he reported it, is slightly broken into bluffs and ravines, but with some large open plains. The day was delightful. The sky was clear, the sun warm and the air transparent as crystal. . .

It is Mr. Thorp's intention to increase the number of stations on his route, a new one about being established at Schwartze's and the journey of nearly one hundred miles from Cheyenne to Fort Laramie will be made between six in the morning and seven in the evening. The stage line is conducted with energy, the drivers I found to be most good natured and accommodating, and the trip is made with as little inconvenience as possible to passengers.

About the time everything was running smoothly under the new management, a fire destroyed the dwelling maintained by Mr. Thorp at Fort Laramie. All of the contents were burned, despite the efforts of the soldiers to put the fire out.

But the sturdy stage owner took things in his stride, and continued to increase the efficiency of his line in order to meet the demands, which he felt would be made upon it in the coming year.

Passenger travel over the line during the early part of 1884 was heavy, with seats being engaged several days ahead. The roads were bad, largely due to the hauling of heavy freight to the mines near Raw Hide Buttes. The roads north of Fort Laramie were in especially poor condition this season.

On february 1, 1884, the Cheyenne and Black Hills Stage company advertised that its coaches left every day running through to Deadwood, Custer, Battle creek, Rapid, Golden, Gayville, and all mining camps in the Hills, just as they had under the old Gilmer and

Salisbury management. In fact, the advertisement of Mr. Thorp was exactly the same as that used by his predecessors, and he assured his passengers that his line had "first class eating stations" and that "division agents take all pains to secure the comfort of passengers."

Interest in the mines had shifted from the Hartville and Sunrise areas to the Running Water, north of Raw Hide Buttes. In march, Woods and Thompson, freighters, arrived at Running Water with an immense train, loaded with machinery and implements for the Great Western Mining and Milling company at Silver Cliff near the Running Water stage station. Where not so long before there had been only the Running Water ranch, just a "solitary and rudely constructed ranch," there now was a mining camp, bustling with activity. A large boarding house had been built; a store, billiard hall, and saloon were in use by march 20.

Heavy snows in the spring caused the stage coaches to detour often and a particularly heavy twenty-four-hour fall, the latter part of march, sent it on a detour of thirty miles in order to gain eighteen, on its way from Pole creek into Cheyenne. But even with the snow declared to be "belly deep" to the horses, in many places along the road, the coaches went through and almost on time.

Cheyenne, by 1884, had emerged from its pioneer era. It had been using electric lights for some months; its "pioneers" were organizing into a society; and Hubert Bancroft had arrived from California to collect material for the writing of a history of Wyoming territory.

Instead of advertising buckskin underwear, as in previous years, Cheyenne stores now emphasized "Beautiful smoking jackets, silk plush lap robes, and gent's elegant neckwear."

Paola Pavesich, noted designer and interior decorator of Denver, did some of the best work this year in the home of Judge J. M. Carey, frescoing the sitting room ceiling in Italian style, doing the hall in Eastlake mode, completing the library in French design, and patterning the dressing room upstairs "after the Turkish manner."

Early in the year the Cheyenne, Black Hills and Montana railway of which A. H. Swan was president, purchased a block of lots in eastern Cheyenne, just north of lake Minnehaha for depot purposes, and gave every indication that work would be pushed as fast as possible on the construction of the proposed railway. The contemplated route was scheduled to go north from Cheyenne up Crow creek toward Chugwater, thence to the North Platte river, where it was hoped that one branch would go to the Black Hills, and another to Montana.

Scattered through Laramie county, along the Cheyenne and Black Hills stage line, were thirty organized schools.

The "Magic City of the Plains" was mighty proud of its electric arc lights and its six miles of water mains that connected with hydrants, even if it were necessary, in case of fire, to build bonfires to thaw out the hydrants in the "cold snaps." At this time, too, Councilman Hines introduced a bill to prevent the running at large of swine and goats.

Cheyenne's Opera house, which had been opened two years previous with much fanfare and satin perfumed programmes and a grand ball, now offered to the public, at ten dollars a seat, Major Gleason's New York Opera company, starring Gerster. The divine Patti was with the company but did not sing in Cheyenne. A citizens' committee went thirty miles in a special train, equipped with the best obtainable in champagne and cigars, to greet the members of the Opera company en route from Denver. And at the Cheyenne railway station, some two to three thousand residents welcomed the company with the 9th Infantry band, in full dress.

There were now in Cheyenne only twenty-seven places where liquor was sold, as compared with sixty at one time. Eight established churches, with ten different church societies, were maintained by the substantial citizenry. One day during that year of 1884, a service was conducted in St. Mark's Episcopal church by Rev. Sherman S. Coolidge, a full blooded Arapahoe, who some years previous had been rescued from the Crows and reared by Lieutenant and Mrs. Coolidge. Coincident to this service, members of the Reorganized Church of Jesus Christ of Latter-Day Saints were gathered on the banks of Crow creek, at the foot of Eddy street, to officiate at a baptizing.

It must be admitted, of course, that there still was plenty of "gay life" in the little prairie city, and the notorious Gold Room,[79] a miniature gambling palace, paid one hundred and twenty-five dollars a night for electricity. But all such "gaiety" had been lifted from the crude level of the very early days. Even Jake Esselborn advertised: "Elegant rooms for private parties. Ladies parlors. No bums allowed."

With the great range cattle business at its peak, the

[79] Variously located: no. 210 W. 16th street; no. 1610 Carey avenue.

streets of the "Magic City of the Plains" clicked and creaked day and night with the turning of wheels, hundreds upon hundreds, yes, thousands of them. Drawn by some of those wheels Lily Langtree skimmed over prairies in Oelrichs's "drag"; lords and ladies went north to spend weeks as guests of Moreton Frewen in "Frewen's castle" up on Powder river; and hundreds of adventurers continued to flock into the mining districts.

Herman Haas, wagon maker, erected a large iron-clad wareroom that season, in which could be found: phaetons, buggies, buckboards, express wagons, livery wagons, all bearing the stamp of good workmanship and highly finished. Tons of iron, wheels, spokes, and unbuilt parts of vehicles were stored there ready to supply a demand on the shortest notice.

Instead of cowboys riding up and down the streets running over little boys and shooting out window lights, some of the younger "cattle kings" dashed up and down on high bicycles, which they had brought over from England and Scotland. And some of the young blades were so expert in maneuvering the contraptions that they could carry, load, and fire a rifle while sailing along on them.

Cheyenne's fourth of july parades, elaborate with floats, now resembled in character the Mardi Gras.

With the new mining boom on, the "Magic City of the Plains" revived its feverish activity and closely resembled, in many respects, the days of the first big rush to the Black Hills.

Will Visscher, editor of the *Great West* wrote:

Cheyenne is simply wonderful. It has more than doubled in a year and the buildings which have been erected in that time are of imposing and superb character. Now several new blocks are going up and are to be larger and much costlier than those already built. Cheyenne has a strong business pulse; its banks are overflowing with money; it is the greatest cattle centre in the world; it is a delightful place to live; the people are friendly and generous; there is an air of liberality, manliness and respectability about the place, and it has such a start that nothing but an earthquake can stop it.

All during the spring of 1884, Russell Thorp was faced with continual difficulty in keeping the stages on time, because of the high water. In july, patrons of the stage line were delighted with a beautiful new coach, which had been made up according to Thorp's order, by the Cheyenne Carriage company. Named "Wyoming," it was a "model of neatness and suitability." It rolled along beside the Concords.

Mr. Thorp's life as owner-superintendent of the Cheyenne and Black Hills stage line, was one of never-ending variety. Drivers, stock tenders, station keepers, and helpers must be supplied and kept on the job; coaches, harness, and equipment of all kinds must be kept in first class repair; horses had to be shod and kept in the best of health, and driven on the stretches of road to which they were best suited. Portable blacksmith shops must be kept moving up and down the line in "jerkies" or "mud wagons."

The hard living, hardy, outdoor men who held the ribbons, were not averse to imbibing now and then, but drivers who drank on the job were promptly discharged.

Now and then accidents did occur, but rarely were they the fault of those in authority. It seems that one "knight of the reins" who was on the boot of an upbound coach imbibed altogether too much whisky and, according to a press account,

. . . soon became for the most part oblivious to the surroundings and the situation. The coach at the time was pretty well filled with passengers, among whom were two ladies. Without the fact being discovered by the passengers, the inebriated driver fell off the coach to the ground. Some of the passengers noticed that the coach was running along into a very dangerous locality, and finally the horses of their own accord stopped. Two of the passengers got out and found that the institution was without a driver. One of them climbed aboard and took the reins and drove the balance of the way to Pole creek. It is a great wonder that there was not a runaway and a general smash-up, for the leaders of the four-horse coach were fiery and as a general thing disposed to run when they get a chance. . . the driver was promptly discharged.

One of the most skilled and best known drivers on the Cheyenne and Black Hills line during Russell Thorp's ownership, was George A. Lathrop, who had come to the line in the spring of 1880, under Voorhees's management. Lathrop had driven stage in Kansas as early as 1861. He was a real pioneer in every sense (*see plate* 16).

In speaking of his work as a driver on the Cheyenne route, Lathrop said:[80]

I tell you I had some dandy six horse teams. Each horse had his own harness that was not used on any other horse, as the company had a set of harness for each team. When my teams went into the station the harness was thoroughly cleaned as well as the horses. I was usually said to be the best kicker on the route about clean harness and horses. I was always proud of them. Another trouble I had was that all the passengers wanted to ride with the driver. I recollect one morning in loading the coach at Cheyenne, Alex Swan, John Sparks,

[80] Lathrop, George, *Memoirs of a Pioneer* (Lusk, Wyoming, 1915).

G. B. Goodell, and R. S. Van Tassel, all big cattlemen at that time, each telling the other that he had the seat beside the driver engaged and that it made them sea sick to ride inside the coach. There was a man in the crowd by the name of Goldsmith, a cattleman, so they agreed to leave it to Goldsmith to decide who should ride by the side of the driver, each one of the crowd insisting to Goldsmith that he should have the seat, and in their argument they would offer him a cigar and also something out of a bottle. This affected Goldsmith so much that he concluded he was the best man and should have the coveted seat, so he climbed up leaving the crowd to get inside or not go that day.

C. G. Coutant, Wyoming historian, often rode with Lathrop and jotted down innumerable notes about "such doings and accounts of the country" as Lathrop was able to give him. Many of these notes, still preserved by the Wyoming Historical department show plainly the difficulties under which they were written, as the legibility of the handwriting varies according to the depth of the ruts in the road.

By june 1885, there were two hundred men at Running Water or Silver cliff, half of whom were at work in the mines. A camp later was surveyed and subdivided into town lots about a mile and a half east of the stage station barn, which became the town of Lusk, a thriving trade and livestock center.

During the ensuing months, splendid service was rendered to the patrons of the Cheyenne and Black Hills stage line through the untiring efforts of Russell Thorp.

In december, he established a line from Raw Hide and Hat Creek stations to Fort Robinson, Nebraska to connect with the Chadron stage and thus put Cheyenne into direct stage communication with Deadwood, over the Sioux City and Pacific railroad's stageline via Chadron.

By the close of the year, the mines at Running Water were reported to be panning out a little better than had been expected. The mill at the camp was running and the yield of bullion was reported to be "very flattering."

During Russell Thorp's ownership of the stage line, he took a special contract with the government to deliver money for the soldiers, with the paymaster and a special coach and escort. The government was desirous of transporting the money from Cheyenne to Fort Laramie between daylight and dark, and was unable to accomplish this with its mules and ambulances, without establishing relays.

One day some road agents visited the "Hog ranch" at the Three Mile, run by Johnny Owens, and told Owens they intended to hold up the coach with the payroll at Eagle's Nest. Why they disclosed their plans to Owens is not of record, but it was an established fact that Owens had the confidence of the outlaws as well as of law abiding citizens.

He was a good friend of Russell Thorp and knew that Thorp had done favors for him. Owens made up his mind that the coach would not be robbed. Immediately he went on horseback to Chug springs, where he knew the stage would stop to change horses.

The horses were being changed as Owens arrived. George Lathrop and a soldier, who was acting as guard, were on the boot. Owens told Lathrop to tell the soldier to ride inside, that he intended to ride beside the driver. The soldier protested, but Lathrop sensed that there was "something in the wind," so he made him relinquish the seat to Owens. Johnny tied his saddle horse alongside the near wheel stage horse, climbed up beside Lathrop, and laid his gun across his lap, without a word of explanation. He also had his six shooters on.

In less than five minutes, the wheels of the stagecoach rolled ahead. As the coach approached the grey chalk bluffs near Eagle's Nest, a command came to: "Halt! Throw up your hands."

Three agents appeared in the dusk. Owens did not move. Then he waved his hand carelessly and said: "Not tonight, boys."

The agents retired without a word. And the payroll was delivered at Fort Laramie intact. That was the last time the "brake was put on" by any driver of the Concord coaches on the Black Hills line, at the request of the road agents.

In so far as the Cheyenne and Black Hills stage line was concerned, the year 1886 might well have been termed the "railway and settlers" year, as there was a great rush for land filings in the area east of Running Water to the Nebraska border. The Chicago and Northwestern railway, which owned the Fremont, Elkhorn and Missouri Valley railway in Nebraska, decided to extend into Wyoming for a coal supply. It came into the territory, early in the year, as the Wyoming Central railway.

Many of the stage passengers now were homesteaders or those connected with railway construction.

Coaches of the line now left the Union depot in Cheyenne at 6:30 A.M. and arrived at Fort Laramie at 9:30 P.M. They reached Raw Hide at 4 A.M. Trips were made mondays, wednesdays, and fridays from Raw Hide to Lusk and Hat creek. F. E. Longhurst was Thorp's agent in Cheyenne.

In speaking of his trip over the stage line, in the spring of 1886, J. K. Calkins, editor of the Lusk *Herald*, who was called to Cheyenne as a witness in a murder trial, said:

George Lathrop was the driver of the coach on this occasion, and the return trip from Cheyenne was made over the most desolate portion of the route in the night. The mercury stood at about 35 degrees below zero. The other two passengers and myself had filled the swaying body of the big Concord coach with hay, wrapped ourselves in fur coats and robes, and were blissfully sleeping when the rear axletree broke square off at the hub, and down we went, bumping along on the frozen ground, until George brought the six horses to a standstill.

I crawled out and asked George what he proposed to do. His reply was that he would ride one of the horses twelve miles into Raw Hide Buttes station and come back with a jerky to get us passengers, adding that we could keep warm in the hay and robes during his absence. I bethought me of the nice warm fire which I knew would be making the home office of Manager Russell Thorp comfortable, so I asked permission to ride one of the horses in. To this Lathrop readily agreed, and we left the wreck at a little after 2 o'clock in a howling blizzard.

How George and the horses kept the trail, I have never been able to figure out, but in due time we reached Thorp's ranch, where I enjoyed a sleep in a real bed, and was eating a wonderful breakfast of antelope steak, flapjacks, fried potatoes, and coffee, when George Lathrop and the two other passengers arrived and joined me at the table. . . I remember that the horse I rode that twelve miles was a light iron gray in color, and that I never did get all the white hairs out of my black trousers.

Conversation along the stage line began to shift from lodes and tunnels and longhorn steers to corn crops. The crops planted by those who had filed on land near Lusk were reported, in may, to be "looking good."

Mining was on the downgrade. Although several of the mines in the Raw Hide Buttes area had been successfully worked, the cost of procuring coke and the prevailing low price of copper had caused most of the important ones to shut down.

As the railway approached Lusk, more and more settlers came into the country and filed on any and every piece of land found available.

Plans for the opening of a stage line through to Custer during the summer were made by Mr. Thorp, but were not carried out in view of the fact that the railway stages were reaching the Hills from Chadron, Nebraska.

In addition to looking after the regular stage business, the stage manager superintended the putting in of some good bridges on the Raw Hide route.

During the summer, he put on daily coaches between Cheyenne and Fort Fetterman via Bordeaux, as a branch from the main Black Hills line. This branch was in direct competition with the Rock Creek stage line, concerning which there had been many recent complaints.

Cheyenneites were outspoken in their approval of this new venture of Mr. Thorp and commented: "Much of the Fort Fetterman trade will hereafter pass through Cheyenne, and for this our people will be indebted to the foresight and enterprise of Russell Thorpe,[81] proprietor of the stage line."

Even after the Wyoming Central railroad pushed on westward from Lusk to the new town of Douglas, near Fort Fetterman, the mail for a time was carried over Thorp's line from Cheyenne to Lusk, instead of

[81] Originally spelled with the final "e."

via railway. According to the mail contract, which was held by the Patrick Brothers, the mail had to be sent from Douglas to the Union Pacific railroad over the Rock Creek line, thence to Cheyenne, and then north over the Cheyenne and Black Hills stage to Lusk. Later, under a new contract, the mail was transported direct from Douglas to Lusk, by rail.

The laying of the rails on the Cheyenne and Northern's roadbed began on september 28, 1886, when two hundred men and a track laying machine headed out of Cheyenne for Chugwater.

Gradually the rails were closing in, first from one direction and then from another, but the wheels of the stagecoaches kept rolling along, taking care of the necessary travel from the Black Hills and northeastern Wyoming. It was said to be the best and most direct way for all who wished to go south and east, especially from Lusk.

Postal Inspector Waterbury said of the route: "It is the best equipped, and has the finest stock, and the most accommodating drivers and agents of any line I ever passed over. It also has the best record for prompt mails, and no complaint has ever been made against it since Mr. Thorp has been its manager."

After the spring floods that did so much damage to the stage roads in 1886, there came a hot, dry summer, followed by an early winter. Heavy falls of snow were followed by extremely cold weather that crusted the drifts with ice and made it impossible for livestock to reach feed. Blizzard followed blizzard in quick succession, but no Chinook came to bring relief to the stockmen.

That winter of 1886-1887 went down in history as

unprecedented in its severity on cattle and livestock in general. Declining prices added to the tragedies of the weather and helped to ring down the curtain on the great boom days of the cattle kings of the Rocky mountain empire.

And with the passing of the glamor of the old days, oddly enough, came the end of the through Cheyenne to Deadwood stage line.

Early in february 1887, the Cheyenne and Northern rails crept over the last hills into Chugwater, thus writing finis to the southern lap of the Black Hills route which for so many years connected Cheyenne with Deadwood.[82]

On february 19, 1887, a large group of interested citizens gathered in front of the Inter-Ocean hotel in Cheyenne to watch the Black Hills stagecoach pull north on its last regular trip.

"The Wyoming," the coach which had been built especially for the "genial and efficient stageman, Russell Thorp," rolled along Sixteenth street with its old-time sounds. George Lathrop was holding the ribbons for six "as fine horses as were ever headed toward the gold fields of the Black Hills."

A stop was made in front of the Inter-Ocean, when Mr. Thorp announced that the stage was ready to depart. At this, a general rush was made to obtain choice seats, and within a minute the coach was crowded and some six or eight gentlemen occupied places on top. Trunks were strapped upon the rear boot and there

[82] As the rails advanced, Russell Thorp shifted the southern terminus of the stage line: first to Chugwater until september 1887; then to Bordeaux; and lastly to Wendover. He continued in the stage business as long as there was need for wagon wheels to connect with the rails.

was every evidence that the parties seated were prepared for a long, tedious, and tiresome journey. The
team tramped impatiently, as if anxious to start. Lathrop gave the outfit a few graceful turns around the
principal business blocks and then pulled up in front
of the Inter-Ocean to allow C. D. Kirkland, photog-
rapher, to take a picture of "The last coach out."

As the picture taking was finished, Lathrop tight-
ened the lines and started the horses on a brisk trot.
The crowd cheered and waved. Soon the horses in the
usual hitch reached a quicker trot and headed out along
the road toward Nine Mile, Schwartze's and Goodwin's, just as they had been doing since 1876. Keepers
and stock tenders were on hand to make the quick
changes of horses for this Black Hills stage that was
rolling by for the last time (*see plate* 17).

As the dust from this last coach, swaying on its
leather thoroughbraces, settled upon the thoroughfare
called "Hill street," the citizens of Cheyenne changed
its name to "Capitol avenue."

Said the editor of the Cheyenne *Tribune:*

The country north is free from the Indian pests; the road agents
are no more and the country is settled up with happy, prosperous
people. Railroads are pushing through and the fertile valleys are
being utilized and the mountains of ages commanded to give up their
hidden wealth. Such is the change of a few years and for the result
we are much indebted to the energy and enterprise of a citizen well
respected by all—a gentleman of sterling qualities and one who has
ever labored for the advancement of our every interest. We refer to
Mr. Russell Thorp, who will hereafter run his line of stages from
Chugwater instead of from Cheyenne. He carries with him the best
wishes of the people of this city.

Later George Lathrop said: "It was a great day for

me. I would not have exchanged places with Grover Cleveland. It was a great day."

And that "great day," february 19, 1887, brought Cheyenne's early pioneer era to an end. On that day the clicking of the spinning stagecoach wheels echoed for the last time through the portals of the "Magic City of the Plains."

Stagefaring Men

The stagefaring men, who kept the wheels turning over the Cheyenne and Black Hills trail were men of vision, ingenuity, courage, and daring.

The owners: Jack Gilmer, Monroe Salisbury, Mathewson T. Patrick, and Russell Thorp, sr., were all men of wide pioneer experience in the west. They were respected, substantial, successful businessmen, with confidence in the development of the Black Hills and with the ability to keep the stages moving in the face of great odds. They were excellent judges of human nature and employed men who they knew had the necessary stamina to stick to their jobs.

In addition to the general superintendent, Luke Voorhees, and his various division agents, there were drivers, stock tenders, blacksmiths, freighters, station masters, and shotgun messengers, all of whom worked as one great unit to transport the passengers, the mail, and the express safely, and with all speed possible.

To those who traversed the Cheyenne to Deadwood routes, the stage drivers or so-called "knights of the reins, or lines, or ribbons," or by some "jehus," were significant of the stage line itself. They were the epitome of romance, skill, and daring. They knew just how to ease the brake so that the lines would slacken and the horses would miss a badger hole or a bad chuck hole in the road; or how to swing the six-horse team around a sharp, blind curve without having them plunge headlong over a cliff. They faced blizzards, hail storms, and terrific lightning, cloudbursts, road agents, or Indians on the warpath, with equal nerve and resourcefulness.

Most of the drivers were quiet spoken men, keen-eyed and capable of perfect muscle coordination. Their wrists were like small steel cables and the muscles of their shoulders were like knots of iron. It was often said that the faculty of being a good horseman was born in a man and no amount of training or education would help to make a good driver, if he were not "born to the reins."

The experienced driver knew so well how to handle the brake, that just the sound of it filled the passengers with confidence. The more dangerous the route, the better some of the drivers liked it. With numerous unforeseen and unavoidable delays always occurring, their hours of eating and sleeping were often most irregular. And many a time they reached their home stations with ice-crusted eyebrows and mustaches, or with rings of bites from buffalo gnats where their hat-bands snugged their foreheads. But they took things as they came, in a good-natured, dry-humored, matter-of-fact way. Buckskin gloves, often of a gauntlet style and fringed, plus a Stetson hat in warm weather and a Scotch cap in the winter time, and often a buffalo coat, belted with a three-buckle eight-inch leather belt, were as much the part of a driver's wardrobe, as were chaps and boots a part of a cowboy's paraphernalia.

The stagemen knew their horses, their habits, names, and dispositions. In fact, they knew practically every horse on the line, or at least, in their division. They would "stand up on their hind legs and fight" anyone who mistreated a horse. They were not given to "chin music" because they were too occupied with watching the road, their horses, and the weather. They knew the rise and roll of every hill and just how deep the snow probably would be in the next gully along their run.

The scout, the guide, the fur trader, the freighter, and the emigrant, the miner, the cowman, the homesteader, the pioneer teacher, the pioneer preacher, the surveyor, the contractor, and the stage driver, all have played their parts in bringing civilization to the west, but none is deserving of more praise than the stage driver.

These drivers were adored by the youngsters at the isolated ranches or stations and in the towns, not only because they were colorful figures, but because often there were packages of firecrackers, candy, or gum in their pockets for the small fry.

After the days of staging to the Black Hills were over, many of the drivers worked for smaller Wyoming stage lines running to Encampment, Keystone, Lander, Sundance, Snake river, or through the Yellowstone National park. Some of the younger, sturdier ones handled teams on construction crews building new highways, railway grades, or reservoirs in Wyoming.

Many of the "old bachelors" went to work on cattle ranches and lived out their days in some mud-daubed, log bunkhouse. They were the experts with the hay mower and stacker in the big hay fields, or were top stock tenders.

Now and then down through the years one of these drivers would lapse into a reminiscent mood and tell of the days when "Little Reddy," Dunc Blackburn, or

Jack Wall ran rampant along the Black Hills trail. But for the most part, the story of the glorious days of adventure which they knew, passed on into oblivion, when these gallant trail-blazers caught the last coach and crossed the Great Divide.

A descriptive list of some of these stagefaring men follows in appendix A.

Appendix A
Owners and Some Employees
Cheyenne & Black Hills Stage Company

BAKER, AL. Driver. Winter of 1886-87.

BARNETT, GENE. Driver. Was on coach when it was held up four miles from Eagle's Nest, october 5, 1877. Had just been relieved from duty on upper end of road. Driver of Treasure Coach when it was held up at Canyon springs, september 26, 1878.

BARTLETT, W. F. Agent. In charge of stage office at Cheyenne from march 1876, to june 17, 1877. Transferred to Deadwood. Very efficient. On december 6, 1877, he drove to Cold Spring ranch to meet treasure coach that was laid up there. Despite an upset, held the ribbons during a trip of 30 miles, with mercury far below zero.

BENHAM, ALEX. Division agent. On september 23, 1877 took the place of division superintendent of northern division, with head-quarters in Deadwood. One of the best stage men in the country. Had been road superintendent for Wells, Fargo & Co. Had worked for Ben Holladay on the Overland route. General super-intendent of the Sweetwater Stage Co., 1870, running between Bryan, Wyo., and South Pass City.

BENT, E. C. Agent. At Deadwood about a month in 1876. Said to be a "young and popular Cheyenne Medicine man."

BINGHAM, JOHN T. Driver. Later worked for Gilmer, Salisbury & Co., in Montana. He was the driver of the last coach over the Bozeman-Helena route on june 20, 1883. The driver, coach, six-horse team were all decorated with red, white, and blue bunting, flags, and evergreens presented by women of Belford.

BLACK, THOMPSON (TOM). Stock tender and station master. At Raw Hide buttes, 1882-1886. Born, Brooklyn, N.Y., june 2, 1861.

Was a Mason, A.F. & A.M. Took up a ranch called Willow. Died, 1932.

BOWEN. Blacksmith. At Raw Hide buttes, 1882.

BRACE, SID. Driver. On the boot in 1883 when cowboys had fracas at the Pole creek ranch.

"BRAVO." Driver. Said to have persisted in making trips from Fort Laramie to Custer, august 1876, during Indian troubles.

BRAY, AL. Driver.

BRENNAN, JOHN. Agent. Rapid City. Assisted both the Cheyenne and Sidney lines.

BRISTOL, W. (BILLIE) L. Agent. At Fort Laramie.

BROWN. Driver. In 1883.

BROWN, JESSE. Shotgun messenger. Scott Davis said: "Jesse Brown was a true-blue friend, known as the man that was in the right place at the right time. We fought a good many Indian fights together and road agent fights and I always found him Johnny-on-the-spot." Born, august 24, 1844, Washington county, Tenn. Whacked bulls along Oregon trail to Fort Laramie. Freighted Bozeman trail, 1865.

BROWN, H. E. (STUTTERING). Division superintendent. An old stage driver and manager from Salt Lake City. Killed on northern division, april 1876, by Persimmon Bill or Indians.

BROWN, J. H. C. Manager of Rustic Hotel, Fort Laramie.

BULLOCK, SETH G. Sheriff. U.S. marshal, Deadwood, D.T. Helped to run down road agents molesting the stage line.

BURNS, J. W. Pony Express rider. Ft. Laramie-Indian Agencies, 1876.

CAMPBELL, DONALD. Stock tender.

CHAPMAN, GEORGE. Driver. On boot during holdup, october 9, 1877.

CHASE, HENRY. Agent and postmaster. At Raw Hide Buttes. A very remarkable man. Graduate of Dartmouth college and had studied astronomy, medicine, civil engineering. It was at his home in Virginia that Harriet Beecher Stowe wrote "Uncle Tom's Cabin." After his wife died, Chase came west and worked for the stage line for years. Just before entering the services of the line he had a ranch on Pole creek. In a skirmish with Indians he had a horse shot out from under him. He was a great reader of Byron, Tennyson, and Shakespeare. An expert carpenter. Tutored his brother, George, who graduated from West Point and became a lieutenant in the Third Cavalry. Lieutenant Chase was active in ridding stage line of road agents.

CLARK, CHARLES. Stock tender, driver, and mail carrier. At Fort Laramie. Murdered by Indians, may 17, 1876, ten miles west of Red Cloud agency, while on duty for stage line.

COCHRAN, JOHN. Shotgun messenger. Later a deputy sheriff, Deadwood.

COFFIN, TOM. Driver. Headquartered at Raw Hide Buttes, 1881.

COLOSKY, JO. Sub-contractor to carry mail. Began carrying on february 15, 1879, at $500 per month from Raw Hide Buttes to Hat creek, three times a week. Paid to january 14, 1880, cash, $5275.00. – Voorhees *Diary*.

COLE, DICK. Driver.

COOK, ED. A. Stock tender and driver. At Raw Hide Buttes.

COOPER, THOMAS. Driver. Known as "Uncle Tom," "Colonel Tom," and "Owl-Eyed Tom." Born, New York City, november 15, 1850. Enlisted in the 17th Illinois Cavalry, in Civil War, at 13. After the war, served as courier over Smoky Hill trail from the Missouri to Kansas outposts. Worked on a construction crew for the Union Pacific railroad, 1867, then saw five years of service with Dr. F. V. Hayden's geological survey. In 1876, Cooper was with General Crook as a guide, together with Big Baptiste. Following Crook's campaign he went to work for Voorhees. Robert Strahorn said: "Thomas Cooper is one who can handle six horses to a Concord coach, equal to the best known in the Rocky mountain country. Mr. Voorhees considers Tom Cooper his most reliable driver on the Black Hills lines." According to Scott Davis: "Thomas Cooper was recognized as being the best six-horse stage driver in the United States. Cooper drove the night route from Jenney Stockade to Hat creek station. The nights were never too dark nor the roads too rough for Owl-Eyed Tom. He had a great appetite. His co-workers said he would 'eat a stage horse broiled on toast every morning for breakfast.'" After Voorhees left the Black Hills line, "Big Tom" drove for him on a star route to Leadville, Colo. There he was injured in a stagecoach accident, so returned to Cheyenne to make his home. In 1887, he became a guard on a treasure train for the Union Pacific railroad. Later for many years he was depot master of the U.P. station in Cheyenne.

Cooper died, january 18, 1915, a few months after he had driven the six-horse hitch at the Wyoming State fair, in a portrayal of the Canyon springs robbery. Tears trickled down the old stage driver's cheeks as he held the lines over a fine six-horse team that he had selected himself.

CRAFT, JOHN G. Driver. On Merino-Sundance run for a time. Last driver for Russell Thorp. Later worked at Raw Hide Buttes ranch.

CRETH, DAVE. Driver. Cheyenne-Fort Laramie. Later was a cab driver in Cheyenne and Chugwater.

CUNNINGHAM, H. B. Driver. Died, Woodville, Miss., 1938.

DAVIS, SCOTT. Captain of the shotgun messengers. Called "Quick Shot" Davis. Born, october 2, 1854, Kinsman, Ohio. Grew up on Platte river near Fremont, Neb. When only fifteen he struck out on his own, freighted across the plains. Arrived in Denver, 1868. Worked on the U.P. construction and also on railway construction in Texas. Went to work for Cheyenne and Black Hills Stage Co., in april 1876. Was fearless. Davis was 5 feet 9 inches tall, rather stocky and well built. After leaving the stage work, he became a special guard for the U.P.R.R. and then its livestock inspector for 30 years. His wife, Celia Jeanette Bryant, was a sister of Mrs. M. V. Boughton. Davis died, april 4, 1927. Buried in Denver, Colo.

DENNY, JOHN. Driver and shotgun messenger. On coach when it was attacked near Hat creek station, september 26, 1877. Denny drove big coaches at the Columbian World's fair, Chicago, 1893.

Dow, E. P. Stock tender. At Jenney Stockade. Pioneer freighter.

DRAKE, GEORGE. Driver. An experienced New England stage driver.

DUFFY, TOM. Driver. Drove the old Concord coach for Buffalo Bill on his tour of Europe with Wild West show. Spent his last days driving in Yellowstone National park. Married a wealthy woman and settled in Lander, Wyoming, where he died. While a Black Hills driver, had the Cheyenne to Chugwater run.

EARP, WYATT. Special messenger. Spring of 1877.

EDSON, JOHN. Driver.

ERNEST, TOM. Station master. At Running Water.

FEATHERSTUN, JOHN. Division agent. Northern division. Member of Vigilantes in Montana. Killed in runaway, may 21, 1877.

FELTON, W. J. (California Bill).   Stock tender.   At Hat creek station.

FLAHERTY, JOHN.   Driver.

FORD, JOHN W.   Agent.   Telegraph operator.   At Fort Laramie. Appointed U.S. commissioner at the fort, november 1877.

FOSS, FRANK.   Telegraph operator and station agent.   Chugwater. Born, Hiram, Maine, september 7, 1852. Died 1938. Was with Crook, 1876.

"FRENCHY."   Stock tender.   Beaver station.

FRIDAY.   Chinese cook.   Raw Hide Buttes station. Later became quite a gambler. Made money and bought ranch near Custer, S.D. Wore a long queue.

GEIS, LEWIS.   Stock tender.   At Ten Mile (Englewood).

GILMER, JOHN (JACK) THORNTON.   Owner.   One of the most popular stage men in the west. Senior member of the firm of Gilmer, Salisbury and Patrick. He said he "turned the first wheel" of the Wells, Fargo Overland stage line across the plains. Was in that company's services ten years. Freighted with mules and oxen for Russell, Majors and Waddell. Drove on the Central, Overland, California and Pike's Peak Express company's line for Ben Holladay. Agent at Bitter creek division for Wells, Fargo, 1864. Was a self-made man. Energetic, resourceful, high-minded and inherited common sense from a line of Scottish and English ancestors. Born, Quincy, Ill., february 22, 1841, the son of Charles Meriwether Gilmer and Mary Ann Ratliffe Gilmer. His mother died when he was about fourteen. Young Jack left home, crossed the plains, and drifted to California. In less than two years he had accumulated $3,000 and started home, but he spent the money on the way, so hired out as a stage driver. In 1866, he married Mary Vance of Tennessee and made a home at Fort Bridger. In 1869, when railway was completed, he moved family to Salt Lake City. Bought Montana stage lines with Monroe Salisbury.
It was said of Gilmer's ability to organize that, "In a staging enterprise of large magnitude, he would distribute stock and men to their respective places; carrying the whole scheme in his head with such precision and accuracy as immediately to give such form to a large organization as to enable passengers and mail to be moved without interruption or delay."

Gilmer understood human nature. He was a horseman, a reinsman, and an indefatigable worker. On one occasion he reprimanded a stage driver for being behind time. The driver invited Gilmer to a fist fight. For a moment Gilmer regarded him contemptuously and then said, "If I should whip you, it would be no credit to me. If I should be whipped by you, I would be everlastingly disgraced." He dismissed the subject by reminding the man not to be impertinent again.

Gilmer had mining and staging interests all over the west from Dakota to California. He gave much time and thought to matters of government and was distressed at the fear that the country might be falling under the control of small and unworthy men. John T. Gilmer was the father of eleven children, eight sons and three daughters. He died in 1892, survived by his widow and six children.

GODARD, HARRY. Mail carrier-driver. Said to have carried first mail over trail from Fort Laramie to Custer winter of 1875-76. The trip probably was made "on his own."

GRAVES, GEORGE. Driver.

GRAY, ISAAC H. Agent. At Deadwood, october 1876-july 16, 1877. Resigned to go into mining. Voorhees: "Honest and square in everything.

GREENE, F. C. Agent.

HARKER, JACK. Driver-carrier. Hat creek to Red Cloud. Killed 1876.

HART, B. A. Trader's clerk. Fort Laramie.

HAWK, GEORGE. Station master. Eagle's Nest and Fort Laramie.

HAWK, TOM. Station master. Eagle's Nest and Fort Laramie.

HAWLEY, CY. Driver. Wounded during holdup, Cheyenne river, 1877.

HAYES, CHARLEY. Shotgun messenger.

HIGBY, JOHN. Driver. Known as the "swift man." One of the fastest six-horse stage drivers in the U.S. He had years of experience in driving stage in New York state before he came to Wyoming. Was influential in getting R. S. Van Tassel to come to Wyoming. No team of six horses could trot fast enough for John, so he generally went on his route in a wild, reckless run. But he was a safe driver. He always hit the bridges and grade roads in such a way that he kept his coach right side up. His brother, Anson Higby, a resident of Deadwood, helped bury Calamity Jane.

HIGH, WILLIAM. Clerk. Cheyenne. Third asst. clerk, Cheyenne headquarters of the stage line, november 1878.

HILL, GALEN E. Shotgun messenger. In 1873, Hill had charge of a freight outfit for Joe Small of Cheyenne. Was said to be the "right man in the right place." Wounded in treasure coach hold-up, 1878. In 1880 was a deputy to Sheriff John Manning of Deadwood. Postal Inspector Furay said of Hill, "He is a gentleman in his instincts and deportment."

HOGEL, JIM. Station keeper. Ran Rustic hotel for Collins in 1876. Later he was at Lusk, Wyo.

HOMER, JOE. Freighter. A mule skinner who hauled for stage company.

HOPKINS, FRED. Driver. Drove stage for Ben Holladay in Nebraska, then for Wells, Fargo & Co. Drove from Deadwood to Cheyenne and also on the Sidney route for Gilmer, Salisbury & Patrick. He was on the boot when Jack Gilmer tied himself to the rear boot and took a load of treasure through to Cheyenne. Hopkins said that Gilmer was "second only to Ben Holladay."

HULL, JOE. Mule skinner. Drove freight and supply outfit for Cheyenne and Black Hills stage company.

HYNDS, HARRY. Blacksmith. Had the heavy end of the line from Cheyenne to Fort Laramie. Had a jerky rigged up with blacksmith tools, with bellows in rear boot so he could do emergency work. He inspected the last coach for its final run north from Cheyenne and pronounced it "fit for any trip." Born, Morris, Ill., 1860. Took special training in blacksmithing and could do fancy things at the forge. When about 18 he went to Idaho, then to Colorado, and on to Cheyenne. Began work for Herman Haas, then went into partnership with man named Elliott. Later went into business for himself and took over the stage work. He fought two professional fights at Rawlins, Wyoming. In the first one he whipped Jack Lavin, but in the second fight his opponent, John B. Clough, a veteran of the ring, pulled the old shoestring trick on young Hynds. When Hynds woke up the next day he was cured of professional fighting. Hynds opened a saloon and later a restaurant known as the Capitol grill, in Cheyenne. He had a boxing ring in the rear of the saloon with a big sign over it which read "Knock Out All Comers in Four Rounds or Give 'em $100." Hynds was successful in business. He opened the Plains hotel in Cheyenne in 1911 and later built the Hynds building. He made a fortune in oil, and bought the A. R. Converse home in Cheyenne, where his widow now resides.

IDDINGS, H. A. Agent. At Cheyenne, june 1877-february 1879, then went to Helena, Mont., in employ of Gilmer and Salisbury.

JOHNSON. Driver. Between Raw Hide and Hat creek, 1880-81.

KEARNEY, LUKE. Driver.

KETCHUM, FRANK. Telegraph operator. Raw Hide, Running Water, Silver cliff, Lusk. Was sent to the penitentiary for the killing of George McFadden near Igoe creek.

KINNEY, PETE. Stock tender. At Jenney Stockade. Occasionally served as a shotgun messenger. Accompanied McReynolds on one trip with a gold shipment.

LAWRENCE, BILLY. Mail carrier. Cheyenne-Red Cloud agency, october 1876.

LAFFERTY, JOHN. Shotgun messenger.

LATHROP, GEORGE. Driver. Born, Pottsville, Penn., december 24, 1830. Was at Cherry creek (Colorado) in 1859, and began driving stage in Kansas as early as in 1861. Arrived at Fort Laramie in 1865 and after whacking bulls in central Wyoming, went to California. Then back to Nevada, where he met Luke Voorhees near White Pine, a great silver mining camp. In 1879, upon learning that Gilmer and Salisbury intended to send a herd of cattle through to Wyoming for Luke Voorhees, Lathrop asked for the trail herd job and delivered the cattle at Raw Hide Buttes in the fall of 1879. In 1881 he began to drive one of the large six-horse passenger, mail and treasure coaches between Raw Hide Buttes and Fort Laramie, for Voorhees. When the stage line changed hands, he went to work for Russell Thorp. He was little given to talk. He was honorable and reliable. After the stage line was abandoned for the railway, Lathrop went to Muskrat canyon to take charge of copper mines owned by Voorhees and Gill. He spent the last years of his life at Tom Black's ranch at Willow, where he jotted down much of the material that later was published by Jim Griffith of Lusk, in "Memoirs of a Pioneer." According to Russell Thorp, jr., "He was one of the best calf ropers I ever saw in a

branding corral. I remember well the last day I saw him rope.
It was at the George Voorhees ranch on the Running Water.
Lathrop roped the entire day, making 98 per cent clean catches,
all by the hind legs. He was then past 70 years of age." Lathrop
died on december 24, 1915 and his remains were interred at Man-
ville, Wyoming. Later he was reburied along the old Cheyenne-
Deadwood trail. A large monument was erected to his memory
and to the memory of the pioneer stagefaring men. George Lathrop was a man among men, faithful and fearless. He was one of
the type and class of men who helped the west grow. He drove the
last coach north from Cheyenne in february 1887.

LOGAN, E. A. Driver. Born in Illinois, october 21, 1857, and came
with his parents to Camp Carlin (Cheyenne depot) in 1871. His
father was a gunsmith in the ordnance depot there. In the winter
of 1875, Logan was a teamster for the construction crew that rebuilt the telegraph line from Fort D. A. Russell to Fort Laramie.
Three years later he helped to deliver 100 horses to General Miles
at Fort Reno, in eighteen degrees below zero weather. In 1881,
Luke Voorhees hired him to carry mail from Raw Hide to Hat
Creek. Later he drove the Fort Laramie "swing." During the
'eighties he worked on a number of big Wyoming ranches. He was
an expert artisan in gold, silver, copper, leather, brass, steel, and
horse hair. He fashioned spurs, bridles, conchas, and many other
things for the cowmen. In 1891, Logan opened a curio store in
Cheyenne and his shop became the mecca for collectors of western
Americana. In addition to books he carried fine Indian blankets
and relics of the range. He passed away in Cheyenne in 1944.

LONGHURST, F. E. Agent.

LUDDY. Teamster, mule skinner. Hauled supplies for stage company.

MADDEN, JACK. Station agent. At Running Water.

MANCHESTER, O. R. Driver.

MAY, D. BOONE. Shotgun messenger and station agent. At Robbers' Roost on Cheyenne river for a time. Was called "quite a
character." He was vigorous and fearless.

McFADDEN, GEORGE. Telegraph operator. At Raw Hide and Running Water. Killed by Ketchum at Igoe creek. Buried next to
"Old Mother Feather Legs."

McKAY, PETER. Agent. Custer City, 1877. One of the first residents of Cheyenne. Worked for U.P.R.R. Was active in development of mining in Hills and was said to be a man of "good judgment and veracity."

McREYNOLDS, ROBERT. Shotgun messenger.

MILLS, PONY. Driver. 1878.

MINER, WILLIAM. Stock tender. Canyon springs, 1878.

MITCHELL, THOMAS. Division agent. Fort Laramie-Deadwood, 1877.

MONROE, JOHN. Driver.

MOORE, M. M. Shotgun messenger.

MORSE, CALVIN A. Station agent. Lusk. Came to Wyoming for his health in early 'eighties. A graduate of Amherst college. Worked for Frank Lusk as a cowboy and round-up cook, then became station agent for stage line. The cowboys called him "Professor" because he wrote their letters for them. In later years he ran the Vendome at Leadville and then became manager of the Brown Palace hotel in Denver. Later was manager of the Cosmopolitan hotel, Denver.

MOULTON, G. B. Agent. Custer City. 1876.

MURPHY, P. G. Blacksmith. 1878.

NAPAY, Mail carrier.

NEFF, JACK. Driver. Began to drive in Nebraska when only fourteen years old. Drove from Cheyenne to Deadwood, then from Deadwood to Bismarck. On his last trip out the citizens decorated the big coach with flags and accompanied it with three bands.

NEWCOMB, RACE. Hotel manager. Rustic hotel, Fort Laramie.

NUNAN, JOHN. Driver. Bugler John Nunan (or Neenan), called "Uncle John," was quite old when in the employ of the stage company. He drove a two-horse jerky with express. Was scheduled to take the last coach out of Cheyenne, because he was the oldest driver, but "celebrated" too soon and was not able to handle the ribbons.

O'HAVER, TOM. Blacksmith. On northern division with headquarters at Raw Hide. Had a long, black beard. Was a miner and prospector. One of first to discover copper in Muskrat canyon.

PARTRIDGE, CHARLES E. Telegraph operator. Hat creek station. Used to repair the telegraph line down Indian creek, through Red canyon to Custer City, when Indians were on warpath. Came to Wyoming from Wisconsin. Made considerable money in horses.

His daughter, Bernice, married George Voorhees, son of Luke Voorhees.

PATRICK, ED. Division agent. Northern division, summer of 1877. Transferred to Sidney line, september 1877.

PATRICK, EDWIN LEGRAND. Stock tender and telegraph operator. Born, july 1, 1857, Omaha, Neb. Stock tender at Chugwater, 1878. Was employed in 1882 by T. Edward Hambleton of Baltimore, Md., who bought the Portugee Phillips ranch at Chugwater. In 1883 Patrick was telegraph operator at Raw Hide Buttes. The next year he worked for Luke Voorhees on the LZ ranch and later homesteaded on Raw Hide creek. Survived by: Carrie E. (Mrs. Albert B. Bartlett), Le Grand, Edwin H., William Bryan, Helen L. (Mrs. Jos. Ross), Robert K., Arthur G., Hugh, and Luke Voorhees Patrick.

PATRICK, ALGERNON S. Proprietor. According to Brown's *Omaha Directory*, 1876, p. 227, he was one of the proprietors of the Cheyenne and Black Hills stage and fast freight line. Wyoming records do not show that he took active part in the Cheyenne to Deadwood line, of which his brother, Matt, was an owner. He did, however, associate himself with his brother and Gilmer and Salisbury in the Sidney to Deadwood line. Later he was one of the proprietors of the Rock creek, Wyoming to Echeta, Mont., (Fort Custer) stage line.

PATRICK, MATHEWSON T. Owner. Born, Pittsburgh, Penn., february 7, 1834; moved with his family to Uniontown, Penn., when very young. After acquiring his education in the common schools there, became a merchant. In 1856, he located in Omaha and entered the general merchandise and lumber business. With the outbreak of the Civil war, young Patrick organized Co. A, First Nebraska Vol. Cavalry, which was absorbed in the Fifth Iowa Vol. Cavalry, of which he was appointed lieutenant colonel. At the time he was mustered out of the service he was in command of a brigade under Rousseau and Kilpatrick. Upon his return to Omaha, he was appointed Indian agent for the Sioux, Cheyennes, and Arapahoes, and served four years. He resigned to accept the marshalship of Utah territory. He continued in that office until 1873, when he was made superintendent of a mine belonging to an English company. In 1876 he formed a copartnership with J. T. Gilmer and Monroe Salisbury and organized the Cheyenne and Black Hills

Stage and Express line. Colonel Patrick was extremely active in the affairs of the company, until his withdrawal in the autumn of 1878. He was interested in the Sidney to Deadwood line, as well as in the Cheyenne route.

After leaving the stage company, Patrick joined his brother, Al, in running a stage line from the U.P.R.R. at Rock Creek, Wyoming, north to Fort McKinney, Fort Custer, and the Yellowstone river. He had ranching interests in northern Wyoming. The Patrick Brothers ran a stage line from Laramie City to North Park during the mining boom. Colonel Patrick was married in Worcester, Mass., august 16, 1881, to Miss Eliza S. Burdette, daughter of the author and critic, Charles Burdette. M. T. Patrick died in 1899. He is survived by one daughter, Edith Mathewson, now the wife of Myles Standish, of Omaha. Colonel Patrick was one of the most substantial builders of the west.

PAWNEE BILL. Driver. Cheyenne to Deadwood, 1876.

PHILLIPS, TOM. Stock tender. Raw Hide Buttes station, 1882.

POULTON. Stock tender. Raw Hide Buttes, 1880's; Chug springs, 1886.

RAFFERTY, WILLIAM. Shotgun messenger. october 1, 1878-january 22, 1879. Killed at Deadwood by accidental discharge of his pistol, when unloading stage.

RAYMOND, RED. Driver.

RENNECKE. Telegraph operator. Fort Laramie and Chugwater. Became a division superintendent for Colorado and Southern railroad.

ROBERTS. Shotgun messenger. Was in holdup at Cheyenne river, 1877.

SALISBURY, MONROE. Owner and Manager. Brother of O. J. Salisbury. Was a partner of Jack Gilmer in various mail contracts in Nevada, Wyoming, Idaho, Montana, and Dakota Territory. Gilmer had worked for Russell, Majors and Waddell. With Gilmer, Salisbury purchased some mines near Deadwood and at one time owned an interest in the Homestake at Lead, Dak. Ter. Monroe Salisbury evidently was responsible for sending H. E. (Stuttering) Brown, an experienced stage driver and manager, from Salt Lake City to Cheyenne, to scout relative to the establishment of a stage line. He actively supervised the launching of the Cheyenne and Black Hills

Stage and was identified with its development during its earliest years. Later he was connected with Wadsworth and Boomer of California. In that state he owned some exceptionally fine race horses.

In 1884 he offered for sale a "Montana horse ranch ... Consisting of about 2,000 geldings, mares and colts, 500 acres of patented land, controlling the water supply for many thousand acres of pasturage, several thousand acres of fenced pasturage, and fencing material on the ground for some 15 miles more of fence, good barns, corrals, and comfortable house, hay, grain and supplies for one year, farming utensils, wagons, harness, a few cows. Everything necessary or required to carry on the business of house or cattle raising on a large scale." His address then was: 320 Sansome street, San Francisco, California.

SALISBURY, ORANGE J. Wealthy stageman. Made his home in Salt Lake City for years. Brother of Monroe Salisbury. Had large interests in mail and freighting contracts in the entire Rocky Mountain West. Was prominently identified with the First National Bank of Deadwood and the Lead City Bank, S. D. in the early days.

SAMPLE, BILLY. Shotgun messenger. Worked with Jesse Brown, 1878.

SHERMAN, WILLIAM. Driver and bullwhacker. Civil War veteran. Died at Sheridan, Wyo., 1918 at age of 82.

SKINNER, C. A. Shotgun messenger. Had charge of first freight teams to reach Deadwood for Gilmer and his partners.

SLAUGHTER, JOHNNY. Driver. Killed by road agents, march 1877.

SMITH, EUGENE S. Shotgun messenger. In several holdups in 1878.

SOUR DOUGH DICK. Stock tender. Old Woman's creek station.

SULLIVAN, FRED. Driver. Born in Wisconsin. Shot in arm by an arrow during Indian attack, 1876. In 1879 was fireman on the steamer, "Black Hills" under Capt. Tim Burley from Yankton to Fort Benton. Worked in trader's store at Fort Laramie, 1880. Buckboard driver on Black Hills line, 1884-86. Died in Lusk, Wyo., september 28, 1941.

TATE. Special mail carrier. Ft. Laramie to Red Cloud agency. Killed by Indians, december 1876.

TEETER, JAKE. Ran the Ten Mile ranch (Englewood), a relay station.

THORP, RUSSELL, SR. Owner. Bought the Cheyenne and Black Hills stage line from Gilmer, Salisbury and Company, may 16, 1883. Born in New York state in 1846. Served as a private in the Union army until his discharge at Clouds Mill, Va., in 1865. Then journeyed to St. Joseph, Missouri, where he accepted employment freighting potatoes with mule teams from that point to Salt Lake City, Utah. He continued freighting on the Overland trail for several years, and while thus engaged, located and filed on a seam of coal which outcropped near Casement's construction camp called Bear River City, or "Beartown," on the westward-building Union Pacific railroad. When the rails reached the camp, Thorp was "ready to do business." The Union Pacific offered him $50,000 for the coal, but the young adventurer held out for $100,000, whereby the railway changed its survey and went around the "seam" and the coal owner's vision of sudden wealth went with it. Thorp, did, however, sell some coal to the railway at a good price, and according to Brown's "Gazeteer of the Union Pacific railroad, 1869": "The first engine was furnished coal from Thorp, Head & Street's mine, december 3, 1868. Mr. Russell Thorp discovered these two veins of coal as early as the spring of 1868 . . ." Some years later, a short-lived coal camp called Spring Valley, operated the veins.

In Bear River City, Russell Thorp went into store-keeping in partnership with J. K. Moore, who later pioneered at Fort Bridger and Fort Washakie. Shortly after setting up business, Thorp was one of the citizens who protected Beartown against the attacks of a mob of 300 lawless invaders from adjacent railway camps, who stormed the place to free some prisoners from the local calaboose. The mob burned the jail and *Frontier Index's* newspaper plant. Thorp and his fellow citizens armed themselves and fired into the gang, killing twenty-five and wounding fifty or sixty. Beartown was placed under martial law, soldiers were summoned from Fort Bridger nearby, and within twenty-four hours "tranquility" had been restored.

As the Union Pacific progressed to Evanston, Wyo., Thorp moved there to engage in the livery business. Love of fine horse flesh was one of his outstanding characteristics. When the first territorial legislature of Wyoming divided Carter county into Uinta and

Sweetwater counties and designated Merrill as the county seat of
Uinta, Governor John D. Campbell appointed temporary officers.
Although then only twenty-three years old, Russell Thorp was
named as one of the first county commissioners of Uinta county.
In 1873, he married Josephine C. Brooks, daughter of L. D.
Brooks, one of the oldest settlers of Wisconsin. Miss Brooks, a
pioneer teacher at Omaha, Nebraska, and the first gentile teacher
at Corinne, Utah, had been teaching for two years at Evanston.
She organized the first grade school there and at the time of her
marriage was principal of the Evanston grade school. Two years
later the family moved to the "Magic City of the Plains," where
a son, Russell, jr., was born. There Mr. Thorp engaged in the
buying, selling, and handling of livestock. In the spring of 1877,
he was one of the most enthusiastic endorsers of a proposed Stock
Association and Jockey club, with a view to holding a territorial
fair. In 1882 he purchased the Atkins ranch at Raw Hide Buttes
and made his home there. He was known as one of the most efficient
and best stagemen in the west.

In addition to running the main through-line of the Cheyenne and
Black Hills stage company from 1883 to 1887, Mr. Thorp managed a number of branch lines, including the so-called "Douglas
Shortline," which he established from Wendover to Douglas in
1888. He soon sold this to the Cheyenne and Northern Stage company. A tri-weekly line which he operated from Wendover to Lusk,
ran by the way of Fairbanks and Hartville. His last stage route
was between Merino, a terminus of the Chicago, Burlington, and
Quincy railroad and Sundance, in northeastern Wyoming.

After selling his interests in stage lines and mines, Mr. Thorp
turned his attention to cattle ranching. Super horseman though he
was, he met his death in a runaway accident, a mile from Lusk,
Wyoming on september 8, 1898, at the age of 52 years.

THORP, RUSSELL, JR. Son of owner. Driver. Born in Cheyenne,
but moved to Raw Hide Buttes ranch when five years old. There
he learned every phase of the stage business from making whips
and repairing harness to shoeing a horse. When only fourteen years
of age, young Thorp drove a four-horse hitch in an emergency on
the Merino to Sundance run of his father's stage line. He was
taught the art of a reinsman by the best stage drivers on the Black

Hills system. His first lessons in how to manipulate the lines were taught by George Lathrop, who drove six pegs into the ground and attached strings to them for "practice lines."

Many an hour young Thorp listened to the drivers and station attendants tell of the days of the road agents and outlaws. From Luke Voorhees, Scott Davis, Captain Willard and others, he heard the details of the Canyon springs (Cold springs) robbery and of the capture of Dunc Blackburn and Wall. It was no guesswork with this young westerner that "Mother Feather Legs" had red hair, because he and a playmate once did some scouting on Demmon hill and dug into a pile of rocks to verify the story of the old woman. A wisp of red hair was sufficient proof!

As president of the Wyoming State fair at Douglas, Wyoming in 1914, Russell Thorp enlisted the aid of Dr. B. F. Davis, Charlie Carey and others, and brought together the old-time stage drivers and employees as well as friends of the old Cheyenne and Black Hills stage company to re-enact the Canyon springs robbery, of 1878. A replica of the old barn at the stage station was erected on the fair grounds, and every detail of the robbery was carried out, in as far as was possible. A special set of harness was obtained; matched horses were used on the old Concord. A perfect team and a yellow-wheeled buggy were obtained for Luke Voorhees. Old stagemen came from all over the west.

Russell Thorp also was active in assisting in the erection of the fine monument to George Lathrop, near Lusk, Wyo. For many years he was engaged in the cattle business near Lusk, and in Montana. Since 1930 he has been executive secretary and chief inspector of the Wyoming Stock Growers association. His search at old ranches, deserted stage stations, and elsewhere for paraphernalia used by the old stage company has produced rich results. He now has perhaps the finest collection of Black Hills stage material in existence, including records, reminiscences, scrapbooks, rough locks, harness, telegraph instruments, handforged kingbolts, a treasure box from an old Concord coach, and innumerable fine photographs. He has kept alive the traditions of the old Cheyenne to Deadwood stage. He has one son, Dietz, now an officer in the u.s. Army.

TOBEY, W. S. Agent. Cheyenne, july 1879.

TUCKER, FRANK. Driver.

TYSON, BILL (POISON BILL). Driver. Emergency driver for Voor-

hees between Fort Laramie and Cheyenne. Came to Wyoming in
1862. Later trailed cattle from Texas.

UTTER, STEVE. Stock tender. Raw Hide Buttes station.

VAN HENSON, SAM. Driver.

VOORHEES, LUKE. Superintendent and part owner. Born, Belvi-
dere, New Jersey, 1835. Came from Salt Lake City to Cheyenne,
february 17, 1876 to organize the Cheyenne and Black Hills Stage
and Express line. He moved with his parents to Michigan when
he was two years old. His last schooling was at a small academy
at Pontiac, Michigan. Started west in 1857, hunted buffalo on the
plains of Kansas, then followed the Pike's Peak gold rush in 1859,
going to Clear creek. Mined in Colorado until the spring of 1863,
then went to Alder Gulch, Montana and on into Saskatchewan,
British Columbia, where he discovered the Kootenai diggings.
After a few months he returned to Virginia City, Montana and
from there followed the mining business in Utah and Nevada.
Attended the driving of the last spike at Promontory, Utah, which
connected the rails of the Union Pacific and the Central Pacific,
on may 10, 1869.

In 1871, Voorhees bought a herd of cattle in Texas and trailed
them to a ranch in Utah. He married Florence Celia Jenks in
Salt Lake City on april 16, 1874. About two years later he was
engaged by Gilmer, Salisbury and Patrick, as superintendent of
the Cheyenne and Black Hills stage line and moved to Cheyenne.
He continued in that position until 1883, when he organized a
large cattle company. In that year and the previous one he was
grazing 12,000 head of mixed cattle near Raw Hide Buttes under
the LZ brand. After suffering heavy losses in the cattle business,
Voorhees returned to the mining game for several years.

As territorial treasurer he was the first official to occupy the new
capitol in Cheyenne. Later he was elected receiver of public moneys
and disbursing agent of the U.S. land office at Cheyenne. He died
january 16, 1925, at the age of 90. Voorhees was a pioneer in every
sense of the word. Quite typical of his own life, Luke Voorhees
once said: "A man likes to be a creator of circumstances, not
altogether a creature of circumstances."

The Daughters of the American Revolution at Lusk, Wyoming
named their chapter in his honor, the Luke Voorhees Chapter.

WARD, W. M. Hotel keeper and division superintendent. Hotel keeper at Custer City. Superintendent of the northern division with headquarters in Deadwood. Once owned a livery stable in Cheyenne as a partner of Mason. Helped John Featherstun lay out and build a road from Custer to Deadwood by way of Gillette's ranch and Reynolds. At one time was interested with Parshall and Company in a sawmill. One of the first Cheyenne men to go into the Hills.

WAGONER. Mailcarrier. Attacked by Indians and wounded on august 11, 1876, while carrying mail between Fort Laramie and Red Cloud.

WATT, FRANK. Driver. In later years was a guard at the Colorado state penitentiary, Canon City, Colo. Quiet, fearless, and most dependable.

WELCH, BILL. Driver.

WILDE, JOE. Station agent. At Rustic hotel, Fort Laramie, 1879. Freighted in early days. Came to Cheyenne from Chicago, 1875.

WILLARD, CAPTAIN A. M. Shotgun messenger. One of the most outstanding men who served the stage line in that capacity. Later served as deputy under Seth Bullock at Deadwood, and was also u.s. marshal. Co-author with Jesse Brown of "The Black Hills Trail." Sheriff of Custer county. Shotgun messenger with the Northwestern Stage company. .

WILLSIE, M. Agent.

WOODS, SAM. Driver.

ZEANER, JOHN. Stock tender. Chugwater, 1881.

ZIMMERMAN, JOHN. Shotgun messenger. On the coach during several holdups.

Appendix B

Coaches

The following old coaches, used on the Cheyenne to Deadwood route, are still in existence. Some of the wheels now and then turn on dress parade, but only a few tints of light pink are left to suggest the resplendent shiny red coaches, with their flashing yellow spokes:

DISTRICT OF COLUMBIA. Washington. U.S. Post Office department's museum. Said to have been the coach used by William F. (Buffalo Bill) Cody. In 1883, Cody telegraphed to Luke Voorhees for a coach to use in his Wild West show. Voorhees sent one to him that had originally cost $1,800. Cody had ridden in it just after he had the fight with Yellow Hand. This stage was at one time abandoned, after being attacked by Indians. It lay neglected near Indian creek for three months. Later it was repaired and put back into service on the Black Hills line. It also saw service in Colorado, on the North Park line. At the time Cody visited Berlin, he had as his guests in the coach, old Emperor Wilhelm and three kings, who were guests of the emperor at the time. After the ride the emperor remarked: "Colonel Cody, I do not suppose that this is the first time you have ever held four kings."

"No, Your Majesty," returned the quick witted scout, "but this is the first time I ever held four kings and a royal joker at the same time." *(Sheridan Press,* december 29, 1900)

SOUTH DAKOTA, DEADWOOD. An old coach often used in parades.

WASHINGTON, TACOMA. Museum of the Washington State Historical society. Coach was presented to Secretary W. P. Bonney by Mr. Fletcher of Split Rock, Wyoming.

WYOMING, CODY. Old coach at the Cody museum.

WYOMING, CHEYENNE. Coach enclosed in small cabin in grounds at Union Pacific depot.

WYOMING, LUSK. Small log museum houses coach presented to Lusk Lions club by Russell Thorp, jr. This four-horse Concord mail wagon is the last survivor of thirty coaches used on the Cheyenne and Black Hills stage and express line. It was shipped around Cape Horn from Concord, N.H., in the 1850's, used in California and Nevada, and then placed in continuous service on the Black Hills lines and other routes in Wyoming, 1876-1890.

WYOMING, ROCK RIVER. Old coach under a small shed on U.S. 30, at eastern entrance to town. This coach, used on Black Hills trail where it received bullet holes in two holdups, was later on the Rock creek to Junction City, Montana line. Afterward it was owned by Jack Linscott of Laramie, and Frank Cluggage and Sam White of Rock River. Before his death, White sold the coach to the Rock River First National bank. When that institution closed its doors the stagecoach, with other effects was up for sale. It was about to be shipped to a buyer in New Jersey, when the citizens of Rock River learned of the deal. The idea of the old coach being sent east was unthinkable. Led by Dr. Florence Patrick, citizens bought the coach, in the name of the children of Rock River.

WYOMING, YELLOWSTONE NATIONAL PARK. Coach no. 259, on the portico of the museum at Mammoth Hot springs, was one of the "big shipment" of coaches from Abbot and Downing to Wells, Fargo in 1868.

Appendix C

Diary of George V. Ayres

In the spring of 1876, George Vincent Ayres and William H. Leacock, of Nebraska, made arrangements with William Brower of Cheyenne, who had a four-horse outfit, to take a party of six to Custer City. Payment was made in advance of $15.00 per hundred-weight on equipment and men.

After outfitting in Cheyenne, the party pulled out on the afternoon of march 8, arriving at Pole creek at eight o'clock that night.

Ayres kept a diary on the trip and in consulting it in later years said:

> Here (at Pole creek) we found no timber, but fortunately we had added a few sticks to our load which enabled us to make coffee and fry some "sow belly" (fat pork). Shortly after making camp, the weather changed to colder and it began to snow and blow a gale, which continued all night. We were poorly equipped for this kind of weather, – not having a tent in the outfit, and it was pretty rough for a bunch of tenderfeet sleeping out in the open and there was some talk of returning to Cheyenne to wait for better weather, but the majority was for going ahead.
>
> In the morning the wind died down and it stopped snowing, but continued cold. We left Pole creek at 8:30 A.M. and arrived at Horse creek about noon. Here we found no wood, but stopped to feed and rest the horses, and we ate a cold lunch. Left Horse creek at half-past one and arrived at Bear springs about 4 o'clock and camped for the night. Here we paid a dollar each for the privilege of spreading our blankets on a dirt floor and sleeping in a log house.

Left Bear springs about 10 o'clock the next morning. The weather continued cold and I frosted my ears and nose. Arrived at Jack Phillips's ranch on Chugwater creek and camped for the night. Here we found wood and a barn to sleep in. The weather continued very cold during the night but cleared up in the morning and we pulled out from Phillips ranch at 8 o'clock A.M. with fine weather, but it did not last long. About 10 o'clock it began to snow and blow so hard that we had to pull down into the timber along the Chugwater and made camp until the storm stopped. Broke camp the next morning and arrived at Chimney Rock P.O. at 10 o'clock. Left Chimney Rock P.O. at 1:30 arriving at J. Hunton's about 3 o'clock P.M. and camped for the night. Weather very cold. Left Hunton's at 8 o'clock the next morning. Arrived at Eagle's Nest about 1 o'clock P.M. and Six Mile ranch about 5 P.M. where we camped for the night. Weather continued very cold. Left Six Mile ranch about 8 o'clock the next morning and arrived at Fort Laramie at 10:30 A.M. Left Fort Laramie about 12 o'clock and crossed the Platte river. Here we left all settlements and entered the Indians' country.

Our next camp was in Cottonwood canyon. Here we were snowed in for a day, from here we went to Government farm (no buildings or sign of habitation). There we camped for the night. At this point we commenced to stand guard every night and from there to Raw Hide Buttes, where we camped for the night. Here our horses got away, and we lost a half day rounding them up. From Raw Hide Buttes we reached Indian creek, arriving in a heavy snow storm late in the evening and made camp in the timber without knowing other campers were there. The next morning a man rode to our camp and informed us that about five hundred Indians were camped up the creek and advised us to bunch up with the other outfits for better defense in case of attack.

We took his advice, but owing to deep snow and severe cold weather the Indians did not molest us. However, as soon as it stopped snowing we moved out and made camp that night on the prairie where we would have a better chance in case of attack. Our next camp was on Hat creek and from there we reached the Cheyenne river, crossed over opposite the mouth of Red canyon and made camp. Here were a number of parties camped along the river. About 3 o'clock the next morning a party of Indians rode along the full length of the camps yelling and firing at each camp as they passed by. We all jumped out of bed, grabbed our guns and took positions behind the trees, expecting a return attack, but the Indians did not return and the only damage was a bad scare and cold feet as the snow was over a foot deep and we did not stop to put on our boots. That morning we moved up into Red canyon and camped at a spring, where I think the Metz family was massacred a little later. Here it was my turn to stand guard and while I was not scared, I was nervous and mighty glad when daylight came.

The next day we moved up to the head of the canyon and camped for the night as our teams had become so tired and worn out that we could only make a few miles a day. We had all been walking most of the way from Cheyenne and sometimes hitched a rope to the tongue and helped pull the wagon out of the mud hole or wait for some other party to come up and help us out. The next day we moved to Pleasant valley and camped for the night. Here it commenced to snow and continued all of the following day, but we broke camp and arrived in Custer City in a big snow storm at 3 o'clock P.M. saturday, march 25, 1876, having been on the trail from Cheyenne seventeen days and it had snowed ten of the seventeen. . . At that time Custer City was made up of a conglomerate mass of people. . . There were but few houses completed, but many under construction. The people were camped all around, up and down French creek, in wagons, tents, and temporary brush houses or wickiups. The principal business houses were saloons, gambling houses and dance halls, two or three so-called stores with very small stocks of general merchandise and little provisions. Most of the business was being done in tents. . . The only law and order organization at that time was the Minute Men organized by Captain Jack Crawford, the "Poet Scout," and they were organized to repel Indian attacks.

Appendix D

Markers along Cheyenne-Deadwood Routes

1. Plaque on grave of Johnny Slaughter, Lakeview cemetery, Cheyenne.
2. One beyond the intersection of Carey avenue and a gravel road to Lake Absarraca, Cheyenne.
3. Chugwater, Wyoming erected by Wyoming landmark commission.
4. Lathrop monument, two miles from Lusk, Wyo. Erected by a committee comprised of: Tom Black, E. B. Willson, Russell Thorp, jr., R. I. Olinger, George Voorhees, J. B. Griffith, and Al Lundquist. More than $600 was raised for the marker through the sale of Lathrop's "Memoirs of a Pioneer." With the cooperation of the Wyoming landmark commission, the monument was unveiled on may 30, 1930. Many of the west's eminent men and women attended to pay tribute to this old-time stage driver and to the memory of the owners and employees of the Cheyenne and Black Hills stage line.
5. Hat Creek station monument on Sage creek, bears a bronze plaque presented by the Luke Voorhees chapter of the D.A.R.
6. Memorial at site of Jenney Stockade on LAK ranch east of Newcastle, Wyo. Unveiled, august 31, 1940.
7. The old Jenney Stockade cabin has been rebuilt in Newcastle, Wyoming as a museum.
8. Monument at Sundance, Wyo., commemorating the passage of the Custer expedition to the Black Hills, 1874.

White stakes have been placed in the ruts of the old Black Hills trail near the Lathrop monument. In the vicinity of Raw Hide Buttes some of the ruts of the old trail are knee-deep, cut in the sandstone by the wheels of the old coaches and stage wagons. Eroding winds have helped to dig some of the ruts deeper, but for the most part, the winds of Wyoming have drifted loose soil into the ruts, or farmers have plowed them under, completely obliterating them from the landscape.

Bibliography

AIKMAN, DUNCAN. Calamity Jane and the Lady Wildcats (New York, 1927)

ANDREAS, A. T. History of the state of Nebraska (Chicago, 1882)

AYRES, GEORGE V. Diary, 1876 (unpublished) Deadwood, South Dakota.

BANCROFT, HUBERT H. History of Nevada, Colorado and Wyoming, 1540-1888 (San Francisco, 1890)

BANNING, CAPT. WILLIAM and George H. Six Horses (New York, 1930)

BARD, ISAAC. Account books; Diaries, 1867-1876 (unpublished) Cheyenne, Wyoming

BARTLETT, I. S., ed. History of Wyoming, 3 vols. (Chicago, 1918)

BEARD, FRANCES (Birkhead) ed. Wyoming from territorial days to the present (Chicago, 1933)

BENNETT, ESTELLINE. Old Deadwood days (New York, 1928)

BLACK HILLS ENGINEER. Custer expedition number, november, 1929 (Rapid City, South Dakota School of Mines)

BRONSON, EDGAR B. Reminiscences of a ranchman (Chicago, 1910)

BROWN, JESSE, and A. M. Willard. The Black Hills trails (Rapid City, South Dakota, 1924)

BROWN, CHARLES EXERA. Brown's gazetteer of the Chicago and Northwestern railway and branches, and of the Union Pacific railroad (Chicago, 1869)

BURNETT, BRIG.-GEN. FRANK C. Letter to Agnes W. Spring dated november 9, 1939

[CANARY, MARTHA JANE] Life and adventures of Calamity Jane by herself (Privately printed, about 1896)

CASPER (Wyoming) Daily Tribune, 1922

CENTRAL CITY (South Dakota) Register, 1878

CHEYENNE Daily Leader, 1867-1890
————— Sun, 1877-1890
[CHEYENNE] Wyoming Eagle, 1942
————— Wyoming Tribune, 1903-38
CLEMENS, SAMUEL L. [Mark Twain] Roughing it (Hartford, 1886)
CLOUGH, WILSON O. "A French picture of Cheyenne, Wyoming, in 1867" in The Frontier magazine, march 1930 (Missoula, Montana)
COLLINS, JOHN S. Across the plains in '64 (Omaha, 1904)
CONKLING, ROSCOE P. and Margaret B. The Butterfield overland mail (Glendale, Calif., The Arthur H. Clark Co., 1947)
COOK, JOHN W., compiler. Hands up, or thirty-five years of detective life in the mountains and on the plains: reminiscences by Gen. D. J. Cook (Denver, 1897)
COUTANT, C. G. History of Wyoming (Laramie, 1899)
————— Notes and manuscript material in Wyoming Historical Society (unpublished)
CRAWFORD, LEWIS F. Rekindling campfires, the exploits of Ben Arnold Connor (Bismarck, North Dakota, 1926)
————— The Medora-Deadwood stage line (Bismarck, North Dakota, 1925)
CULLUM, GEORGE W. Biographical register of officers and graduates of the U.S. Military academy, 2 vols. (New York, 1868)
CUSTER, ELIZABETH B. Boots and saddles (New York, 1885)
DAVID, ROBERT B. Malcolm Campbell, sheriff (Casper, Wyoming, 1932)
[DEADWOOD, South Dakota] Black Hills Daily Times, 1877-78
————— BLACK HILLS PIONEER, 1882
DEADWOOD (South Dakota) resident directory, 1878-79
[DENVER] Rocky Mountain News, 1875-78
DODGE, LT.-COL. RICHARD I. The Black Hills (New York, 1876)
FRANK LESLIE's Illustrated Newspaper, 1877 (New York)
FREDERICK, J. V. Ben Holladay, the stagecoach king (Glendale, Calif., The Arthur H. Clark Co., 1940)
FRONTIER Magazine, march 1930, vol. 10, pp. 240-43 (Missoula, Montana)
FURAY, JOHN B. Letters (unpublished) New York City

GRINNELL, GEORGE BIRD. Two great scouts (Cleveland, The Arthur H. Clark Co., 1928)

GUERNSEY, CHARLES A. Wyoming cowboy days (New York, 1936)

HAFEN, LeRoy R. The overland mail (Cleveland, The Arthur H. Clark Co., 1926)

———————— and Francis M. Young. Fort Laramie (Glendale, Calif., The Arthur H. Clark Co., 1938)

HARLOW, ALVIN F. Old waybills (New York, 1934)

HARPER'S WEEKLY, 1875 (New York)

HEBARD, GRACE R. Washakie (Cleveland, The Arthur H. Clark Co., 1930)

HEITMAN, FRANCES B. Historical register and dictionary of U.S. army, 2 vols. (Washington, 1903)

HOLT, GEORGE L. Holt's map of Wyoming (New York, Colton, 1883)

HOWARD, J. W. "Doc" Howard's memoirs (Denver, 1931)

HUESTON, ETHEL P. Calamity Jane of Deadwood gulch (New York, 1937)

HUGHES, RICHARD B. Autobiography (unpublished) Rapid City, South Dakota

HULBERT, ARCHER BUTLER, ed. Crown collection of American maps. Series V, The great western stage coach routes. Vol. I, The Deadwood trails (Colorado Springs, 1930)

HUNTON, JOHN. Scrapbook (unpublished) Public library, Torrington, Wyoming.

JENNEY, WALTER P. Mineral wealth, climate, rain-fall and natural resources of the Black Hills of Dakota (44th Cong., 1 sess., Senate ex. doc. no. 51, Washington, 1876)

KUYKENDALL, W. L. Frontier days (Privately printed, 1917)

LATHROP, GEORGE. Memoirs of a pioneer (Lusk, Wyoming, 1917)

LEADVILLE (Colo.) Herald-Democrat, august 19, 1937

LEEDY, C. I. Scrapbooks (unpublished) Rapid City, South Dakota

LUSK (Wyoming) Herald, 1886-87

MAJORS, ALEXANDER. Seventy years on the frontier (Chicago, 1893)

McCLINTOCK, JOHN S. Pioneer days in the Black Hills (Deadwood, South Dakota, 1939)

McGILLYCUDDY, JULIA B. McGillycuddy: agent; biography of Dr. Valentine McGillycuddy (Stanford University, 1941)

———————— Dr. Valentine T. Notebook, 1876-77 (unpublished)

NEBRASKA Historical society. Nebraska historical magazine, april-june, 1927 (Lincoln, Nebraska)

NEW YORK Tribune, 1878

NYE, EDGAR W. Bill Nye and Boomerang (Chicago, 1881)

OMAHA Bee, 1876

PARKER, DAVID B. A Chautauqua Boy in '61 and afterward; reminiscences (Boston [1912])

PARSHALL, A. J. Scrapbook (unpublished) owned by Mrs. C. J. Ohnhaus, Cheyenne, Wyoming.

PATRICK, ED. Diaries, 1880-83 (unpublished) Cheyenne, Wyoming

PELZER, LOUIS. The cattlemen's frontier (Glendale, Calif., The Arthur H. Clark Co., 1936)

PRICE, WILLIAM. Diary, 1876 (unpublished) Cheyenne, Wyoming

[RAWLINS, WYOMING] Carbon County Journal, 1878-1893

ROOT, FRANK A., and W. E. Connelley. The overland stage to California (Topeka, 1901)

SOUTH DAKOTA Historical society. Collections, vol. XIII (Pierre, South Dakota, 1926)

SPEED, JOHN GILMER. The Gilmers, 1731-1897 (Privately printed, New York, 1897)

SPRING, AGNES WRIGHT. Seventy Years, a panoramic history of the Wyoming Stock Growers association (Cheyenne, 1942)

——————— Biography of William C. Deming (Glendale, Calif., The Arthur H. Clark Co., 1944)

——————— CASPAR COLLINS (New York, 1927)

STONE, ELIZABETH ARNOLD. Uinta county, its place in history (Laramie, 1924)

STRAHORN, ROBERT. Handbook of Wyoming, and guide to the Black Hills and Big Horn regions (Cheyenne, 1877)

STUART, GRANVILLE. Forty years on the frontier, edited by Paul C. Phillips. 2 vols. (Cleveland, The Arthur H. Clark Co., 1925)

TALLENT, ANNIE D. The Black Hills (St. Louis, 1899)

THORP, RUSSELL, SR. Account books, papers, 1883-87 (unpublished) in Thorp Black Hills collection, Cheyenne, Wyoming

——————— Russell, jr. Scrapbook (unpublished) in Thorp Black Hills collection, Cheyenne, Wyoming

TIBBALS, Z. N. Diary, 1877 (unpublished) Big Piney, Wyoming

TOPONCE, ALEXANDER. Reminiscences of Alexander Toponce (Ogden, 1923)

TRIGGS, J. H. History of Cheyenne and northern Wyoming (Omaha, 1876)
———— History and directory of Laramie City (Laramie, 1875)
———— A reliable and correct guide to the Black Hills, Powder river, and Big Horn gold fields (Omaha, 1876)
UNITED STATES Department of the Interior. Annual report of the secretary, 1875-80 (Washington, D.C.)
———— War Department. Annual report of the secretary, 1876-80 (Washington, D.C.)
VOORHEES, LUKE. Notebooks (unpublished) Cheyenne, Wyoming
———— Personal recollections of pioneer life (Privately printed, 1920)
WAKELEY, ARTHUR C. Omaha: the gate city and Douglas county, Nebraska (Chicago, 1917)
WARE, EUGENE F. The Indian war of 1864 (Topeka, 1911)
WYOMING Historical society. Collections, vol. 1 (Cheyenne, 1897)
———— Miscellanies, vol. 1 (Cheyenne, 1919)
———— Quarterly bulletin, vols. 1-2 (Cheyenne, 1923-25)
———— Annals of Wyoming, vols. 3-20 (Cheyenne, 1925-1948)
WYOMING, state of. Council journal, 1877, 1878
———— House journal, 1877, 1878
———— Session laws, 1869, 1877-79

PLATE 2

Dyer's hotel, Cheyenne, and the hotel bus, 1876

PLATE 3

JOHN THORNTON GILMER

ORANGE J. SALISBURY

COL. MATTHEWSON T. PATRICK

RUSSELL THORP, SR.

PLATE 4

LUKE VOORHEES
Superintendent, Cheyenne and Black Hills Stage company.

PLATE 5

A COWBOY FRACAS AT POLE CREEK STATION, FRED SCHWARTZE'S RANCH

From a contemporary woodcut

PLATE 6

CHUGWATER STAGE STATION AT HI KELLY'S RANCH

PLATE 7

POST SUTLER'S STORE, FORT LARAMIE

In 1865 the prospectors brought gold here in cans.
Here Jim Bridger told tales of gold in the Black Hills.

PLATE 8

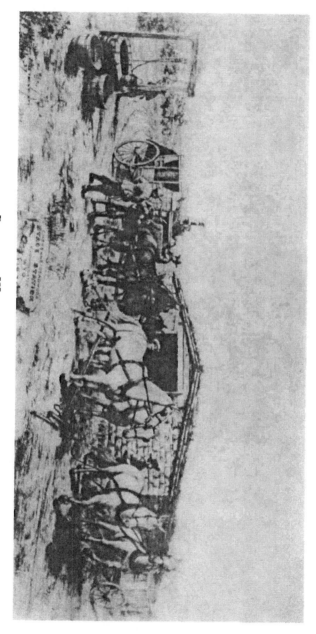

RUNNING WATER STAGE STATION
From a sketch by E. E. Stevens.

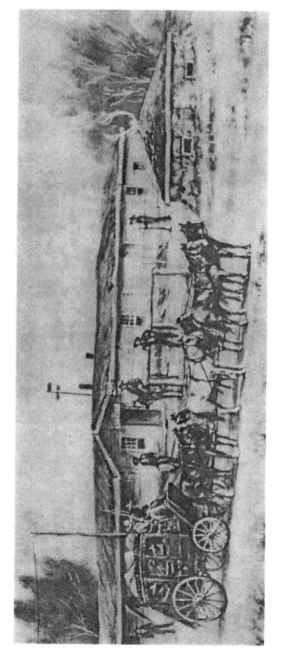

HAT CREEK STATION ON SAGE CREEK

A reproduction of an original water color by William H. Jackson for the Russell Thorp collection; now in Denver public library, Western collection.

PLATE 9

PLATE 10

TELEGRAPH SCRIP ISSUED BY THE CHEYENNE AND BLACK
HILLS TELEGRAPH LINE

PLATE II

FREIGHTING OUTFITS LOADED FOR THE BLACK HILLS

In Cheyenne, 1876. Note the man on the near wheel horse driving jerk line.

PLATE 12

A JERK LINE TEAM ON THE ROAD

PLATE 13

HOLE-IN-THE-WALL

Hide-out of cattle rustlers and outlaws in the 'eighties and 'nineties.
From a sketch by Merritt D. Houghton.

PLATE 14

CALAMITY JANE
With C. S. Stobie (Mountain Charlie)
and Capt. Jack Crawford of the "Minute Men."

PLATE 15

RAW HIDE BUTTES, RANCH AND STAGE STATION
From a sketch by Merritt D. Houghton.

PLATE 16

GEORGE LATHROP
One of the best drivers on the line.

PLATE 17

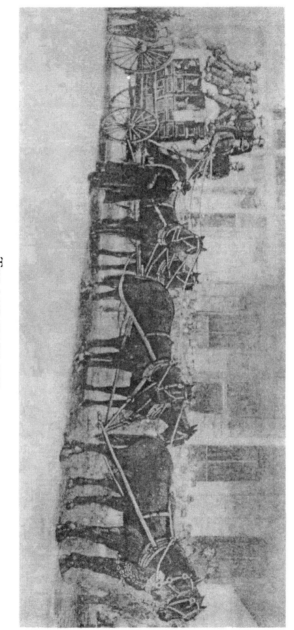

THE LAST COACH OUT

Departure from Cheyenne of the last trip by stagecoach.
From a contemporary woodcut.

Index

Kearney (Neb.): 41

Keating, George W: 263

Kelly, Hiram B: ranch, *plate* 6, 105-07; wife, 105-06; Raw Hide Buttes, 118; Indians, 150, 158

Kent, T.A: cattleman, 218, 315

Ketchum, Frank: 121, 348

Key, Postmaster-Gen: 255

"The Kid": *see* Pelton, Ryan, Osborn, Condon

Kirkland, C.D: 335

Kuykendall, Judge William L: expedition, 25-26; road bill, 75; to Deadwood, 145; mail, 155

LANCE CREEK STAGE STATION: 127, 207, 234, 250, 254, 259

Land: homestead filings, 330

Langrishe, Jack: 151

Laramie City: on Hills route, 41, 135, 238, 239, 246, 285, 286

Laramie county: 76; commissioners, 224; road agents, 261; schools, 323

Laramie Kate: 216

Laramie peak: 110, 114

Laramie river: 32, 36, 111, 114

Lathrop, George: *plate* 16, 91, 304, 327, 328, 329, 331; "Last Coach," 334-36, 348-49; monument, 364

"Laughing Sam": *see* Hartman

Lawrence county (Dak.): 239

Leach, M.F: arrests suspect, 243, 279

Lead City (Dak.): founded, 160, 253, 276, 295; weather, 302

Leadville: *Herald-Democrat*, 284; horse market, 315; hotel, 350

Lee, Edward M: 35

Lehane, Dr. James: 77

Lemmon, G.E: 192

Liberman, A: 249-50

Lightning Creek stage station: 56, 251, 290, 300

Lincoln (Neb.): penitentiary, 239, 279, 281

Lincoln Territory: 243

Little Bear stage station: 102-03; 311

Little Big Horn: 149; battle, 153

Little Big Man: 70-71

Little Meadow: 129

Livestock: *Cattle* – ranches, 36, 353; 48; Laramie plains, 51, 78, 98, 102, 104, 105, 106, 107, 108, 111, 112, 121; first herd, 144; drivers, 223, 225; in storm, 245, 275, 280; Hat Creek area, 292, 295, 299, 300, 306; brands, 207, 313, 324. *Sheep* – ranch, 98; in storm, 245

Llewellyn, W.H: 300-01

Lodge Pole creek: *see* Pole

Log Cabin House station: 126

Logan, Ernest A: 216, 311, 312

London, John: 116

Lone Tree (Neb.): 274

Loomis, Abner: 106

Lost Cabin mine: 24

Louisiana: 298

Lowrey, Mr. and Mrs. Amasa: 120, 303

Lusk, Frank: 121

Lusk (Wyo.): established, 121; editor quoted, 331; railway, 332; mail, 333; coach, 360; marker, 364

MADDEN, JACK: 121

Mail: overland, 32; Fort Laramie, 33, 44-45; Spotted Tail Agency, 44, 46, 55, 81; freighters, 76; Red Cloud, 81; via Inyan Kara, 129; suspended, 146; horseback, 154, 155; stage, 156; envelopes, 162; Custer City, 165; bid, 165; to Hills, 166; schedule, 197, 246; branch route, 243; robbed, 251; registered, 255; route, 298-99, 303; Colorado, 304; "star route" investigation, 310-11; Fort Fetterman, 332; Lusk, 333; contracts, 33, 44, 81, 165, 197, 291, 304

Maine: sends expedition, 189

Mallory, T.H: 71

Manchester, O.R: 228

Manning, Sheriff: 271

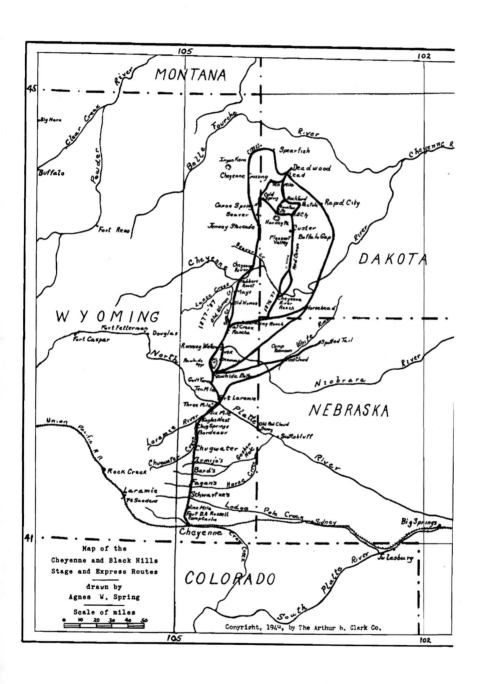

Map of the
Cheyenne and Black Hills
Stage and Express Routes

drawn by
Agnes W. Spring

Scale of miles

Copyright, 1949, by The Arthur h. Clark Co.

CPSIA information can be obtained at www.ICGtesting.com
Printed in the USA
BVOW03s1416141013

333699BV00007B/63/P